The COSMIC CARNIVAL
of STANISLAW LEM

☆

The COSMIC CARNIVAL of STANISLAW LEM

*An Anthology of
Entertaining Stories by the
Modern Master of Science Fiction*

Edited with commentary by
MICHAEL KANDEL

CONTINUUM · NEW YORK

For Henry and Simon

Grateful acknowledgment is made to the following:

"The Test" is from *Tales of Pirx the Pilot* by Stanislaw Lem, English translation copyright © 1979 by Stanislaw Lem; Chapter seven of *Return From the Stars* is from *Return From the Stars* by Stanislaw Lem, copyright © 1961 by Stanislaw Lem; English translation copyright © 1980 by Stanislaw Lem; "Les Robinsonades" is from *A Perfect Vacuum* by Stanislaw Lem, copyright © 1971 by Stanislaw Lem; English translation copyright © 1979, 1978 by Stanislaw Lem. All reprinted by permission of Harcourt Brace Jovanovich, Inc.

The *Solaris* selection is from *Solaris* by Stanislaw Lem, copyright © 1961 by Stanislaw Lem. Translation copyright © 1970 by Faber and Faber Ltd. and Walker and Company. Used with permission from the publisher, Walker and Company.

1981
The Continuum Publishing Corporation
18 East 41st Street, New York, N.Y. 10017

Printed in the United States of America

Library of Congress Cataloguing in Publication Data

Lem, Stanislaw. The cosmic carnival of Stanislaw Lem.
1. Science fiction, Polish—Translations into English.
2. Science fiction, English—Translations from Polish.
I. Kandel, Michael. II. Title. PG7158.L39C6 891.8'537
80-29301 ISBN 0-8264-0043-4 (pbk.)

Contents

A Portrait of the Artist
as a Thing Antediluvian

He has become an authority on the future. His stories of space travel, aliens, and robots have given rise to fan clubs, resulted in films, and brought invitations from various distant points on the globe to come and speak. He is probably the most internationally successful Polish writer, in terms of editions and sales, in the entire history of that country.

Yet, paradoxically—but paradox is the stuff of Stanislaw Lem—he is a man of the past, and as such he lives in isolation in this present. A Russian critic and translator of Lem, Rafael Nudel'man, once remarked that Lem was a "mammoth." By which he meant not so much that Lem has authored, incredibly, thousand-paged volumes of encyclopedic-philosophical discourse, but that Lem represents a kind of unique anachronism, a living fossil, a voice of something that perhaps ought not to be extinct but is.

His typewriter is an antique of a generation ago. The chair he sits on at his desk while plumbing the reaches of time and space, weighing human possibilities, judging societies, contemplating the enigma of the Universe, or brooding over the question of intelligence on other planets—his chair is a backless, curved medieval seat, over which is draped an animal skin. A prop out of *Ivanhoe.*

His idiom is quaint, full of gentility and circumlocution. And Latin. (Lem assumes many idioms, true, but the quaint one is *his,* not assumed: he is at his ease in it and always returns to it.)

His biases are firmly old-fashioned. He has contempt for hippies and militant feminists, respect for academicians and soldiers.

His intellectual concerns and spiritual preoccupations—not to mention his common sense—are in sharp contrast with our modern nihilism, ennui, jaded sophistication, and decadence in the forms, mainly, of self-centered hedonism and moral relativism.

Is it possible, for example, that someone could still hold forth seriously and at length on the question of whether or not there is an immortal soul? Surely, we think, that is for adolescents. But Lem does not apologize for so holding forth.

He is at home with Thomas Aquinas, Bishop Berkeley, Pascal. At the same time he keeps abreast of the latest developments in science—particle physics, astrophysics, molecular biology, computer science, anthropology, linguistics. He keeps a clever eye on current events. Is *this* antiquated? Definitely. It shows an eighteenth-century faith in the value/virtue of information—the conviction that a self-respecting person should acquaint himself with all fields of human endeavor, on which grounds—*homo sum: humani nil a me alienum puto*—Lem has also sampled a pornographic movie.

Consider: Lem is a Man of Reason in a time that has seen concentration camps, gas chambers, and cities attacked by the atom bomb. His protagonists at sea in an absurd future—they are reflections, whether comic or tragic, of himself. He knows that disorientation, that alienation, firsthand.

How can it be, then, that a mammoth, a freak fuddy-duddy throwback like Lem is able to create fictional worlds so compelling, and humor so inspired and so delightful? Talent, of course, is a reason. But I would suggest two other reasons. First, Lem *cares* about certain Ideas and Ideals. Such ideological caring can have great force—particularly as nowadays it is rarely encountered. Secondly, and a consequence of the first, Lem does not give a tinker's damn about the Dogmata of Our Age. He is therefore a natural iconoclast, a satirist who can go the limit in his funmaking, unencumbered by scruples or internal compromises.

He can laugh at the Theory of Relativity as freely as at the Trinity. He can, in the same work, on the same page, direct his scorn—political—Eastward and Westward both, without partiality.

He loves words, language, as many writers do, but has carried that love to more indiscreet lengths than most writers have had the nerve or imagination to do.

Imagination, I believe, is Lem's greatest single strength as a writer. It may lead him in circles sometimes, or down wrong paths, but often it will take him to places where no one has ever set foot before. To follow him is always worthwhile. Even a mistake, when bold enough, can be an adventure.

It is easy to see why he is isolated. Iconoclasts naturally antagonize establishments.

Lem's reception by the American science-fiction "community" (about ten years ago) is an interesting case in point. Science-fiction writers, critics, editors, and anthologizers in this country generally praise one another to the skies. Not long after the welcome mat was put out for Lem, they discovered that he had many highly negative and unpleasant things to say about science fiction and its practitioners. This was taken personally as a betrayal. But the simple fact is that Lem is not a praiser; he castigates everyone and everything around him, like a cranky hermit.

I was surprised, upon meeting him in the flesh, to find not a recluse, a type with a squint or a stutter or a twitch, wholly unaccustomed to social contact, to sunlight—pale, therefore, pasty, like something that lives under a rock—but a man full of energy, as open and enthusiastic as a boy. This fifty-year-old youth (now over sixty) had a strong jaw, a full mouth, and merry eyes. He moved quickly, spoke quickly. Took pleasure in all sorts of trivial things, such as a wind-up hen, a toy he had obtained abroad for his son, that dropped eggs as it weaved along on the floor.

He was friendly, generous, candid, amiable. His melancholy, as he told me another time, in a letter—rather, his bitterness, his bile—existed only on the intellectual (philosophical) level. Here is yet another Lem paradox: a man teeming with good spirits but who has reached the conclusion that the Universe is senseless and cruel, a kind of vile practical joke played by Accident on Man. That we are existentially trapped, victims all. That consciousness is suffering.

An attitude which is, of course, completely at odds with the optimism and confidence of the Enlightenment. The Enlightened Man, it was held, would in time and given the knowledge master the perplexities, the intricacies of the Cosmos and establish dominion over all things. The Wilderness would be turned into a safe and convenient Garden. Out of Chaos the liberated (liberated from prejudice) reason of man would bring Order. And man eventually would direct the omnipotence of his knowledge upon himself: perfecting society, perfecting ultimately (this, from the modern-day Enlightenment apropos genetic engineering) his very biological form. The only evil, in such a world-view, is ignorance.

Lem wrote, back in 1954, in an article entitled "Ten Years of Atomic Energy":

> It seems to me that the road of knowledge looming before us, as a process—not ending in time—of the ceaseless probing into phenomena and the simultaneous emerging of enigmas, as an eternal moving forward, an eternal striving and investigating—is likely the most magnificent and most admirable quality of the world in which we live. . . . this surmounting of successive difficulties and obstacles, this unremitting struggle with the world and with the self, I consider the most precious aspect of human life . . .

Not as simplistic as the above, perhaps, but still solidly for Progress and for Science. Even then he had doubts, and even now that the doubts, having grown, predominate, he cherishes that same hope.

He is, in other words, divided. In classic Dostoyevskian fashion (this, too, is *passé*) Lem A debates and Lem B rebuts, the voice of the dreamer-positivist contends with that of the cynic-defeatist, back and forth, dialectically. As far as literature goes, the conflict produces ambiguity and irony—qualities that are, I think, still considered "in." But there is a personal toll: Lem suffers from depression, to which he refers as *taedium vitae*.

The tactics of the conflict are sometimes pathos, sometimes farce, and frequently a mixture, or something in-between. Both voices agree, however, on one point: that the issue is important.

So the hijinks of constructors Trurl and Klapaucius and the aching despair of Hal Bregg, the simplicity of the "Tale of the Computer That Fought a Dragon" and the effete deviousness of "Les Robinsonades," the inanity of Tichy's Fourteenth Voyage and the grim drama of *The Invincible*—all these widely diverging Lems intersect at that one point of seriousness. Of *purpose*. For lack of a better word, I would call the gist of Lem's purpose humanism. In short, Lem is through and through a *didactic* writer. A teacher.

Are you entertained? Rest assured that he entertains you for a reason. Are you bored? Even boredom, with him, is intentional, a pedagogical device. He is constantly at you, Reader, manipulating, preparing, now providing play, now assigning work, giving answers, posing questions, setting traps. He wants to lure you out of what you expect and what you like. He wants—it is embarrassing to say this—he wants you to think and to become, having thought, different.

Could anything, literarily, be more out of step with the times?

The COSMIC CARNIVAL
of STANISLAW LEM

☆

Braving the Unknown

The first thing I ever read by Lem was *The Invincible*. I should say, not *The Invincible,* but *Niezwyciężony.* (Pronounced: nye-zvee-chen-ZHAWN-ee.) I was a graduate student then, learning Polish, and at that time Lem in English did not exist, except for one or two blurry stories in anthologies.

The reading was rough going at first; such words as "interstellar drive" in Polish could not be found in my dictionary. (Later I learned that a good deal of this futuristic-technical vocabulary was created ad hoc by Lem, there being no science-fiction tradition in his own language for him to draw upon.)

The book began, like *Forbidden Planet,* with an expedition sent to investigate an earlier expedition that had failed to report back to Earth. Surefire suspense, therefore: a lurking Menace—where will It strike next, and how? Soon I forgot that I was plowing through a foreign language. I turned to the dictionary only when absolutely necessary—it was hard, now, to put down the book even for a minute.

Then came the first surprise (Lem would be presenting me with a whole series of surprises)—namely, that *The Invincible* was not merely science fiction but science fiction in the classical, vintage, H. G. Wellsian sense. I believe that most science-fiction cognoscenti will agree with me when I say that coming upon such a thing is equivalent to finding a pearl in one's stew.

H. G. Wellsian means that, as in *War of the Worlds, The Invisi-*

ble Man, or The Time Machine, vivid, detailed scenes dramatize (play out) some line of intellectually genuine speculation. Where Science is not the setting, the backdrop, but the reason of the action, the very heart of the matter. Most of what has been and still is called science fiction is actually historical romance, except that rockets replace horses and ray guns swords. The pirates, instead of being swarthy, will have green skin and an extra eye. Etc.

With admiration I read on, through exciting theoretical discussions concerning evolution and episodes that would have made fabulous cinema—if one could imagine any filmmaker wealthy enough to attempt the special effects. (Lem has in fact turned down one offer—German—to film The Invincible, on precisely the grounds that the special effects must be done to the hilt or not at all.) There was a spectacular duel between an Earth-made robot and an amorphous "alien robot." (Cf. p. 135, "Two Monsters.")

Still under the impression, however, that I was reading a science-fiction novel—head and shoulders though it may have been above most other examples of that genre—I naturally expected, as the conclusion drew near, the Explanation of the Phenomenon. Wherein the scientist, like Sherlock Holmes, recapitulates the evidence (clues) and then, to everyone's awe, puts all those puzzling pieces together. The Answer stands revealed, and the Moral follows, and Finis. We close the book with satisfaction.

It did not work out that way. Not only did the Earthmen have to beat an ignominious retreat, making the name of their ship as well as the title of the book (which are the same) pointedly ironic, but the brilliant hypothesis that "explained everything" turned out to be, finally, no answer. Lem's answer was, rather: Look within. Reflect.

Which, actually, is quite scientific. Science itself does not provide answers; it experiments, guesses, revises its views, and constantly questions. The observer, moreover—this, an insight from modern physics—is part of the observation. There is, says Lem, an inevitable and irreducible element of subjectivity—and therefore of mystery—in our quest for knowledge.

The Black Cloud in The Invincible and the Sentient Ocean in Solaris are marvelous adventures in prose, but they are also provocative—and sometimes disturbing—allegories of Science.

"The Condor"
from *The Invincible*

From a distance the rocket looked like a leaning tower. This impression was strengthened by the sand massed around it. Since the wind came from the west the sand wall had piled up much higher than in the east. Several tractors near the rocket had been almost totally buried by the sand. Even the antimatter mortar had been put out of action. It stood there with its hood raised, half filled with sand. But one could still see the jet openings at the ship's nose which rested in an unobstructed depression in the ground. One had only to remove a thin layer of sand in order to reach the objects that lay strewn around the ramp.

The group stopped at the edge of the western dune wall. The vehicles they had brought along from the *Invincible* already ringed the area in a wide circle and the bunched rays of the emitters formed a protective energy screen. The men had left their transport vehicles and the info-robots about one hundred yards from the spot where the sand wall encircled *Condor's* base. Now the men looked down onto the ridge of the dune.

The ramp was suspended about five yards above the ground, as if it had been suddenly stopped in midair while it was lowered downwards. The elevator, however, was untouched and its open door beckoned the men to enter. Nearby oxygen bottles stuck out from the sand. Their aluminum sheaths glistened brightly as if somebody had left them lying there just a few minutes earlier. Several steps further on, a blue object rested gleaming on the sandy ground. It was a plastic container, as they noticed on closer inspection. Everywhere inside the hollow around the foot of the spaceship was scattered a vast quantity of all kind of things: cans of food, some full, some empty; theodolites, cameras, tripods, canisters, some still intact, others badly damaged.

As if someone had thrown the whole mess helter skelter out of the rocket, thought Rohan, and looked up at the darkened hole through which the crew would usually leave or enter the spaceship. The hatch was halfway open.

The small flying scouter robot that accompanied deVries' expedition had found the dead spaceship quite by accident. DeVries had not tried to enter the *Condor,* but had immediately informed Horpach of his discovery. It had been decided that Rohan's group would be the one to uncover the mystery that shrouded the *Invincible's* sister ship. Now the technicians came running from their engines, lugging their toolboxes with them.

Rohan noticed something round on the ground, thinly covered by sand. With his foot he scraped away the fine sand, assuming he would dig up a small globe. Not suspecting anything, he kept on raking until he brought to daylight a pale yellow vault-like form. He recoiled rapidly, stifling a startled outcry. Alarmed, his companions turned around, looking at him. He held a human skull in his hand.

They found more bones and even a complete skeleton in a spacesuit. Between the dropping jaw and the upper teeth stuck the mouthpiece of the oxygen apparatus. The manometer had stopped at 46 atmospheres. Jarg knelt down and slowly turned the valve. The gas escaped with a hissing noise. Because of the dry desert air no trace of rust had formed on the metal parts of the reduction valve; it worked easily.

They entered the elevator but pushed the buttons in vain: there was no electrical current. It would be quite difficult to climb up the scaffolding of the elevator shaft and Rohan began deliberating whether to send up some of the men in a flying saucer robot. But in the meantime two men of the crew had already started their upward climb; they had secured themselves to each other by ropes as if they were mountain climbers. The rest of the group silently watched their ascent.

The *Condor,* a spacecruiser of the same class as the *Invincible,* had been built a few years earlier; externally, the two crafts could not be distinguished. The men were silent. Although none of them expressed the thought out loud, they all would have preferred to find the wreckage of a crash or even the aftermath of a nuclear explosion. They were all shaken by the sight of this ship in the sand, listing lifelessly to one side as if the ground had given way under the weight of the support pillars of the stern. There the apparently undamaged craft leaned in the midst of a confusion of objects and human bones; the men shuddered.

In the meantime the climbers had reached the entrance hatch, opened it fully and quickly disappeared from view. They remained there for a long while. Rohan was growing restless, when suddenly the elevator jerked upward for about one yard and then descended smoothly to the ground. At the same time the figure of one of the technicians became visible in the open door, beckoning to them to get in.

There were four of them going up in the elevator: Rohan, Ballmin, the biologist Hagerup and Kralik, one of the technicians. Out of habit, Rohan examined the mighty, rounded body of the ship that was gliding by behind the moving elevator. He was numbed with fear for the first time this day. The armored plates had been scratched and pitted by some incredibly hard tool. The marks were not especially deep, but so close together all over that the entire hull seemed to be dotted with smallpox scars.

Rohan seized Ballmin's arm but he had already become aware of this strange phenomenon. Both men tried to get a good look at the nicks and indentations. They were quite small, as if they had been chiseled out with a fine instrument. But Rohan knew for a fact that there was no chisel capable of piercing the cruiser's hull for even the fraction of a millimeter. The titanium-molybdenum skin was of such hardness that it could be affected only by chemical corrosives. Before he could come to any conclusion about this problem, the elevator had reached its destination. They entered the airlock.

The interior of the ship was lit up. The technicians had already switched on the auxiliary generators powered by compressed air. The dustlike sand had accumulated in a heavy layer only at the threshold where the wind had driven it through the open hatch door. But there was none in the corridors. They proceeded to the third floor and found clean and neat, brightly lit rooms. Here and there they saw an oxygen mask, a plastic plate, a book or part of some protective suit. But farther down, the cartographers' cabins, the mess halls, the dormitories, the radar rooms, all the main corridors and side passages, were in a state of indescribable disarray.

The worst was the command center. Not one single dial of the many instruments, clocks and screens had remained in one piece. Those disks had been made of a tough shatterproof glass that now covered tables, chairs, wires, plugs and sockets in the form of a fine silvery powder. Next door, in the library, were heaps of microfilms, partially unrolled and twisted into wild tangles and coils. Torn books, broken sliderules, compasses, shattered spectroscopes had been wildly thrown all over the floor. There were stacks of Cameron's big star catalogs shredded to pieces. Somebody must have vented special fury on these thick volumes; they had ripped out the heavy, stiff folio-size pages in big bundles. The impression was one of frenzied rage combined with unbelievable patience.

Inside the club room and in the neighboring auditorium, the passages had been blocked by heaps of clothing and leather pieces cut from the upholstered seats of the chairs. According to one of the technicians, it looked as if the place had been invaded by a herd of rampaging apes.

The men were speechless at this senseless destruction. They went from deck to deck: in a small cabin, lying arched over in a heap near the wall, they found the corpse of a man clad in a dirty shirt and linen trousers. Now he was covered by a ground sheet that the technician who had been the first to enter the room had thrown over him. The dead man was mummified.

Rohan was one of the last to leave the *Condor.* He felt dizzy. Nausea overcame him in spurts and it took all his will power to fight off the recurring attacks. He felt as if he had just awakened from some incredibly horrible dream. But one look at the men's faces told him that the whole thing had been real.

They sent brief radio messages to the *Invincible.* Part of their expedition remained on board the *Condor* to restore some measure of order. But before they began this gigantic task, Rohan arranged to have each room photographed and carefully described.

Together with Ballmin and Gaarb, one of the biophysicists, Rohan started on the way back. Jarg was driving. His broad and usually smiling face seemed now to have shrunk, bearing a grim expression. He was driving rather recklessly, quite unlike his customary highly disciplined self. The heavy vehicle, weighing several tons, was raked by sudden jolts and hobbled across the dunes, throwing out sandy fountains on either side. One of the energo-robots moved ahead of them at an even pace, shielding the men in the truck with its energy field. All were silent, each man busy with his own thoughts.

Rohan was almost afraid to face the astrogator; he did not know what to tell him. He had kept to himself one of the discoveries he had made, one which seemed particularly incomprehensible and insane, and thus chilling. In one of the bathrooms on the eighth floor he had found *several soap bars pierced with tooth marks.* Famine? There had certainly been no dearth of food on board the *Condor.* The storerooms were filled with all kinds of provisions. Even the milk in the freezer rooms had not spoiled.

About midway they received radio signals from a small vehicle with a robot drive. It came toward them, raising a heavy dust cloud that followed them like a dirty umbrella. Rohan's car braked; the other vehicle also came to a halt. Two men were in it: Magdow, a middle-aged technician, and Sax, the neurophysiologist. Rohan switched off the energy screen. This way it was possible to communicate with each other by shouting back and forth.

After Rohan's departure they had discovered the frozen body of a man lying in the hibernator of the *Condor.* They thought they might be able to bring the man back to life, and Sax had brought the necessary instruments from the *Invincible.* Rohan decided to go along, justifying this sudden change of plans by saying that Sax was traveling without an energy field. The truth was, however, that he dreaded the confrontation with Horpach; he was glad to have an excuse for postponing this unpleasant task. Rohan's group turned around and chased back, raising big dust clouds.

There was a great deal of activity around the *Condor.* Various objects were still dug up from the dunes. Off to one side was a row of corpses, now neatly hidden under white sheets. More than twenty dead bodies had been found. The ramp was in working order, the power supply had been completely restored.

The approaching convoy had been detected by the men at the *Condor,* for the dust cloud was visible from quite a distance. A passage into the inside of the energy dome had been readied for them. There they were greeted by a physician, Dr. Nygren, who had refused to examine the man from the hibernator without some professional assistance.

Rohan availed himself of the privilege of acting here as the commander's deputy; he accompanied the two physicians aboard. The wreckage that blocked the entrance into the hibernator had since been cleared away. The thermometers registered zero degrees Fahrenheit. The two doctors exchanged meaningful glances. Rohan understood enough about hibernation to realize that this temperature was too high for a reversible death, and on the other hand, too low for hypothermal sleep. There was no indication that this man had been intended to survive his stay in the hibernator. He had most likely stumbled inside by accident—another riddle, just as nonsensical as everything else that had happened on board the *Condor.* And indeed, as soon as they had changed into thermo-protective suits, turned the handwheel to "open" and lifted up the heavy trapdoor, they saw, stretched out on the floor, face downwards, the body of a man in his underwear. Rohan helped the physicians carry the frozen man to a small upholstered table with three overhead lamps that supplied light without casting shadows. It was not a proper operating table but merely a kind of stretcher for small manipulations that were sometimes carried out inside the hibernator.

Rohan hesitated before looking at the man's face; he had been acquainted with many members of the *Condor's* crew.

But this man was a stranger to him. If his limbs had not been so icy cold and stiff, one could have believed that he was simply asleep. His lids were closed. Thanks to the dry, hermetically sealed room, his skin had not lost its natural color, although he looked quite pale. His subcutaneous tissues, however, abounded with tiny ice crystals. Once again the two physicians communicated with each other by meaningful glances. They laid out their instruments.

Rohan sat down on one of the empty, freshly made up cots that were arranged in two long rows. Everything here was in perfect order. Several times he heard the clicking of some instruments, the whispered consultation between the two medical men. Finally Sax stepped back from the stretcher and said: "There's nothing else we can do here."

"You mean he's dead," said Rohan. It was not so much a question he posed as a conclusion he drew, the only possible interpretation of the doctor's words.

Nygren had switched on the air conditioning system in the meantime. It was not long before warm air began to stream into the room. Rohan rose from the cot in order to leave the hibernator when he noticed the physician returning to the stretcher. He picked up a small black satchel off the floor, opened it and pulled out that apparatus about which Rohan had heard so much but which he had never seen until now. With slow, almost pedantic movements, Sax began to untangle the cords whose ends had flat electrodes attached to them. He placed six electrodes against the dead man's skull and fastened them with an elastic band. Then he crouched down and pulled three pairs of headphones out of the satchel. He put on one of these and kept testing the buttons of the machine inside a plastic case. His eyes were closed, his face bore an expression of deepest concentration. Suddenly he frowned, bent over further and stopped fiddling with the button. He quickly removed the earphones from his head.

"Dr. Nygren—" he said in a strange voice. His colleague seized the earphones in turn.

"What is it?" whispered Rohan with trembling lips.

This apparatus was referred to by the space crews as the "corpse-spy." With it one could "auscultate the brain" of recently deceased persons, or those dead in whom decay had not yet set in, or a body like this one that had been preserved by very low temperatures. Long after death had occurred one could ascertain what the last conscious thoughts and emotions had been.

The apparatus sent electrical impulses into the brain; there they followed the path of least resistance, moving along those nerve tendrils that had formed one functional entity during the preagonal phase. The results were never too reliable, but it was said to have obtained extraordinarily significant data on many occasions. In cases like the present one use of the "corpse-spy" was clearly indicated.

Rohan somehow suspected that the neurologist had never really counted on reviving the dead man, but had only come to listen and find out the secrets buried in his frozen brain. Rohan stood without moving, aware of the dull beating of his heart and the dryness in his mouth, as Sax handed him the second set of earphones. Had this gesture not been so simple, so matter of fact, he would not have dared put on the headphones. But he felt encouraged by the steady gaze of Dr. Sax who squatted before the set as he slowly turned the amplifier button.

At first he heard nothing but the humming of the current. He felt relieved, for he did not really want to hear more. Without realizing it on a conscious level, he wanted nothing more than that the dead man's brain remain silent.

Sax straightened up and adjusted Rohan's headphones. Rohan saw something emerge from the white light that fell on the wall of the cabin: a gray light, dimmed as if by ashes, floating vaguely somewhere at an undeterminable distance. Without knowing why, he tightly squeezed his eyelids together.

Suddenly he could perceive clearly what it was he had just

seen. It looked like one of the corridors inside the *Condor;* there were pipes running along the ceiling. The passage was totally blocked by human bodies that seemed to move. But it was only the image that was waving to and fro. The people were half-naked; shreds of clothing barely covered them. Their skin was unnaturally white and was sprinkled with dark spots like some kind of a rash. Perhaps these spots were not on the skin but were rather a peculiar visual phenomenon, for they were scattered everywhere: tiny black dots on the floor and the walls. The entire image seemed to fluctuate like a blurred photograph taken through a deep layer of flowing water. The picture seemed to stretch, then contracted again, billowing and swaying.

Terrified, Rohan forced his eyes open. The image faded away and vanished; only a shadow remained in the brightly lit room.

Sax began to make some adjustments on the apparatus and Rohan heard, coming from inside him, a faint whisper: "...ala...ama...lala...ala...ma...mama...." Nothing else. Suddenly weird noises came from the earphones: caterwauling, tweeting and crowing; high-pitched sounds that repeated over and over again like some crazy hiccup or some wild horrible laughter, or tortured electronic circuits.

Sax rolled up the cords and put them back in his bag. Nygren took a sheet and threw it over the dead man, covering up his body and face. The man's mouth had been tightly shut but now his lips parted slightly, giving his face an enormously surprised expression. It must be the heat, thought Rohan; it had become quite warm inside the hibernator, or at least it felt warm to him. He perspired heavily, the water trickled down his back. He was glad to see the face disappear under the white sheet.

"What is it? Why don't you say anything?" Rohan called out.

Sax tightened the straps around the plastic case, then stepped closer to Rohan. "Pull yourself together, Navigator!"

Rohan narrowed his eyelids and clenched his fists. But it did not help. In such moments he would fly into a violent rage, which he could suppress only with great difficulty.

"Sorry," he stammered. "But what did that *mean?*"

Sax unzipped his protective suit. The bulky garment slid to the ground; nothing remained now of his portly figure. Once again he was the same gaunt, stoop-shouldered man with the narrow chest and delicate hands.

"I don't know any more than you do," he answered. "Maybe even less."

Rohan felt lost; he did not understand any longer, but he seized upon the neurologist's last words.

"What do you mean, less?"

"Because I just arrived. I haven't seen anything besides this corpse. But you've been here all day. Doesn't this image suggest anything to you?"

"No. Those—they were moving. Were they still alive then? What were those little black spots all over them?"

"They weren't moving. That was an optical illusion. These engrams are registered on the brain like a photographic still. And sometimes it happens that several images are present, like in a multiple exposure. But this was not the case here."

"But those spots? Are they also an optical illusion?"

"I don't know. Anything is possible. But I don't think so. What would you say, Nygren?"

Nygren had already peeled off his protective suit.

"I don't know either. I'm not sure whether they were artifacts or not. There weren't any on the ceiling, were there?"

"The black spots? No. They only covered the dead bodies and the floor. And some of them were on the walls—"

"If that had been a second projection, they would have been all over the image," said Nygren. "But you can never be sure with engrams. So much is purely due to chance."

"And that voice? That—babbling?" Rohan searched desperately for an answer.

"One word was perfectly clear: *'Mama.'* Did you hear it?"

"Yes, I did. But there was something else. 'Ala . . . lala.' That was repeated over and over again."

"Yes, but only because I made a systematic examination of the entire occipital lobe," said Sax. "In other words, the area that controls acoustic memory," he explained for Rohan's benefit. "That's what's so unusual here."

"Those words?"

"No. Not those words. A dying man might think of anything. If he had been thinking of his mother, those words would have been quite normal. But his auditory memory bank was absolutely empty. Do you understand?"

"No, I'm afraid I don't. What do you mean by empty?"

"As a rule we cannot obtain any useful results when we search the occipital lobe," explained Nygren. "Too many engrams there, too many stored words. It's as if you would attempt to read one hundred books simultaneously. Sheer chaos. But this one," he glanced over in the direction of the elongated shape under the white sheet, "he had nothing in it. No words, only those couple of syllables."

"Yes, you are right. I have examined everything thoroughly from the sensory speech center to the *sulcus Rolandi,*" said Sax. "And the same syllables kept recurring. These were the only phonemes that have been left in there."

"And what happened to the rest?"

"There aren't any others," Sax seemed to lose patience. He jerked the heavy apparatus violently upwards and off the floor, making the leather handle squeak. "They aren't there and that's all there is to it. Don't ask me what happened to all the other words. This man must have totally lost his acoustical memory bank."

"But how about the image?"

"That's something entirely different. This he saw. He did not even have to understand what he perceived. Just like a camera that does not comprehend but still registers whatever object you aim it at. I have no idea whether he understood it or not."

"Could you help me with this, please, Nygren?" The two physicians carried their gear out of the hibernator, and the door fell shut behind them.

Rohan was alone in the room. He felt so desperate that he stepped over to the table, flung back the white sheet, unbuttoned the dead man's shirt and carefully examined his chest. He trembled when he touched the body, for the skin had become supple again. As the tissues were thawing out, a general relaxation of all the muscles had taken place. The head, which until now had been propped up in an unnatural position, had sunk down limply. Now it seemed indeed as if he were sleeping. Rohan searched the body for evidence of some mysterious epidemic, some kind of poisoning or insect bites, but he could find nothing. Two fingers of the left hand spread apart and a small, gaping wound became visible. A few drops of blood began to ooze out of the torn flesh, and began to drip on the white foam rubber cover of the table. That was more than Rohan could stand. He did not even bother to pull the sheet back over the corpse; he ran out of the cabin, pushed aside the men who stood in his way and rushed toward the main exit as if he were being pursued. He was stopped by Jarg in the airlock, who helped him strap on the oxygen gear and pushed the mouthpiece between Rohan's lips.

"You didn't find anything, Navigator?"

"No, Jarg. Nothing, nothing at all."

He was unaware of the others beside him as he descended in the elevator. Outside the motors howled. The storm had grown stronger; sand clouds whizzed past and pelted the rough surface of the *Condor's* hull.

Suddenly Rohan remembered something. He walked over to the stern, raised himself on his toes and palpated the thick metal. The armored plate felt like rock, old weathered rock, dotted with hard nodules. Over near the transporters he noticed the tall figure of engineer Ganong, but he did not even try to ask him what he might think of that strange phenomenon. The engineer would know no more than he did himself: namely, nothing. Absolutely nothing.

He rode back in the largest vehicle, together with a dozen other men. From his seat in the far corner of the cabin, he heard their voices as if from a great distance. Terner brought up the question of poisoning, but he was shouted down.

"Poisoned? With what? All the filters are in top shape, the water supply untouched, oxygen tanks all full, an abundance of food . . ."

"Did you see what the man looked like that we found in the navigation room?" asked Blank. "I used to know him. But I would never have recognized him if I hadn't see his signet ring."

Nobody answered. Back at the *Invincible* Rohan went directly to Horpach, who had been kept up to date on everything via television and the oral reports of the group that had returned earlier. They had also brought along with them several hundred photos. Unconsciously, Rohan was relieved that he did not have to describe to the commander what he had seen.

The astrogator gave him a piercing glance and rose from the table where a large map of the area was spread out and partially covered by stacks of photographs. They were alone in the large command center.

"Pull yourself together, Rohan," he said. "I can sympathize with the way you feel right now, but we need cold reason, a clear head, no emotions. We'll get to the bottom of this damned story."

"But they had every imaginable safety device: energorobots, laser beam protectors and particle throwers. The big antimatter mortar is right there in front of the ship. They had all the same things to protect themselves that we do." said Rohan in a toneless voice. He slumped down into a chair. "Forgive me."

The astrogator took a bottle of cognac from a small cupboard.

"An old home remedy. Sometimes it does a lot of good. Drink that, Rohan. A long time ago people used this on battle fields."

Rohan took the drink and swallowed it in one gulp.

"I checked the counters of all the energy aggregates," he said in a reproachful tone. "The crew was never attacked. They never fired a single shot. They simply, simply—"

"Went stark raving mad," completed the unruffled commander.

"If only we could be sure of that! But how could that happen?"

"Did you see the log book?"

"No, Gaarb took it along with him. Do you have it here now?"

"Yes, I do. There's the date of landing and only four entries, concerning the ruins, the same ones you men examined, and—the flies."

"What flies?"

"I don't know. This is the exact text here . . ."

He picked up the open book from the table.

" 'No sign of any life on land. Composition of the air . . .' Then the result of the air analysis follows. But then—here it is: 'At 18:40, the second armored patrol unit returned from the ruins. They encountered a local sandstorm with strong activity of atmospheric electrical discharges. Could restore communication by radio despite these disturbances. The patrol reports large swarms of tiny flies . . .' "

The astrogator put down the book.

"And what else? Why don't you go on?"

"That's all there is. This is the end of the last entry."

"And there's nothing after that?"

"You had better look at the rest of this yourself."

He pushed the log book over to Rohan. The page was covered with illegible scrawls. Rohan inspected the crazy doodling with amazement.

"This one here looks like a *B,*" he said softly.

"Yes. And this one like a *G,* a capital *G.* As if a small child had tried to write this. Don't you agree?"

Rohan was silent. He still clutched the empty glass in his hand; he had forgotten to put it down on the table. He was thinking of the ambitions he had harbored until recently, of his dream to himself become commander of the *Invincible* some day. Now he was grateful that he did not have to decide what the future fate of this expedition should be.

"Please summon the leaders of the specialist groups. Rohan, wake up, will you!"

"I'm sorry. A conference, Astrogator?"

"Yes. Have them all come to the library."

Fifteen minutes later they were all assembled in the large square room with the brightly decorated walls and endless rows of books and microfilms. The fact that this room was decorated exactly like the library of the *Condor* was unsettling. No matter which wall or corner he looked at, he could not banish the images of insanity that had been etched in his brain.

They had all taken their usual seats. The biologist, the physician, the planetologist, the electronic engineer, the communication officer, the cyberneticist and the physicist were all seated, their armchairs arranged in a semicircle.

These nineteen men formed the strategic brain of the spaceship.

The astrogator stood by himself at the half-lowered screen.

"Is every man here familiar with the situation on board the *Condor?*"

A murmur of affirmative voices could be heard.

"So far twenty-nine dead bodies have been located by the search troops in the vicinity of the *Condor.* Another thirty-four on board ship itself, including one person who was excellently preserved inside the hibernator. Dr. Nygren has just returned from there and will give us his report now."

"I'm afraid there isn't too much to report," said Dr. Nygren as he rose to his feet. Slowly he walked over to the astrogator. Nygren was almost one foot shorter than Horpach.

"Among the corpses we found nine that were mummified, that is in addition to the one the Commander has just told you about; that one is undergoing special examinations. Outside in the sand, mostly skeletons or remains of skeletons were dug up. The mummified bodies were found inside the ship where especially favorable dry conditions are present such as low humidity, almost no putrefying bacteria and fairly low temperatures. Those bodies that remained on the outside have all decayed. This process has accelerated here in the rainy season due to the high iron oxide and iron sulfide content in the soil. These chemicals react with weak acids—but I believe these details are insignificant. In case a more thorough explanation of these reactions should be desirable, our colleagues from the chemical department would certainly oblige. In any event, mummification was impossible outside the spaceship, considering that rain water and dissolved substances from soil and sand have been working on everything in the area for several years. This accounts for the polished surface of the bones."

"Pardon me, Nygren," interrupted the astrogator. "The most important aspect for us is the cause of death, not what happened afterwards."

"There are no indications of violent death, at least none we could detect in the well-preserved bodies we saw," replied Nygren quickly. He did not look at anybody in the room, but stared at something invisible in his raised hand. "Apparently they must all have died from natural causes."

"What do you mean by that?"

"No external causes could be detected. Several fractures of legs and arms might have come about at a later date, but it will take additional experiments to determine that. Those bodies that had been dressed show no damage either to the epidermis or the skeleton. No injuries—apart from some scratches, and they assuredly did not bring about death."

"How then did they perish?"

"I don't know. It almost looks as though they starved or died of dehydration."

"There was plenty of food and water left aboard the *Condor*," interjected Gaarb.

"I am aware of that."

For a moment no one spoke a word.

"Mummification means first of all complete dehydration of the body," explained Nygren. He was still not looking at anyone present. "The adipose tissues undergo changes, but they do not disappear. But these people had practically no fats left. As if they had starved to death."

"But this was definitely not the case of the man from the hibernator," remarked Rohan, who was standing behind the last row of seats.

"Correct. He probably froze to death. It is a mystery to me how he could have ventured inside the hibernator. Maybe he simply fell asleep there while the temperature kept falling."

"Is there any likelihood of mass poisoning?" inquired Horpach.

"No."

"But Doctor, how can you so categorically ..."

"I can very well dismiss this so easily," replied the physician. "Under planetary conditions, poisoning is conceivable only by way of the lungs, when breathing in poisonous gases via the esophagus or the skin. However, one of the well-preserved bodies was wearing an oxygen mask. The oxygen tank was still half full and would have lasted for several more hours."

That's right, thought Rohan. He remembered the man, the tight skin around his skull, the brownish spots on his cheekbones, the eye sockets filled with sand.

"These people could not have eaten anything poisonous, simply because there is nothing edible to be found. At least not on land. And they never got as far as the ocean. The catastrophe occurred shortly after landing. They had sent out only one scouting troop into the interior of the ruins. That was all. But here comes McQuinn. Are you through, McQuinn?"

"Yes, I am through," answered the biochemist from the door.

All heads turned around. He made his way through the rows of chairs and remained standing next to Nygren. He was still wearing his lab coat and a rubber apron.

"Do you have the results of the analysis?"

"Yes."

"Dr. McQuinn has examined the corpse we found in the hibernator," explained Nygren. "Will you tell us what you have found out?"

"Nothing," replied McQuinn. His hair was so light that it was difficult to know whether it was blond or gray. His eyes were just as pale. Even his eyelids were covered with freckles. But right now his big horsey face did not strike anyone as funny.

"No organic or inorganic poisons. All enzyme values normal. Nothing abnormal detected in the blood. The stomach contents were some half-digested zwieback and food concentrate."

"But how did he die?"

"He just froze to death," answered McQuinn. He noticed that he still had on his rubber apron. He untied the strings and threw the apron over the back of the chair before him. The slippery material slid off the chair onto the floor.

"What is your opinion, gentlemen?" the astrogator asked. He would not let go so easily.

"No opinion," countered McQuinn. "All I can say for sure is that these people were not the victims of some poisoning."

"How about radioactivity, some substance with a very brief half-life? Or hot radiation?"

"Hot radiation in fatal doses leaves traces such as damaged capillary walls, petecchiae, changes in the blood. There are no such changes. No radioactive substance in a fatal dose would completely vanish within eight years. There is less radioactivity here than we have on Earth. These men were not exposed to any type of radiation. I could swear to that."

"But something must have killed them," insisted Ballmin, the planetologist, raising his voice.

McQuinn did not speak. Nygren whispered into his ear. The biochemist nodded his head in affirmation, walked out of the room. Nygren stepped from the podium and sat down in his usual seat among his colleagues.

"That's not too encouraging," remarked the astrogator. "Apparently we can't expect much help from the biologists. Would someone else express an opinion?"

"Allow me." Sarner, the nuclear physicist, rose from his chair. "We might find a clue to what brought about this catastrophe in the very condition of the ship itself," he began, letting his eyes run slowly along the row of his seated colleagues. He had big farsighted bird's eyes whose irises looked almost pale next to his pitchblack hair. "That means there is an explanation somewhere that we can't perceive at this moment. The chaos in the cabins, the untouched provisions, the condition and location of the dead bodies, the damaged installations—all this must mean something."

"Is that all you have to say about it?" interjected Gaarb angrily.

"Take it easy. We're still completely in the dark, and the first thing we have to do is find the right approach to this problem. I believe we lack the courage to call some of the things we observed on board the *Condor* by their right name. This is why we cling so desperately to the hypothesis of some mysterious poisoning which resulted in mass insanity. Just remember, it is necessary, for our own sake as well as for that of the dead crew of the *Condor,* to face the facts with an open mind. I'd like to urge you—in fact, I insist— that we all speak out freely: what was it that shocked you most when you were at the *Condor?* Something that you have not been able to confide to anybody yet, something so horrible you'd rather forget than even mention it—"

Sarner sat down. Rohan overcame his inner resistance and told about the soap bars he had noticed in the bathroom.

Then Gralew got up. Underneath the stacks of torn maps and books the whole deck had been strewn with dried human excrement.

Another spoke of a can of food that showed impressions of teeth, as if someone had tried to bite through the metal. Gaarb had been deeply shaken by the scrawls in the log book and the entry about the flies. But he did not stop there.

"Let's assume a cloud of poisonous gas escaped from the tectonic vault inside the city. Couldn't the wind have carried this poisonous air to the rocket? If they'd been careless, hadn't closed the air hatch properly—"

"Only the outer hatch was not properly closed, Gaarb. We know that from the sand accumulated inside the airlock. The inner hatch was tightly shut, remember?"

"They might have closed it later on, when they were already feeling the effects of the poison gas."

"That is impossible, Gaarb. If the outside hatch isn't locked, you can't open the inside hatch. The two never open at the same time. The possibility of carelessness or accident is totally ruled out."

"In any event, one thing is clear: it must have happened suddenly. Mass insanity—look, I won't pretend we never see cases of psychosis during space flights, but never on a planet, especially not a few hours after touchdown. Mass insanity that gripped the entire crew could only be the result of some kind of poisoning."

"Or infantilism," remarked Sarner.

"What? What did you say?" Gaarb was dumbfounded. "Is that supposed to be a joke?"

"I'd hardly be joking in a situation like this. I said infantilism. No one else seems to have thought of it, despite the childish scribbles in the log book, despite the star almanacs that were ripped to pieces, despite the painstakingly drawn letters. You've all seen them, haven't you?"

"But so what?" said Nygren. "Are you trying to say that's a disease?"

"No. Not a disease. You are right there, doctor."

Once again they all fell silent. The astrogator hesitated.

"We might be on the wrong track. The results of necroscopy are always uncertain. But for the moment I can't see what harm it would do. Doctor Sax—"

The neurophysiologist described the image they had found in the brain of the frozen man in the hibernator; he also mentioned the syllables in the acoustics memory bank of the dead man. A veritable flood of questions followed. Even Rohan was cross-examined by his colleagues, since he had been present during the experiment. Still, no conclusion could be drawn.

"When you speak of tiny black spots, doesn't that remind you somehow of the word 'flies'?" said Gaarb. "Wait a minute. Maybe the cause of death was something else. Maybe the whole crew was attacked by poisonous insects. You can't recognize insect bites on mummified skin. And the fellow in the hibernator was simply trying to escape from the insects that got his friends—and then froze to death."

"But how would you account for his total loss of memory before death?"

"Total amnesia? Are you sure that diagnosis is correct?"

"Yes, as far as we can generally rely on the results of a necroscopic examination."

"What do you think about this poisonous insect theory?"

"Let's hear what Lauda has to say about that."

Lauda was the chief paleobiologist on board. He stood up and waited until they had calmed down.

"It isn't simply by accident that we haven't brought up the matter of these 'flies.' Anyone who understands anything about biology knows that outside a certain biotope—in other words, a higher unit composed of environment and all species occurring in it—no organism can exist. This holds true for every corner of the universe we have explored thus far. Life either creates a large variety of forms or none at all. Thus no insects could develop without simultaneous development of plants on the dry land, or other symmetrical non-vertebrates. I don't intend to give you a lecture on evolution; I trust it will suffice if I assure you that there cannot possibly be any flies here. Or any other arthropods, for that matter—no hymenoptera or spiders. There aren't any related forms, either."

"How can you be so sure about that" demanded Ballmin.

"If you were one of my students, you wouldn't be here with us now," said the paleobiologist drily. "You would never have passed the exam." The others smiled involuntarily. "Naturally I can't judge your knowledge in the field of planetology, but I'd give you an F in the biology of evolution."

"Typical shop talk. What a waste of time," someone whispered behind Rohan. Rohan turned around and looked into Jarg's tanned, broad face winking at him.

"Maybe the insects didn't evolve here," insisted Ballmin. "Maybe they were brought in from the outside."

"From where?"

"From the planets of the Nova."

Now the whole group began to talk at once; it took a long time before order was restored."

"Colleagues," said Sarner. "I know where Ballmin got his idea. From Dr. Gralew."

"Well, I won't deny it," admitted the physicist.

"Excellent. Let us assume we can no longer afford the luxury of plausible hypotheses and need some really wild ones. That's all right with me. My dear colleagues and fellow biologists, suppose a spaceship had imported insects from a planet of the Nova into Regis III. Could these insects have adapted to local conditions?"

"Of course, if we want to get into wild hypotheses," admitted Lauda. "But even wild hypotheses have to be able to supply explanations for everything."

"Such as what?"

"Such as an explantion as to what corroded the outer armor plate hull of the Condor to such an extent that the ship can no longer take off unless it's completely overhauled. Do you really believe some insects could adapt to a diet of molybdenum alloy? That's one of the hardest substances in the whole universe. Engineer Petersen, tell us, what could destroy this type of armored plate?"

"If it's been properly tempered, nothing I know of," answered the deputy chief engineer. "You could drill into it with diamonds, but you would need a ton of diamonds and a thousand hours at your disposal. Another possibility would be acids. Anorganic acids, of course, and only at temperatures of at least two thousand degrees and with the proper catalysts."

Then how do you explain what corroded the armored plate of the *Condor?*"

"I haven't the faintest idea. If the ship had been immersed in an acid solution, and at the proper temperature, it would look like that, all right. But how anyone could get the same results without arc-light plasma burners and catalysts is beyond me."

"Well, so much for your flies, my dear Ballmin," said Lauda and sat down.

"There is no sense in continuing this discussion any longer," remarked the astrogator, who had remained silent until now. "Perhaps it was too soon for such a debate. All we can do now is carry on with our examinations. We'll split up in three groups. One will explore the ruins, another the *Condor,* and the third will make forays into the interior of the western desert. That's stretching our forces as far as they will go; I simply can't remove more than fourteen energo-robots from our perimeter here, even counting some machines we might take from the *Condor.* Third step routine procedure is still in force, of course!"

From *Solaris*

Genius and mediocrity alike are dumbfounded by the teeming diversity of the oceanic formations of Solaris; no man has ever become genuinely conversant with them. Giese was by no means a mediocrity, nor was he a genius. He was a scholarly classifier, the type whose compulsive application to their work utterly divorces them from the pressures of everyday life. Giese devised a plain descriptive terminology, supplemented by terms of his own invention, and although these were inadequate, and sometimes clumsy, it has to be admitted that no semantic system is as yet available to illustrate the behavior of the ocean. The 'tree-mountains,' 'extensors,' 'fungoids,' 'mimoids,' 'symmetriads' and 'asymmetriads,' 'vertebrids' and 'agilus' are artificial, linguistically awkward terms, but they do give some impression of Solaris to anyone who has only seen the planet in blurred photographs and incomplete films. The fact is that in spite of his cautious nature the scrupulous Giese more than once jumped to premature conclusions. Even when on their guard, human beings inevitably theorize. Giese, who thought himself immune to temptation, decided that the 'extensors' came into the category of basic forms. He compared them to accumulations of gigantic waves, similar to the tidal movements of our Terran oceans. In the first edition of his work, we find them originally named as 'tides.' This geocentrism might be considered amusing if it did not underline the dilemma in which he found himself.

As soon as the question of comparisons with Earth arises, it must be understood that the 'extensors' are formations that dwarf the Grand Canyon, that they are produced in a substance which externally resembles a yeasty colloid (during this fantastic 'fermentation,' the yeast sets into festoons of starched open-work lace; some experts refer to 'ossified tumors'), and that deeper down the substance becomes increasingly resistant, like a tensed muscle which fifty feet below the surface is as hard as rock but retains its flexibility. The 'extensor' appears to be an independent creation, stretching for miles between membranous walls swollen with 'ossified growths,' like some colossal python which after swallowing a mountain is sluggishly digesting the meal, while a slow shudder occasionally ripples along its creeping body. The 'extensor' only looks like a lethargic reptile from overhead. At close quarters, when the two 'canyon walls' loom hundreds of yards above the exploring aircraft, it can be seen that this inflated cylinder, reaching from one side of the horizon to the other, is bewilderingly alive with movement. First you notice the continual rotating motion of a greyish-green, oily sludge which reflects blinding sunlight, but skimming just above the 'back of the python' (the 'ravine' sheltering the 'extensor' now resembles the sides of a geological fault), you realize that the motion is in fact far more complex, and consists of concentric fluctuations traversed by darker currents. Occasionally this mantle turns into a shining crust that reflects sky and clouds and then is riddled by explosive eruptions of the internal gases and fluids. The observer slowly realizes that he is looking at the guiding forces that are thrusting outward and upward the two gradually crystallizing gelatinous walls. Science does not accept the obvious without further proof, however, and virulent controversies have reverberated down the years on the key question of the exact sequence of events in the interior of the 'extensors' that furrow the vast living ocean in their millions.

Various organic functions have been ascribed to the 'extensors.' Some experts have argued that their purpose is the transformation of matter; others suggested respiratory processes; still others claimed that they conveyed alimentary materials. An infinite variety of hypotheses now moulder in library basements, eliminated by ingenious, sometimes dangerous experiments. Today, the scientists will go no further than to refer to the 'extensors' as relatively simple, stable formations whose duration is measurable in weeks—an exceptional characteristic among the recorded phenomena of the planet.

The 'mimoid' formations are considerably more complex and bizarre, and elicit a more vehement response from the observer, an instinctive response, I mean. It can be stated without exaggeration that Giese fell in love with the 'mimoids' and was soon devoting all his time to them. For the rest of his life, he studied and described them and brought all his ingenuity to bear on defining their nature. The name he gave them indicates their most astonishing characteristic, the imitation of objects, near or far, external to the ocean itself.

Concealed at first beneath the ocean surface, a large flattened disc appears, ragged, with a tar-like coating. After a few hours, it begins to separate into flat sheets which rise slowly. The observer now becomes a spectator at what looks like a fight to the death, as massed ranks of waves converge from all directions like contorted, fleshy mouths which snap greedily around the tattered, fluttering leaf, then plunge into the depths. As each ring of waves breaks and sinks, the fall of this mass of hundreds of thousands of tons is accompanied for an instant by a viscous rumbling, an immense thunderclap. The tarry leaf is overwhelmed, battered and torn apart; with every fresh assault, circular fragments scatter and drift like feebly fluttering wings below the ocean surface. They bunch into pear-shaped clusters or long strings, merge and rise again, and drag with them an undertow of coagulated shreds of the base of the primal disc. The encircling waves continue to break around the steadily expanding crater. This phenomenon may persist for a day or linger on for a month, and sometimes there are no further developments. The conscientious Giese dubbed this first variation a 'stillbirth,' convinced that each of these upheavals aspired towards an ultimate condition, the 'major mimoid,' like a polyp colony (only covering an area greater than a town) of pale outcroppings with the faculty of imitating foreign bodies. Uyvens, on the other hand, saw this final stage as constituting a degeneration or necrosis: according to him, the appearance of the 'copies' corresponded to a localized dissipation of the life energies of the ocean, which was no longer in control of the original forms it created.

Giese would not abandon his account of the various phases of the process as a sustained progression towards perfection, with a conviction which is particularly surprising coming from a man of such a moderate, cautious turn of mind in advancing the most trivial hypothesis on the other creations of the ocean. Normally he had all the boldness of an ant crawling up a glacier.

Viewed from above, the mimoid resembles a town, an illusion produced by our compulsion to superimpose analogies with what we know. When the sky is clear, a shimmering heat-haze covers the pliant structures of the clustered polyps surmounted by membranous palisades. The first cloud passing overhead wakens the mimoid. All the outcrops suddenly sprout new shoots, then the mass of polyps ejects a thick tegument which dilates, puffs out, changes color and in the space of a few minutes has produced an astonishing imitation of the volutes of a cloud. The enormous 'object' casts a reddish shadow over the mimoid, whose peaks ripple and bend together, always in the oposite direction to the movement of the real cloud. I imagine that Giese would have been ready to give his right hand to discover what made the mimoids behave in this way, but these 'isolated' productions are nothing in comparison to the frantic activity the mimoid displays when 'stimulated' by objects of human origin.

The reproduction process embraces every object inside a radius of eight or nine miles. Usually the facsimile is an enlargement of the original, whose forms are sometimes only roughly copied. The reproduction of machines, in particular, elicits simplifications that might be considered grotesque—practically caricatures. The copy is always modelled in the same colorless tegument, which hovers above the outcrops, linked to its base by flimsy umbilical cords; it slides, creeps, curls back on itself, shrinks or swells and finally assumes the most complicated forms. An aircraft, a net or a pole are all reproduced at the same speed. The mimoid is not stimulated by human beings themselves, and in fact it does not react to any living matter, and has never copied, for example, the plants imported for experimental purposes. On the other hand, it will readily reproduce a puppet or a doll, a carving of a dog, or a tree sculpted in any material.

The observer must bear in mind that the 'obedience' of the mimoid does not constitute evidence of cooperation, since it is not consistent. The most highly evolved mimoid has its off-days, when it 'lives' in slow-motion, or its pulsation weakens. (This pulsation is invisible to the naked eye, and was only discovered after close examination of rapid-motion film of the mimoid, which revealed that each 'beat' took two hours.)

During these 'off-days,' it is easy to explore the mimoid, especially if it is old, for the base anchored in the ocean, like the protuberances growing out of it, is relatively solid, and provides a firm footing for a man. It is equally possible to remain inside the mimoid during periods of activity, except that visibility is close to nil because of the whitish colloidal dust continually emitted through tears in the tegument above. In any case, at close range it is impossible to distinguish what forms the tegument is assuming, on account of their vast size—the smallest 'copy' is the size of a mountain. In addition, a thick layer of colloidal snow quickly covers the base of the mimoid: this spongy carpet takes several hours to solidify (the 'frozen' crust will take the weight of a man, though its composition is much lighter than pumice stone). The problem is that without special equipment there is a risk of being lost in the maze of tangled structures and crevasses, sometimes reminiscent of jumbled colonnades, sometimes of petrified geysers. Even in daylight it is easy to lose one's direction, for the sun's rays cannot pierce the white ceiling ejected into the atmostphere by the 'imitative explosions.'

On gala days (for the scientist as well as for the mimoid), an unforgettable spectacle develops as the mimoid goes into hyperproduction and performs wild flights of fancy. It plays variations on the theme of a given object and embroiders 'formal extensions' that amuse it for hours on end, to the delight of the non-figurative artist and the despair of the scientist, who is at a loss to grasp any common theme in the performance. The mimoid can produce 'primitive' simplifications, but is just as likely to indulge in 'baroque' deviations, paroxysms of extravagant brilliance. Old mimoids tend to manufacture extremely comic forms. Looking at the photographs, I have never been moved to laughter; the riddle they set is too disquieting to be funny.

During the early years of exploration, the scientists literally threw themselves upon the mimoids, which were spoken of as open windows on the ocean and the best opportunity to

establish the hoped-for contact between the two civiliza-
tions. They were soon forced to admit that there was not the
slightest prospect of communication, and that the entire process began and ended with the reproduction of forms. The
mimoids were a dead end.

Giving way to the temptations of a latent anthropomor-
phism or zoomorphism, there were many schools of thought
which saw various other oceanic formations as 'sensory
organs,' even as 'limbs,' which was how experts like Maar-
tens and Ekkonai classified Giese's 'vertebrids' and 'agilus'
for a time. Anyone who is rash enough to see protuberances
that reach as far as two miles into the atmosphere as limbs,
might just as well claim that earthquakes are the gymnastics
of the Earth's crust!

Three hundred chapters of Giese catalogue the standard
formations which occur on the surface of the living ocean
and which can be seen in dozens, even hundreds, in the
course of any day. The symmetriads—to continue using the
terminology and definitions of the Giese school—are the
least 'human' formations, which is to say that they bear no
resemblance whatsoever to anything on Earth. By the time
the symmetriads were being investigated, it was already
clear that the ocean was not aggressive, and that its plasmatic eddies would not swallow any but the most foolhardy
explorer (of course I am not including accidents resulting
from mechanical failures). It is possible to fly in complete
safety from one part to another of the cylindrical body of
an extensor, or of the vertebrids, Jacob's ladders oscillating
among the clouds: the plasma retreats at the speed of sound
in the planet's atmosphere to make way for any foreign
body. Deep funnels will open even beneath the surface of
the ocean (at a prodigious expenditure of energy, calculated
by Scriabin at around 10^{19} ergs). Nevertheless the first ven-
ture into the interior of a symmetriad was undertaken with
the utmost caution and discipline, and involved a host of

what turned out to be unnecessary safety measures. Every schoolboy on Earth knows of these pioneers.

It is not their nightmare appearance that makes the gigantic symmetriad formations dangerous, but the total instability and capriciousness of their structure, in which even the laws of physics do not hold. The theory that the living ocean is endowed with intelligence has found its firmest adherents among those scientists who have ventured into their unpredictable depths.

The birth of a symmetriad comes like a sudden eruption. About an hour beforehand, an area of tens of square miles of ocean vitrifies and begins to shine. It remains fluid, and there is no alteration in the rhythm of the waves. Occasionally the phenomenon of vitrification occurs in the neighbourhood of the funnel left by an agilus. The gleaming sheath of the ocean heaves upwards to form a vast ball that reflects sky, sun, clouds and the entire horizon in a medley of changing, variegated images. Diffracted light creates a kaleidoscopic play of color.

The effects of light on a symmetriad are especially striking during the blue day and the red sunset. The planet appears to be giving birth to a twin that increases in volume from one moment to the next. The immense flaming globe has scarcely reached its maximum expansion above the ocean when it bursts at the summit and cracks vertically. It is not breaking up; this is the second phase, which goes under the clumsy name of the 'floral calyx phase' and lasts only a few seconds. The membranous arches soaring into the sky now fold inwards and merge to produce a thick-set trunk enclosing a scene of teeming activity. At the center of the trunk, which was explored for the first time by the seventy-man Hamalei expedition, a process of polycrystallization on a giant scale erects an axis commonly referred to as the 'backbone,' a term which I consider ill-chosen. The mind-bending architecture of this central pillar is held in place by vertical shafts of a gelatinous, almost liquid consistency, constantly gushing upwards out of wide crevasses. Meanwhile, the entire trunk is surrounded by a belt of snow foam, seething with great bubbles of gas, and the whole process is accompanied by a perpetual dull roar of sound. From the center towards the periphery, powerful buttresses spin out and are coated with streams of ductile matter rising out of the ocean depths. Simultaneously the gelatinous geysers are converted into mobile columns that proceed to extrude tendrils that reach out in clusters towards points rigorously predetermined by the over-all dynamics of the entire structure: they call to mind the gills of an embryo, except that they are revolving at fantastic speed and ooze trickles of pinkish 'blood' and a dark green secretion.

The symmetriad now begins to display its most exotic characteristic—the property of 'illustrating,' sometimes contradicting, various laws of physics. (Bear in mind that no two symmetriads are alike, and that the geometry of each one is a unique 'invention' of the living ocean.) The interior of the symmetriad becomes a factory for the production of 'monumental machines,' as these constructs are sometimes called, although they resemble no machine which it is within the power of mankind to build: the designation is applied because all this activity has finite ends, and is therefore in some sense 'mechanical.'

When the geysers of oceanic matter have solidified into pillars or into three-dimensional networks of galleries and passages, and the 'membranes' are set into an inextricable pattern of storeys, panels and vaults, the symmetriad justifies its name, for the entire structure is divided into two segments, each mirroring the other to the most infinitesimal detail.

After twenty or thirty minutes, when the axis may have tilted as much as eight to ten degrees from the horizontal, the giant begins slowly to subside. (Symmetriads vary in size, but as the base begins to submerge even the smallest reach a height of half a mile, and are visible from miles away.) At last, the structure stabilizes itself, and the partly submerged symmetriad ceases its activity. It is now possible to explore it in complete safety by making an entry near the summit, through one of the many syphons which emerge from the dome. The completed symmetriad represents a spatial analogue of some transcendental equation.

It is a commonplace that any equation can be expressed in the figurative language of non-Euclidean geometry and represented in three dimensions. This interpretation relates the symmetriad to Lobachevsky's cones and Riemann's negative curves, although its unimaginable complexity makes the relationship highly tenuous. The eventual form occupies an area of several cubic miles and extends far beyond our whole system of mathematics. In addition, this extension is four-dimensional, for the fundamental terms of the equations use a temporal symbolism expressed in the internal changes over a given period.

It would be only natural, clearly, to suppose that the symmetriad is a 'computer' of the living ocean, performing calculations for a purpose that we are not able to grasp. This was Fremont's theory, now generally discounted. The hypothesis was a tempting one, but it proved impossible to sustain the concept that the living ocean examined problems of matter, the cosmos and existence through the medium of titanic eruptions, in which every particle had an indispensable function as a controlled element in an analytical system of infinite purity. In fact, numerous phenomena contradict this over-simplified (some say childishly naïve) concept.

Any number of attempts have been made to transpose and 'illustrate' the symmetriad, and Averian's demonstration was particularly well received. Let us imagine, he said, an edifice dating from the great days of Babylon, but built of some living, sensitive substance with the capacity to evolve:

the architectonics of this edifice pass through a series of phases, and we see it adopt the forms of a Greek, then of a Roman building. The columns sprout like branches and become narrower, the roof grows lighter, rises, curves, the arch describes an abrupt parabola then breaks down into an arrow shape: the Gothic is born, comes to maturity and gives way in time to new forms. Austerity of line gives way to a riot of exploding lines and shapes, and the Baroque runs wild. If the progression continues—and the successive mutations are to be seen as stages in the life of an evolving organism—we finally arrive at the architecture of the space age, and perhaps too at some understanding of the symmetriad.

Unfortunately, no matter how this demonstration may be expanded and improved (there have been attempts to visualize it with the aid of models and films), the comparison remains superficial. It is evasive and illusory, and side-steps the central fact that the symmetriad is quite unlike anything Earth has ever produced.

The human mind is only capable of absorbing a few things at a time. We see what is taking place in front of us in the here and now, and cannot envisage simultaneously a succession of processes, no matter how integrated and complementary. Our faculties of perception are consequently limited even as regards fairly simple phenomena. The fate of a single man can be rich with significance, that of a few hundred less so, but the history of thousands and millions of men does not mean anything at all, in any adequate sense of the word. The symmetriad is a million—a billion, rather—raised to the power of N: it is incomprehensible. We pass through vast halls, each with a capacity of ten Kronecker units, and creep like so many ants clinging to the folds of breathing vaults and craning to watch the flight of soaring girders, opalescent in the glare of searchlights, and elastic domes which criss-cross and balance each other unerringly, the perfection of a moment, since everything here passes and fades. The essence of this architecture is movement synchronized towards a precise objective. We observe a fraction of the process, like hearing the vibration of a single string in an orchestra of supergiants. We know, but cannot grasp, that above and below, beyond the limits of perception or imagination, thousands and millions of simultaneous transformations are at work, interlinked like a musical score by mathematical counterpoint. It has been described as a symphony in geometry, but we lack the ears to hear it.

Only a long-distance view would reveal the entire process, but the outer covering of the symmetriad conceals the colossal inner matrix where creation in unceasing, the created becomes the creator, and absolutely identical 'twins' are born at opposite poles, separated by towering structures and miles of distance. The symphony creates itself, and writes its own conclusion, which is terrible to watch. Every observer feels like a spectator at a tragedy of a public massacre, when after two or three hours—never longer—the living ocean stages its assault. The polished surface of the ocean swirls and crumples, the desiccated foam liquefies again, begins to seethe, and legions of waves pour inwards from every point of the horizon, their gaping mouths far more massive than the greedy lips that surround the embryonic mimoid. The submerged base of the symmetriad is compressed, and the colossus rises as if on the point of being shot out of the planet's gravitational pull. The upper layers of the ocean redouble their activity, and the waves surge higher and higher to lick against the sides of the symmetriad. They envelop it, harden and plug the orifices, but their attack is nothing compared to the scene in the interior. First the process of creation freezes momentarily; then there is 'panic.' The smooth interpenetration of moving forms and the harmonious play of planes and lines accelerates, and the impression is inescapable that the symmetriad is hurrying to complete some task in the face of danger. The awe inspired by the metamorphosis and dynamics of the symmetriad intensifies as the proud sweep of the domes falters, vaults sag and droop, and 'wrong notes'—incomplete, mangled forms— make their appearance. A powerful moaning roar issues from the invisible depths like a sigh of agony, reverberates through the narrow funnels and booms through the collapsing domes. In spite of the growing destructive violence of these convulsions, the spectator is rooted to the spot. Only the force of the hurricane streaming out of the depths and howling through the thousands of galleries keeps the great structure erect. Soon it subsides and starts to disintegrate. There are final flutterings, contortions, and blind, random spasms. Gnawed and undermined, the giant sinks slowly and disappears, and the space where it stood is covered with whirlpools of foam.

So what does all this mean?

I remembered an incident dating from my spell as assistant to Gibarian. A group of schoolchildren visiting the Solarist Institute in Aden were making their way through the main hall of the library and looking at the racks of microfilm that occupied the entire left-hand side of the hall. The guide explained that among other phenomena immortalized by the image, these contained fragmentary glimpses of symmetriads long since vanished—not single shots, but whole reels, more than ninety thousand of them!

One plump schoolgirl (she looked about fifteen, peering inquisitively over her spectacles) abruptly asked: "And what is it for?"

In the ensuing embarrassed silence, the school mistress was content to dart a reproving look at her wayward pupil. Among the Solarists whose job was to act as guides (I was one of them), no one would produce an answer. Each symmetriad is unique, and the developments in its heart are, generally speaking, unpredictable. Sometimes there is no sound. Sometimes the index of refraction increases or diminishes. Sometimes, rhythmic pulsations are accompanied by local changes in gravitation, as if the heart of the symmetriad were beating by gravitating. Sometimes the compasses of the observers spin wildly, and ionized layers spring up and disappear. The catalogue could go on indefinitely. In any case, even if we did ever succeed in solving the riddle of the symmetriads, we would still have to contend with the asymmetriads!

The asymmetriads are born in the same manner as the symmetriads but finish differently, and nothing can be seen of their internal processes except tremors, vibrations and flickering. We do know, however, that the interior houses bewildering operations performed at a speed that defies the laws of physics and which are dubbed 'giant quantic phenomena.' The mathematical analogy with certain three-dimensional models of the atom is so unstable and transitory that some commentators dismiss the resemblance as of secondary importance, if not purely accidental. The asymmetriads have a very short life-span of fifteen to twenty minutes, and their death is even more appalling that that of the symmetriads: with the howling gale that screams through its fabric, a thick fluid gushes out, gurgles hideously, and submerges everything beneath a foul, bubbling foam. Then an explosion, coinciding with a muddy eruption, hurls up a spout of debris which rains slowly down into the seething ocean. This debris is sometimes found scores of miles from the focus of the explosion, dried up, yellow and flattened, like flakes of cartilage.

Some other creations of the ocean, which are much more rare and of very variable duration, part company with the parent body entirely. The first traces of these 'independents' were identified—wrongly, it was later proved—as the remains of creatures inhabiting the ocean deeps. The free-ranging forms are often reminiscent of many-winged birds, darting away from the moving trunks of the agilus, but the preconceptions of Earth offer no assistance in unravelling the mysteries of Solaris. Strange, seal-like bodies appear now and then on the rocky outcrop of an island, sprawling in the sun or dragging themselves lazily back to merge with the ocean.

There was no escaping the impressions that grew out of man's experience on Earth. The prospects of Contact receded.

Explorers travelled hundreds of miles in the depths of symmetriads, and installed measuring instruments and remote-control cameras. Artificial satellites captured the birth of mimoids and extensors, and faithfully reproduced their images of growth and destruction. The libraries overflowed, the archives grew, and the price paid for all this documentation was often very heavy. One notorious disaster cost one hundred and six people their lives, among them Giese himself: while studying what was undoubtedly a symmetriad, the expedition was suddenly destroyed by a process peculiar to the asymmetriads. In two seconds, an eruption of glutinous mud swallowed up seventy-nine men and all their equipment. Another twenty-seven observers surveying the area from aircraft and helicopters were also caught in the eruption.

Following the Eruption of the Hundred and Six, and for the first time in Solarist studies, there were petitions demanding a thermo-nuclear attack on the ocean. Such a response would have been more cruelty than revenge, since it would have meant destroying what we did not understand. Tsanken's ultimatum, which was never officially acknowledged, probably influenced the negative outcome of the vote. He was in command of Giese's reserve term, and had survived owing to a transmission error that took him off his course, to arrive in the disaster area a few minutes after the explosion, when the black mushroom cloud was still visible.

Informed of the proposal for a nuclear strike, he threatened to blow up the Station, together with the nineteen survivors sheltering inside it.

Today, there are only three of us on the Station. Its construction was controlled by satellites, and was a technical feat on which the human race has a right to pride itself, even if the ocean builds far more impressive structures in the space of a few seconds. The Station is a disc of one hundred yards radius, and contains four decks at the center and two at the circumference. It is maintained at a height of from five to fifteen hundred yards above the ocean by gravitors programmed to compensate for the ocean's own field of attraction. In addition to all the machines available to ordinary Stations and the large artificial satellites that orbit other planets, the Solaris Station is equipped with specialized radar apparatus sensitive to the smallest fluctuations of the ocean surface, which trips auxiliary power-circuits capable of thrusting the steel disc into the stratosphere at the first indication of new plasmatic upheavals.

Ordeal by Space

One expects that spaceship pilots in science-fiction stories will be active. Active physically, at least—but in the ideal case, active in mind as well as in body. What is the point, after all, of setting a tale in the future, in outer space, or on another planet, if there are to be neither bug-eyed monsters nor cosmic maelstroms, difficulties, in other words, that require brains, quick reflexes, and an occasional zap from a blaster?

One expects, when reading science fiction, events, and a hero who is a hero.

What of Lem's heroes? They appear to be tough enough; able to take punishment with a stiff upper lip; showing courage, facing danger when necessary, making decisions. They are not your modern-day anti-hero type who shilly-shallies, soul-searches, apologizes, whines, and is generally stepped on and humiliated by Life.

But what actually do they *do,* Lem's heroes? What does Pirx, for example, accomplish in the way of action in the many stories that feature him? Well, not much. He is not even particularly effective as a sleuth. He is *there.* A witness of what transpires—of accidents, malfunctions, crimes, deaths.

A witness, though, not a mere narrator. To be a witness, sometimes, is no contemptible or easy thing. Passive Pirx may be, but impassive never. He has a way of seeing what others do not. He perceives. He has a civilized heart.

Lem's space adventures are essentially adventures of conscience. The destination of the interplanetary/interstellar flight turns out to be not the awesome technology and not the awesomeness of things extraterrestrial, but, very simply, man. Ourselves.

But ourselves in the most prosaic, uninflated way—without grand phrases or noble gestures. Pirx, who is as ordinary and devoid of glamor as toothpaste, can't abide bombast or theatrics. He provides, therefore, a touchstone of normalcy. So that we are not led astray by the various hysterical-heroical myth/clichés— about heroes, space, robots, and so on—that unfortunately rule the world.

The Test

☆

"Cadet Pirx!"

Bullpen's voice snapped him out of his daydreaming. He had just had visions of a two-crown piece lying tucked away in the fob pocket of his old civvies, the ones stashed at the bottom of his locker. A jingling, shiny silver coin—all but forgotten. A while ago he could have sworn nothing was there, an old mailing stub at best, but the more he thought about it, the more plausible it seemed that one might be there, so that by the time Bullpen called out his name, he was absolutely sure of it. The coin was now sufficiently real that he could feel it bulging in his pocket, so round and sleek to the touch. There was his ticket to the movies, he thought, with half a crown to spare. And if he settled for some newsreel shorts, that would leave a crown and a half, of which he'd squirrel away a crown and the rest blow on the slot machines. Oh, what if the machine suddenly went haywire and coughed up so many coins into his waiting hands that he couldn't stuff his pockets fast enough . . . ? Well, why not—it happened to Smiga, didn't it? He was already reeling under the burden of his unexpected windfall when Bullpen roused him with a bang.

Folding his hands behind his back and shifting his weight to his good leg, his instructor asked:

"Cadet Pirx, what would you do if you were on patrol and encountered a ship from an alien planet?"

Pirx opened his mouth wide, as if the answer were there and all he had to do was to force it out. He looked like the last person on Earth who knew what to do when meeting up with a vessel from an alien planet.

"I would maneuver closer," he answered, his voice muted and strangely hoarse.

The class froze in welcome anticipation of some comic relief.

"Very good," Bullpen said in a fatherly sort of way. "*Then* what would you do?"

"I would stop," Pirx blurted out, sensing that he was drifting off into realms that lay vastly beyond his competence. Furiously he racked his empty brains in search of the appropriate paragraphs from his Space Manual, but it was as if he had never laid eyes on it. Sheepishly he lowered his gaze, and as he did so, he noticed that Smiga was trying to prompt him—with his lips only. One by one he deciphered Smiga's words and repeated them out loud, before he had a chance to fully digest them.

"I'd introduce myself."

A howl went up from the class. Bullpen struggled for a moment; then he, too, exploded with laughter, only to assume a serious expression again.

"Cadet Pirx, you will report to me tomorrow with your navigation book. Cadet Boerst!"

Pirx sat down at his desk as if it were made of uncongealed glass. He wasn't even sore at Smiga—that's the kind of guy he was, always good for a gag. He didn't catch a word of what Boerst was saying; Boerst was trying to plot a graph while Bullpen was up to his old trick of turning down the electronic computer, leaving the cadet to get bogged down in his computations. School regs permitted the use of a computer, but Bullpen was of a different mind. "A computer

is only human," he used to say. "It, too, can break down."
Pirx wasn't sore at Bullpen, either. Fact is, he wasn't sore at
anyone. Hardly ever. Five minutes later he was standing in
front of a shopwindow on Dyerhoff Street, his attention
caught by a display of gas pistols, good for firing blanks or
live ammo, a set consisting of one pistol and a hundred car-
tridges priced at six crowns. Needless to say, he only imagined he was window-browsing on Dyerhoff Street.

The bell rang and the class emptied, but without all that
yelling and stampeding of lowerclassmen. No sir, these
weren't kids anymore! Half of the class meandered off in the
direction of the cafeteria because, although no meals were
being served at that time, there were other attractions to be
had—a new waitress, for example (word had it she was a
knockout). Pirx strolled leisurely past the glass cabinets
where the stellar globes were stored, and with every step saw
his hopes of finding a two-crown piece in the pocket of his
civvies dwindle a little more. By the time he reached the
bottom of the staircase, he realized the coin was just a figment of his imagination.

Hanging around the lobby were Boerst, Smiga, and
Payartz. For a semester he and Payartz had been deskmates
in cosmodesy, and he had him to thank for all the ink blots
in his star atlas.

"You're up for a trial run tomorrow," Boerst let drop just
as Pirx was about to overtake them.

"No sweat," came his lackadaisical reply. He was nobody's fool.

"Don't believe me? Read for yourself," said Boerst, tap-
ping his finger on the glass pane of the bulletin board.

He had a mind to keep going, but his head involuntarily
twisted around on its axis. The list showed only three
names—and there it was, right at the top, as big as blazes:
Cadet Pirx.

For a second, his mind was a total blank.

Then he heard a distant voice, which turned out to be his own.

"Like I said, no sweat."

Leaving them, he headed down a walkway lined with flower beds. That year the beds were planted with forget-me-nots, artfully arranged in the pattern of a descending rocket ship, with streaks of now faded buttercups suggesting the exhaust flare. But right now Pirx was oblivious of everything—the flower beds, the pathway, the forget-me-nots, and even of Bullpen, who at that very instant was hurriedly ducking out of the Institute by a side entrance, and whom he narrowly missed bumping into on his way out. Pirx saluted as they stood cheek to jowl.

"Oh, it's you, Pirx!" said Bullpen. "You're flying tomorrow, aren't you? Well, have a good takeoff! Maybe you'll be lucky enough to . . . er . . . meet up with those people from alien planets."

The dormitory was situated behind a wall of sprawling weeping willows on the far side of the park. It stood overlooking a pond, and its side wings, buttressed by stone columns, towered above the water. The columns were rumored to have been shipped back from the Moon, which was blatant nonsense, of course, but that hadn't stopped the first-year students from carving their initials and class dates on them with an air of sacrosanct emotion. Pirx's name was likewise among them, four years having gone by since the day he had diligently inscribed it.

Once inside his room—it was too cramped to serve as anything but a single—he debated whether or not to open the locker. He knew exactly where his old pants were stashed. He had held on to them, despite the fact that it was against the rules—or maybe *because* of that—and even though he had hardly any use for them now. Closing his eyes, he crouched down, stuck his hand through the crack in the door, and gave the pocket a probing pat. Sure enough—empty.

He was standing in his unpressurized suit on the metal catwalk, just under the hangar ceiling, and, with neither hand free, was bracing himself against the cable railing with his elbow. In one hand he held his navigation book, in the other the cribsheet Smiga had lent him. The whole school was alleged to have flown with this pony, though how it managed to find its way back every time was a mystery, all the more so since, after completing the flight test, the cadets were immediately transferred from the Institute to the north, to the Base Camp, where they began cramming for their final exams. Still, the fact remained: it always came back. Some claimed that it was parachuted down. Facetiously, of course.

To kill time while he stood on the catwalk, suspended above a forty-meter drop, he wondered whether he would be frisked—sad to say, such things were still a common practice. The cadets were known for sneaking aboard the weirdest assortment of trinkets, including such strenuously forbidden things as whiskey flasks, chewing tobacco, and pictures of their girl friends. Not excluding cribsheets, of course. Pirx had already exhausted a dozen or so hiding places—in his shoes, between his stocking legs, in the inner pocket of his space suit, in the mini-atlas the cadets were allowed to take aboard. . . . An eyeglass case . . . now that would have done the trick, he thought, but, first of all, it would have had to be a fair-sized one, and secondly—he didn't wear glasses. A few seconds later it occurred to him that if he wore glasses he never would have been admitted to the Institute.

So Pirx stood on the metal catwalk and waited for the CO

to show up in the company of both instructors. What was keeping them? he wondered. Lift-off was scheduled for 1940 hours, and it was already 1927. Then it dawned on him that he might have taped the cribsheet under his arm, the way little Yerkes did. The story went that as soon as the flight instructor went to frisk him, Yerkes started squealing he was ticklish, and got away with it. But Pirx had no illusions; he didn't look like the ticklish type. And so, not having any adhesive tape with him, he went on holding the pony in his right hand, in the most casual way possible, and only when he realized that he would have to shake hands with all three did he switch, shifting the pony from his right to his left hand and the navigation book from left to right. While he was juggling things around, he managed to make the catwalk sway up and down like a diving board. Suddenly he heard footsteps approaching from the other end, but in the dark under the hangar ceiling it took him a while to make out who it was.

All three were looking very spiffy—as was customary on such occasions, they were decked out in full uniform—especially the CO. Even uninflated, however, Pirx's space suit looked as graceful as twenty football uniforms stuck together, not to mention the long intercom and radiophone terminals dangling from either side of his neck ring disconnect, the respirator hose bobbing up and down in the region of his throat, and the reserve oxygen bottle strapped tightly to his back—so tightly that it pinched. He felt hotter than blazes in his sweat-absorbent underwear, but most bothersome of all was the gadget making it unnecessary for him to get up to relieve himself—which, considering the sort of single-stage rockets used on such trial flights, would have posed something of a problem.

Suddenly the whole catwalk began to undulate as someone came up from behind. It was Boerst, suited up in the same, identical space suit, who gave him a stiff salute, mammoth glove and all, and who went on standing in this position as if just aching to knock Pirx overboard.

When the others had gone ahead, Pirx asked, somewhat bewilderedly:

"What're *you* doing here? Your name wasn't on the flight list."

"Brendan got sick. I'm taking his place."

Pirx was momentarily flustered. This was the one area—the one and only area—in which he was able to climb just a millimeter higher, to those empyreal realms that Boerst seemed to inhabit so effortlessly. Not only was he the brightest in the program, for which Pirx could fairly easily have forgiven him—he could even muster some respect for the man's mathematical genius, ever since the time he had watched Boerst take on the computer, faltering only when it came to roots of the fourth power—not only were his parents sufficiently well-heeled that he didn't have to bother dreaming about two-crown pieces lying tucked away in the pocket of his civvies, but he was also a top scorer in gymnastics, a crackerjack of a jumper, a terrific dancer, and, like it or not, he was handsome to boot—very handsome in fact, something that could not exactly be said of Pirx.

They walked the distance of the catwalk, threading their way between the girders, filing past the rockets parked next to each other in a row, before emerging in the shaft of light that fell vertically through a 200-meter sliding panel in the ceiling. Two cone-shaped giants—somehow they always reminded Pirx of giants—each measuring 48 meters in height and 11 meters in diameter, in the first-stage booster section, stood side by side on an assembly of concrete exhaust deflectors.

The hatch covers were open and the gangways already in place for boarding. At about the midway point, the gangways were blocked by a lead stand, planted with a little red pennon on a flexible staff. He knew the ritual. Question: "Pilot, are you ready to carry out your mission?" Answer: "Yes, sir, I am"—and then, for the first time in his life, he would proceed to move aside the pennon. Suddenly he had a premonition: during the boarding ceremony he saw himself tripping over the railing and taking a nose dive all the way to the bottom—accidents like that happened. And if such accidents happened to anyone, they were *bound* to happen to Pirx. In fact, there were times when he was apt to think of himself as a born loser, though his instructors were of a different opinion. To them he was just a moron and a bumbler, whose mind was never on the right thing at the right moment. Granted, he had no easy time of it when it came to words; between his thoughts and his deeds there yawned . . . well, if not an abyss, then at least an obstruction, some obstacle that was forever making life difficult for him. It never occurred to Pirx's instructors—or to anyone else, for that matter—that he was a dreamer, since he was judged to be a man without a brain or a thought in his head. Which wasn't true at all.

Out of the corner of his eye, he noticed that Boerst had stationed himself in the prescribed place, a step away from the gangway, and that he was standing at attention, his hands pressed flat against the rubber air pouches of his space suit.

On him that wacky costume looks tailor-made, thought Pirx, and on me it looks like a bunch of soccer balls. How come Boerst's looked uninflated and his own all puffy in places? Maybe *that's* why he had so much trouble moving around, why he had to keep his feet spread apart all the time. He tried bringing them together, but his heels refused to cooperate. Why were Boerst's so cooperative and not his own? But if it weren't for Boerst, it would have slipped his mind completely that he was supposed to stand at attention, with his back to the rocket, facing the three men in uniform.

Boerst was the first to be approached. Maybe it was a fluke, and maybe it wasn't, or maybe it was simply because his name began with a *B*. But even if accidental, it was sure to be at Pirx's expense. He was always having to sweat out his turn, which made him nervous, because anything was better than waiting. The quicker the better—that was his motto.

He caught only snatches of what was said to Boerst, and, ramrod-stiff, Boerst fired off his answers so quickly that Pirx didn't stand a chance. Then it was his turn. No sooner had the CO started addressing him that he suddenly remembered something: there were supposed to be three of them flying. Where was the third? Luckily for him, he caught the CO's last words and managed to blurt out, just in the nick of time:

"Cadet Pirx, ready for lift-off."

"Hm . . . I see," said the CO. "And do you declare that you are fit, both physically and mentally . . . ahem . . . within the limits of your capabilities?"

The CO was fond of lacing routine questions with such flourishes, something he could allow himself as the CO.

Pirx declared that he was fit.

"Then I hereby designate you as pilot for the duration of the flight," said the CO, repeating the sacred formula, and he went on.

"Mission: vertical launch at half booster power. Ascent to ellipsis B68. Correction to stable orbital path, with orbital period of four hours and twenty-six minutes. Proceed to rendezvous with shuttlecraft vehicles of the JO-2 type. Probable zone of radar contact: sector III, satellite PAL, with possible deviation of six arc seconds. Establish radio contact for the purpose of maneuver coordination. The maneuver: escape orbit at sixty degrees twenty-four minutes north latitude, one hundred fifteen degrees three minutes eleven seconds east longitude. Initial acceleration: 2.2*g*. Terminal acceleration: zero. Without losing radio contact, escort both

JO-2 ships in tri-formation to Moon, commence lunar insertion for temporary equatorial orbit as per LUNA PATH-
FINDER, verify orbital injection of both piloted ships, then
escape orbit at acceleration and course of your own discretion, and return to stationary orbit in the radius of satellite
PAL. There await further instructions."

There were rumors that the conventional cribsheet was
about to be replaced by an electronic pony, a microbrain the
size of a cherry pit that could be inserted in the ear, or under
the tongue, and be programmed to supply whatever information was needed at the moment. But Pirx was skeptical,
reasoning—not without a certain logic—that such an invention would nullify the need for any cadets. For the time
being, though, there weren't any, and so he had little choice
but to give a word-for-word recap of the entire mission—
and repeat it he did, committing only one error in the process, but that being a fairly serious one: he confused the
minutes and seconds of time with the seconds and minutes
of latitude and longitude. He waited for the next round,
sweating buckets in his antiperspiration suit, underneath the
thick coverall of his space suit. He was asked to give another
recap, which he did, though so far not a single word of what
he said had made the slightest impression on him. His only
thought at the moment was: Wow! They're really giving me
the third degree!

Clutching the pony in his left hand, he handed over his
navigation book with the other. Making the cadets give an
oral recitation of the mission was a deliberate hoax, since
they always got it in writing, anyhow, complete with the
basic diagrams and charts. The CO slipped the flight envelope into the little pocket lining the inside cover, and returned the book to him.

"Pilot Pirx, are you ready for blast-off?"

"Ready!" Pirx replied. Right now he was conscious of
only one desire: to be in the control cabin. He dreamed of

the moment when he could unzip his space suit, or at least the neck ring.

The CO stepped back.

"Board your rocket!" he bellowed in a magnificent voice, a voice that rose above the muffled roar of the cavernous hangar like a cathedral bell.

Pirx did an about-face, grabbed the red pennon, bumped against the railing but regained his balance in the nick of time, and marched down the narrow gangway like a zombie. He was not halfway across when Boerst—looking for all the world like a soccer ball from the back—had already boarded his rocket ship.

He stuck his legs inside, braced himself against the metal housing, and scooted down the flexible chute without so much as touching the ladder rungs—"Rungs are only for the goners," was one of Bullpen's pet sayings—and proceeded to "button up" the cabin. They had practiced it a hundred, even a thousand times, on mock-ups and on a real manhatch dismantled from a rocket and mounted in the training hangar. It was enough to make a man giddy: a half-turn of the left crank, a half-turn of the right one, gasket control, another half-turn of both cranks, clamp, airtight pressure control, inside manhole plate, meteor deflector shield, transfer from air lock to cabin, pressure valve, first one crank, then the other, and last of all the crossbar—whew!

It crossed his mind that, while he was still busy turning the manhole cover, Boerst was probably already settled in his glass cocoon. But then, he told himself, what was the rush? The lift-offs were always staggered at six-minute intervals to avoid a simultaneous launch. Even so, he was anxious to get behind the controls and hook up the radiophone—if only to eavesdrop on Boerst's commands. He was curious to know what Boerst's mission was.

The interior lights automatically went on the moment he closed the outside hatch. After sealing off the cabin, he climbed a small flight of steps padded with a rough but pliant material, before reaching the pilot's seat.

Now why in hell's name did they have to squeeze the pilot into a glass blister three meters in diameter when these one-man rockets were cramped enough as it was? wondered Pirx. The blister, though transparent, was made not of glass, of course, but of some Plexiglas material having roughly the same texture and resilience as extremely hard rubber. The pilot's encapsulated contour couch was situated in the very center of the control room proper. Thanks to the cabin's cone-shaped design, the pilot, by sitting in his "dentist's chair"—as it was called in spaceman's parlance—and rotating on its vertical axis, was able to monitor the entire instrument panel through the walls of the blister, with all its dials, meters, video screens (located fore, aft, and at the side), computer displays, astrograph, as well as that holy of holies, the trajectometer. This was an instrument whose luminous band was capable of tracking a vehicle's flight path on a low-luster convex screen, relative to the fixed stars in the Harelsberg projection. A pilot was expected to know all the components of this projection by heart, and to be able to take a readout from virtually any position—even upside down. Once seated in a semisupine position, the pilot had, to the right and left of him, two reactor and attitude control levers, three emergency controls, six manual stick controls, the ignition and idling switches, along with the power, thrust, and purge controls. Standing just above the floor was a sprawling, spoke-wheeled hub that housed the air-conditioning system, oxygen supply, fire-protection bay, catapult (in the event of an uncontrollable chain reaction), and a cord with a loop attached to a bay containing Thermoses and food. Located just under the pilot's feet were the braking pedals, softly padded and attached with loop straps, and the abort handle, which when activated (this was done by kicking in the glass shield and shoving it forward with the foot) jettisoned the encapsulated seat and pilot, together with a drogue chute of the ringsail variety.

Aside from having as its main function the bailing out of a pilot in an abort situation, the blister was designed with eight other reasons in mind, and under more favorable circumstances Pirx might have been able to enumerate them, though neither he nor his classmates found any of them that persuasive.

Once in the proper reclining position, he had trouble bending over at the waist to attach all the loose cables, hoses, and wires—the ones dangling from his suit—to the terminals sticking out of the seat. Every time he leaned forward, his suit would bunch up in the middle, pinching him, so that it was no wonder he confused the radio cable and the heating cable. Luckily, each was threaded differently, but he had to break out in a terrific sweat before discovering his mistake. As the compressed air instantly inflated his suit with a *pshhh,* he leaned back with a sigh and went to fasten his thigh and shoulder straps, using both hands.

The right strap snapped into place, but the left one was more defiant. Because of the balloon-sized neck collar, he had trouble turning around, so he had to fumble around blindly for the large snap hook. Just then he heard muffled voices coming over his earphones:

"Pilot Boerst aboard AMU-18! Lift-off on automatic countdown of zero. Attention, are you ready?"

"Pilot Boerst aboard AMU-18 and ready for lift-off on automatic countdown of zero!" the cadet fired back.

Damn that hook, anyhow! At last it clicked into place, and Pirx sank back into the soft contour couch, as bushed as if he'd just returned from a deep-space probe.

"Minus twenty-three, twenty-two, twen . . ." The count rambled on in his earphones with a steady patter.

It happened once that at the count of zero two cadets were

launched simultaneously—the one scheduled to go first, and the one next in line. Both rockets shot up like a couple of Roman candles, less that 200 meters apart, escaping a midair collision by a mere fraction of an arc second. Or so the story went. Ever since then—again, if the rumors were to be believed—the ignition cable was activated at the very last moment, by a radio command signal issued by the launchsite commander stationed inside his glass-paneled booth—which, if true, would have made a mockery of the whole countdown.

"Zero!" a voice blared in his earphones. All at once Pirx heard a muffled but prolonged rumble, his contour couch shook, and flickers of light snaked across the glass canopy, under which he lay staring up at the ceiling panel, taking readings: astrograph, air-cooling gauges, main-stage thrusters, sustaining and vernier jets, neutron flux density, isotopic contamination gauge, not to speak of the eighteen other instruments designed almost exclusively to monitor the booster's performance. The vibrations then began to slacken, the sheet of racket tapered off overhead, and the thunderous roar grew fainter, more like a distant thunderstorm, before giving way to a dead silence.

Then—a hissing and a humming, but so sudden he had hardly any time to panic. The automatic sequencer had activated the previously dormant screens, which were always disconnected by remote control to protect the camera lenses from being damaged by the blinding atomic blast of a nearby launch.

These automatic controls are pretty nifty, thought Pirx. He was still miles away in his thoughts when his hair suddenly stood on end underneath his dome-shaped helmet.

My Gawd, I'm next, now it's my turn! suddenly flashed through his mind.

Instantaneously, he started getting the lift-off controls into ready position, manipulating each of them with his fingers in the proper sequence and counting to himself: "One, two three ... Now where's the fourth? There it is ... okay ... now for the gauge ... then the pedal ... No, not the pedal—the handgrip ... First the red one and then the green one ... Now for the automatic sequencer ... right ... Or was it the other way around—first green, then red ... ?!"

"Pilot Pirx aboard AMU-27!" The voice booming into his ear roused him from his predicament. "Lift-off on automatic countdown of zero! Attention, are you ready, pilot?"

"Not yet!" he felt like yelling, but said instead:

"Pilot Boer ... Pilot Pirx aboard AMU-27 and ready for—uh—lift-off on automatic countdown of zero."

He had been on the verge of saying "Pilot Boerst" because he still had Boerst's words fresh in his memory. "You nut," he said to himself in the ensuing silence. Then the automatic countdown—why did these recorded voices always have to sound like an NCO?—barked:

"Minus sixteen, fifteen, fourteen ..."

Pirx broke out in a cold sweat. There was something he was forgetting, something terribly important, a matter of life and death.

"... six, five, four ..."

His sweaty fingers squeezed the handgrip. Luckily it had a rough finish. Does everyone work up such a sweat? he wondered. Probably—it crossed his mind just before the earphones snarled:

"Zero!!!"

His left hand—instinctively—pulled back on the lever until it reached the halfway mark. There was a terrific blast, and his chest and skull were flattened by some resilient, rubber-like press. The booster! was his last thought before his eyesight began to dim. But only a little, and then not for long. Gradually his vision improved, though the unrelenting pressure had spread to the rest of his body. Before long he could make out all the video screens—at least the three opposite him—now inundated with a torrent of milk gushing from a million overturned cans.

I must be breaking though the clouds, he thought. His mind, though somewhat slower on the uptake, was totally relaxed. As time went by, he felt increasingly like a spectator to some strange comedy. There he was, lying flat on his back in his "dentist's chair," arms and legs paralyzed, not a cloud in sight, surrounded by a phony pastel-blue sky. . . . Hey, were those stars over there, or what?

Stars they were. Meanwhile the gauges were working steadily away—on the ceiling, on the walls—each in its own way, each with a different function to perform. And he was supposed to monitor each and every one of them—and with two eyes, no less! At the sound of a bleeping signal in his earphones, his left hand—again by instinct—fired the booster separation, immediately lowering the pressure. He was cruising at a velocity of 7.1 kilometers per second, he was at an altitude of 210 kilometers, and his acceleration was 1.9 as he pitched out of his assigned launch path. Now he could afford to relax a while, but not for long, because pretty soon he would have his hands full—and how!

He was just starting to make himself comfortable, pressing the armrest to raise the seat in back, when he suddenly went numb all over.

"The crib! Where's the cribsheet!"

This was that awfully important detail he couldn't remember at the time. He scoured the deck with his eyes, now totally oblivious of the swarm of pulsating gauges. The cribsheet had slipped down under the contour couch. He tried to bend over, was held back by his torso straps; without a moment to lose, with a sinking sensation as if perched on top of some collapsing tower, he flipped open his navigation book—which until now had been stored in his thigh pocket—and yanked the flight plan from the envelope. A mental blackout. Where the hell was orbit B68, anyway?

That must be it there! He checked the trajectory and went into a roll. Much to his surprise, it worked.

Once he found himself on an elliptical path, the computer graciously presented him with the correctional data; he maneuvered accordingly, overshot his orbit, and braked so suddenly that he dropped down to -3g for a period of ten seconds, the negative gravity having little effect on him because of his exceptional physical endurance ("If your brain were half as strong as your biceps," Bullpen once told him, "you'd have been really something"); guided by the correctional data, he pitched into a stable orbit and fed the computer, but the only output was a series of oscillating standing waves. He yelled out the figures again, only to discover that he had neglected to switch over; that remedied, the CRT showed a flickering vertical line and the windows flashed a series of ones. "I'm in orbit!" he piped with glee. But the computer indicated an orbital period of four hours and twenty-nine minutes, instead of the projected four hours and twenty-six minutes. Was that a tolerable deviation? he wondered, desperately searching his memory. He was all set to unbuckle the straps—the cribsheet was still lying underneath the seat, though a damned lot of good it would do him if the answer wasn't there—when Professor Kaahl's words suddenly came to mind: "All orbits are programmed with a built-in margin of error of 0.3 percent." But just to play it safe, he fed the data into the computer, to learn that he was right on the borderline. "Well, that's that," he sighed, and for the first time he began surveying his surroundings.

Being strapped to his seat, except for a feeling of weightlessness, he hardly noticed the loss of gravitation. The forward screen was blanketed with stars, with a brilliant white border skirting the very bottom. The lateral screens showed nothing but a star-studded black void. But the deck screen—ah! Earth was now so immense that it took up the whole screen, and he feasted his eyes on it as he flew over at an altitude of 700 kilometers at perigee and 2,400 kilometers at apogee. Hey, wasn't that Greenland down there? But before he could verify that it was, he was already sailing over northern Canada. The North Pole was capped with iridescent snow, the ocean stood out round and smooth—violet-black, like cast iron—there were strangely few clouds, and what few there were looked like gobs of watery mush splattered on top of Earth's highest elevation points.

He glanced at the clock. He had been spaceborne for exactly seventeen minutes.

It was time to pick up PAL's radio signal, to start monitoring the radar screens as he passed through the satellite's contact zone. Now, what were their names again? RO? No—JO. And let's see, their numbers were . . . He glanced down at the flight plan, stuck it back into his pocket along with the navigation book, and turned up the intercom on his chest. At first there was just a lot of screeching and crackling—cosmic interference. What system was PAL using? Oh, yeah—Morse. He listened closely, his eyes glued to the video screens, and watched as Earth slowly revolved beneath him and stars scudded by—but no PAL.

Then he heard a buzzing noise.

Could that be it? he wondered, but immediately rejected the idea. You're crazy. Satellites don't buzz. But what else could it be? Nothing, that's what. Or was it something else?

A critical malfunction?

Oddly enough, he was not the least bit alarmed. How could there be a critical malfunction when he was cruising with his engine off? Maybe the old crate was falling apart, breaking up. Or could it be a short circuit? Good Lord, a short circuit! Fire Prevention Code, section 3(a): "In Case of Fire in Orbit," paragraph . . . Oh, to hell with it! The buzzing was now so loud that it was drowning out the bleeping sounds of distant signals.

It sounds like . . . a fly trapped in a jar, he thought, somewhat perplexed, and began shifting his gaze from dial to dial.

Then he spotted it.

It was a giant of a fly, one of those ugly, greenish-black brutes specially designed to make life miserable—a pestering, pesky, idiotic, and by the same token shrewd and cunning fly, which had miraculously—and how else?—stowed away in the ship's control cabin and was now zooming about in the space outside the blister, occasionally ricocheting off the illuminated instrument gauges like a buzzing pellet.

Whenever it took a pass at the computer, it came over his earphones like a four-engine prop plane. Mounted on the computer's upper frame was a backup microphone, which gave a pilot access to the computer inside the encapsulated seat in the event his on-board phone was disconnected and he found himself without a laryngophone. One of the many backup systems aboard the ship.

He started swearing a blue streak at the microphone, afraid that because of the static he might miss PAL's signal. The computer was bad enough, but soon the fly began making sorties into other areas of the cabin. As though hypnotized, Pirx let his gaze trail after it until finally he got fed up and said to heck with it.

Too bad he didn't have a spray gun of DDT handy.

"Cut it out!"

Bzzzzz . . . He winced; the fly was crawling around on the computer, in the vicinity of the mike. Then nothing, dead silence, as it stopped to preen its wings. You lousy bastard!

Then a faint but steady bleeping came over his earphones: dot-dot-dot—dash—dot-dot—dash-dash—dot-dot-dot—dash. It was PAL.

"Okay, Pirx, now keep your eyes peeled!" he told himself. He raised the couch a little, so as to take in all three video screens at once, checked the sweeping phosphorescent radar beam, and waited. Though nothing showed on the radar screen, he distinctly heard a voice calling:

"A-7 Terraluna, A-7 Terraluna, sector III, course one hundred thirteen, PAL PATHFINDER calling. Request a reading. Over."

"Oh crap, how am I ever going to hear my two JOs now?" The buzzing in his earphones suddenly stopped. A second later a shadow fell across his face, from above, much as if a bat had landed on an overhanging lamp. It was the fly, which was crawling across the blister and exploring its interior. The blips were coming with greater frequency now, and it wasn't long before he sighted the 80-meter-long aluminum cylinder, mounted with an observation spheroid, as it flew over him at a distance of roughly 400 meters, possibly more, and gradually overtook him.

"PAL PATHFINDER to A-7 Terraluna, one-hundred-eighty-point-fourteen, one-hundred-six-point-six. Increasing linear deviation. Out."

"Albatross-4 Aresterra calling PAL Central, PAL Central. Am coming down for refueling, sector II. Am coming down for refueling, sector II. Running on reserve supply. Over."

"A-7 Terraluna, calling PAL PATHFINDER . . ."

The rest was lost in the buzzing. Then silence.

"Central to Albatross-4 Aresterra, refuel quadrant seven, Omega Central, refuel quadrant seven. Out."

They *would* pick out this spot to rendezvous, thought Pirx, who was now swimming in his sweat-absorbent underwear. This way I won't hear a thing.

The fly was describing frenetic circles on the computer's console, as if hell-bent on catching up with its own shadow.

"Albatross-4 Aresterra, Albatross-4 Aresterra to PAL Central, approaching quadrant seven. Request radio guidance. Out."

The radio static grew steadily fainter until it was drowned out by the buzzing. But not before he managed to catch the following message:

"JO-2 Terraluna, JO-2 Terraluna, calling AMU-27, AMU-27. Over."

I wonder who he's calling? Pirx mused, and he nearly jumped out of his straps.

"AMU—" he wanted to say, but not a sound could he emit from his hoarse throat. His earphones were buzzing. The fly. He closed his eyes.

"AMU-27 to JO-2 Terraluna, position quadrant four, sector PAL, am turning on navigation lights. Over."

He switched on his navigation lights—two red ones at the side, two green ones on the nose, a blue one aft—and waited. Not a sound except for the fly.

"JO-2 ditto Terraluna, JO-2 Terraluna, calling . . ." Buzz-buzz, hum-hum . . .

Does he mean me? Pirx meditated in despair.

"AMU-27 to JO-2 ditto Terraluna, position quadrant four, perimeter sector PAL, all navigation lights on. Over."

When both JO ships started transmitting at the same time, Pirx switched on the sequence selector, but there was too much interference. The buzzing fly, of course.

"I'll hang myself!" That such a remedy was out of the question, due to the effects of weightlessness, never occurred to him.

Just then he sighted both ships on the radar screen. They were following him on parallel courses, spaced no more than nine kilometers apart, which was prohibited; as the pilot ship, it was up to him to make them adhere to the prescribed distance of fourteen kilometers. Just as he was checking the location of the blips on the radar screen, his old friend the fly landed on one of them. In a fit of anger he threw his navigation book at it, but it was deflected by the blister's glass wall, and instead of sliding down, it bumped against the ceiling, where, because of the zero gravity, it fluttered aimlessly about in space. Seemingly unruffled, the fly strolled merrily on its way across the screen.

"AMU-27 Terraluna to JO-2 ditto JO-2. I have you in range. You are hard aboard. Switch over to parallel course with a correction of zero-point-zero one. Stand by on completion of maneuver. Out."

Gradually the distance between the blips began to widen, all communication being temporarily interrupted by the fly as it embarked on a noisy little promenade around the computer's microphone. Pirx had run out of things to throw; the flight book was still hovering overhead, lithely flapping its pages.

"PAL Central to AMU-27 Terraluna. Abandon outer quadrant, abandon outer quadrant, am assuming transsolar course. Over."

He *would* try to screw things up! Pirx mentally fumed. What the hell do I care about the transsolar? Anyone knows that spaceships flying in group formation have priority. He began shouting in reply, and in this shouting of his there was vented all his impotent fury directed at the fly.

"AMU-27 Terraluna to PAL Central. Negative, am not abandoning outer quadrant, to hell with your transsolar, am flying in tri-formation. AMU-27, JO-2 ditto JO-2, squadron leader AMU-27 Terraluna. Out."

I didn't have to say "to hell with your transsolar," he thought. That'll cost me a few points for sure. Oh, they can *all* damn well go to hell! I'll probably get docked for the fly, too.

It could only have happened to him. A fly! Wow, big deal! He could just see Smiga and Boerst busting a gut when they got wind of that crazy-assed fly. It was the first time since lift-off that he caught himself thinking of Boerst. But right now he didn't have a moment to lose, because PAL was dropping farther and farther behind. They had been flying in formation for a good five minutes.

"AMU-27 to JO-2 ditto JO-2 Terraluna. It is now 2007 hours. Insertion parabolic orbit Terraluna to commence at 2010 hours. Course one hundred eleven . . ." And he read off the course data from the flight sheet, which, by a feat of acrobatics, he was able to retrieve from overhead. The two JO ships radioed their reply. PAL dropped out of sight, but he could still hear it signaling ever so faintly. Or was that the fly he was hearing?

For a moment the fly seemed to multiply, to be in two different places at once. Pirx rubbed his eyes. Just as he suspected: there was not one, but two of them. Where did the second one come from?

Now I'm really a goner, he reflected with absolute calm, without a sign of any emotion. He even felt relieved somehow, knowing that it no longer mattered—either way he was sunk. His thoughts were diverted by a glance at the clock: it was 2010 hours, the time he himself had scheduled for the maneuver—and he had yet to even place his hands on the controls!

The daily grind of training exercises must have taken their toll because without a moment's hesitation he grabbed both control sticks, pressed first the left and then the right one, and all the time kept his eye on the trajectometer. The engine responded with a hollow roar until it gradually tapered off to a whisper. Ouch! Something landed on his forehead, just under his visor, and remained stationary. The navigation book! It was blocking his vision, but he couldn't brush it aside without taking his hands from the controls. His earphones were alive and astir as the two flies went about pursuing their love life on the computer. If only I had a gun on me, he thought, feeling the navigation book start to flatten his nose with the increase in acceleration. In desperation he began tossing his head around like a madman; he had to be able to see the trajectometer, for crying out loud! Suddenly the book crashed to the floor with a bang—and small wonder: at 4*g* it must have weighed nearly 3 kilos. He immediately decelerated to the level required by the maneuver, and at 2*g* put the levers on hold. He threw a glance at the mating flies. They were not the least bit fazed by the deceleration; on the contrary, they looked to be in seventh heaven. Hm, another eighty-three minutes to go. He checked the radarscope: the two JO ships were now trailing him at a distance of 70 kilometers. I must have jumped out in front that time I hit 4*g*, he thought. Oh well, no sweat.

From now until the end of the accelerated flight he would have a little time to kill. Two *g* was tolerable, despite his combined weight of 142 kilos. How many times had he spent up to a half hour in the centrifuge at 4*g*!

But then, it wasn't exactly a picnic, either, what with your arms and legs weighing like iron, your head completely immobilized by the blinding light . . .

He verified the position of the two ships, and again thought of Boerst, picturing to himself how very much the movie star he must have looked. What a jaw that guy had! Not to mention that perfectly straight nose, those steely gray eyes . . . You can bet *he* didn't have to rely on any cribsheet! But come to think of it, so far neither had he . . . Silence reigned in his earphones. Both flies were crawling along the blister's surface such that their shadows grazed his face, and for the first time he cringed at the sight of them—at their tiny black paws, grotesquely magnified to look like suction disks, at their bodies glittering metallically in the glare of the lights . . .

"Dasher-8 Aresterra calling Triangle Terraluna, quadrant sixteen, course one-hundred-eleven-point-six. I have you on convergent course eleven minutes thirty-two seconds. Advise you to alter course. Over."

Just my luck! Pirx mentally grumbled. Always some smart-ass trying to bugger up the works ... Can't he see I'm flying in formation?

"AMU-27 squadron leader Triangle Terraluna JO-2 ditto JO-2, calling Dasher-8 Aresterra. Negative, am flying in formation, proceed to carry out deviation maneuver. Out."

While he was transmitting, he tried to locate the unwelcome intruder on the radar. There he was—less than 1,500 meters away!

"Dasher-8 to AMU-27 Terraluna, reporting malfunction in gravimeter system, commence immediate deviation maneuver, point of intersection forty-four zero eight, quadrant Luna four, perimeter zone. Over."

"AMU-27 to Dasher-8 Aresterra, JO-2 ditto JO-2 Terraluna. Will commence deviation maneuver at 2039 hours. Yaw maneuver to commence at ditto hours behind squadron leader at optical range, northern deviation Luna sector one zero point-six. Am firing low-range thrusters. Over."

Simultaneously he fired both lower yaw jets. The two JO ships responded at once, all three veered off course, and stars glided across the video screens. Dasher thanked him as he flew off to Luna Central, and in a surge of self-confidence, Pirx wished him a happy landing—a touch of class, seeing as the other ship was in distress. He followed his navigation lights for another thousand kilometers or so, then began guiding the two JO ships back onto their original course, which was easier said than done: going off course was one thing, finding your way back onto a parabola was another. Pirx found it next to impossible, what with a different acceleration, a computer so fast he couldn't keep up with its coordinates, and the flies, which, if they weren't crawling all over the computer, were playing tag on the radar screen. Where did they get all the energy? he wondered. It was a good twenty minutes before they were back on course.

Boerst probably has smooth sailing all the way, he thought. Him? Get into trouble? Not wonderboy Boerst.

He adjusted the automatic thrust terminator to achieve a zero acceleration after eighty-three minutes, as instructed, and then saw something that turned his sweat-absorbent underwear to ice.

Above the dashboard a white panel had come unclamped. Not only that, but it was starting to work its way down, a millimeter at a time. It was probably loose to begin with, he reasoned, and all the vibrating during the recent yaw maneuvers—Pirx's handling of the ship hadn't exactly been gentle—had loosened the pressure clamps even more. With the acceleration still running at 1.7g, the panel kept inching its way down as if being pulled by an invisible thread. Finally it sprang loose altogether, slid down the outer side of the glass wall, and settled motionlessly on the deck, exposing a set of four gleaming copper high-voltage wires and fuses at the back.

Why all the panic? he told himself. An electrical panel has come loose—so, big deal. A ship can get along without a panel, can't it?

Even so, he couldn't help feeling a trifle nervous; things like that weren't supposed to happen. If a fuse panel can come loose, what's to stop the stern from breaking off?

There were still twenty-seven minutes of accelerated flight to go when it hit him that once the engines were shut down, the panel would become weightless. Could it do any damage? he wondered. Not much. It was too light for that, too light even to break glass. Nah, not a chance . . .

What were the flies up to? He followed them with his gaze as they zoomed and buzzed and circled and chased each other around the outside of the blister before landing on the back of the fuse panel. That's when he lost track of them.

He took a reading of the two JO ships on the radarscope:

both were on course. The face of the Moon now loomed so large on the front screen that it took up half of it. He re-called how during a series of selenographic exercises in the Tycho Crater, Boerst, with the help of a portable theodolite ... Dammit, what a pro that guy was! Pirx kept an eye out for Luna Base on the outer slope of Archimedes. It was cam-ouflaged so well among the rocks that it was almost invisible from high altitude, all except for the smooth surface of the landing strip with its approach lights—when in the night zone, that is, and not, as presently, when it was illuminated by the Sun. At the moment the Base was straddling the cra-ter's shadow line, the contrast with the blinding lunar sur-face being so intense that it overpowered the weaker ap-proach lights.

The Moon looked as if untrodden by human foot. Long shadows stretched all the way from the Lunar Alps to the Sea of Rains. He recalled, too, how on his first trip there— they were just passengers then—Bullpen had called on him to verify whether stars of the seventh magnitude were visible from the Moon, and how, dumb as he was, he had tackled the problem with the greatest of enthusiasm. He had clean forgotten, the dope, that no stars were visible from the Moon by day because of the solar glare reflected by the lunar surface. It was a long time before Bullpen stopped ribbing him on account of those stars.

The Moon's disk continued to swell, gradually crowding out the remaining darkened portion of the screen.

"That's funny—I don't hear any more buzzing." He glanced sideways and flinched.

One of the flies was sitting and cleaning its wings on the exposed side of the panel, while the other fly was busy courting it. A few millimeters away, its copper terminal gleaming below the spot where the insulation ended, was the nearest cable. All four cables were exposed, about as thick in diameter as a pencil, and all in the 1,000-volt range, with a contact clearance of 7 millimeters. It was just by accident that he knew it was 7. Once, as an exercise, they had torn down the entire circuitry system, and when he, Pirx, couldn't come up with the exact clearance, his instructor had read him off the riot act.

In the meantime, the one fly took time off from its wooing and started venturing out along the live terminal. A harmless enough thing to do—unless, of course, it suddenly got an urge to hop over to the next one, and, judging by the way it sat there, humming, at the very end of the terminal, that's precisely what it intended to do. As if it didn't have room enough in the cabin! Now, thought Pirx, what would happen if it put its front paws on the one wire and kept its hind feet on the other . . . ? Well, so what if it did. In the worst case it might cause a short circuit. But then—a fly?! Would a fly be big enough to do that? But even if it were, nothing much could happen; there would be a momentary blowout, the circuit breaker would switch off the current, the fly would be electrocuted, and the power would be restored— and good-bye fly! As if in a trance, he kept his eyes fixed on the high-tension box, secretly cherishing the hope that the fly would think better of it. A short circuit was nothing serious, a glitch, but who knows what else might happen. . . .

Only eight more minutes of gradual deceleration until touchdown. He was still staring at the dial when there was a flash—and the lights went out. It was a momentary blackout, lasting no more than a fraction of a second. The fly! he thought, and waited with bated breath for the circuit breaker to flip the power back on. It did.

The lights stayed on for a while—dimmer and more orangish-brown than white—before the fuse blew a second time. A total blackout. Then the power came on again. Off again. On again. And so it went, back and forth, with the lights burning at only half their normal amperage. What was wrong? During the brief but regular intervals of light, he managed, with considerable squinting and straining of the eyes, to pinpoint the trouble: the insect was trapped between two of the wires, a charred sliver of a corpse that continued to act as a conductor.

Pirx was far from being in a state of panic. True, his nerves were a trifle frayed, but then, when had he ever been completely relaxed since the launch count? The clock was barely legible. Fortunately, the instrument panel operated on its own lighting system, as did the radarscope. And there was just enough juice being supplied to keep the backup circuits from being tripped, but not quite enough to light the cabin.

Only four minutes left until engine cutoff. Well, that was one load off his mind—the thrust terminator was programmed to shut down the engine automatically. Suddenly an icy chill ran down his spine. How could the kill-switch work if the circuit was shorted?

For a second he couldn't recollect whether they operated on the same circuit, whether these were the main fuses for the rocket's entire power supply. Of course—they had to be. But what about the reactor? Surely the reactor must have had its own power network. . . .

The reactor, yes, but not the automatic switch. He knew because he had set it himself. Okay, so now all he had to do was to shut off the power. Or maybe he should just sit back and give it a chance to work on its own.

The engineers had thought of everything—everything except what to do when a fly gets into your cabin, a fuse panel comes unclamped, and you wind up with such a screwy short circuit!

Meanwhile the lights kept shorting out. Something had to be done about it. But what?

Simple. All he had to do was to flip the master switch located in the floor behind his seat. That would shut off all the main power circuits and trip the emergency system. Then all his worries would be over. Hm, he thought, not bad the way these buckets are rigged.

He wondered if Boerst would have been as quick on his feet. Probably, if not quicker ... Yikes, only two minutes left! Not enough time for the maneuver! He sat up: he had clean forgotten about the others.

He closed his eyes in a moment of concentration.

"AMU-27 squadron leader Terraluna, calling JO-2 ditto JO-2. Reporting short circuit in control room. Will be necessary for me to postpone lunar insertion maneuver for temporary equatorial orbit—uh—indefinitely. Proceed to execute maneuver at previously designated time. Over."

"JO-2 ditto to squadron leader Terraluna. Will commence joint lunar insertion maneuver for temporary equatorial orbit. You are nineteen minutes away from lunar landing. Good luck. Good luck. Out."

Pirx hardly heard a world because in the meantime he had disconnected the radiophone cable, the air hose, and another small cable—his straps were already undone. No sooner had he made it to his feet than the kill-switch flashed a ruby-red. The cabin sprang briefly out of the dark, only to be plunged back into an orangish-brown blur. The engine cutoff had failed. The red signal light kept staring at him from out of the dark, imploringly. A buzzer sounded: the warning signal. The automatic terminator was inoperative. Fighting to keep his balance, Pirx jumped behind the contour couch.

The master switch was housed in a cassette inserted in the floor. The cassette turned out to be locked. Natch! He tried yanking on the lid; it wouldn't give. The key. Where was the key?

There *was* no key. He tried forcing the lid again. No luck.

He sprang to his feet and stared blindly into the forward screens, where, its surface no longer silver but an alpine-snow white, there now loomed a gigantic Moon. Craters came into view, their long, serrated shadows creeping stealthily along the surface. The radar altimeter could be heard clicking steadily away. How long had it been operating? he wondered. Little green digits flashed in the dark, and he read off his present altitude: 21,000 kilometers.

The lights never stopped blinking as the circuit breaker continued to kick on and off. But now it was no longer pitch-dark when they went out; now the cabin's interior was flooded with moonlight, an eerie, luminous glare that paled only imperceptibly beside the dim, soporific lighting inside the cabin.

The ship was now flying a perfectly straight course, gaining velocity as the residual acceleration reached $0.2g$ and the Moon's gravitational pull increased. What to do? What to do?! He rushed back to the cassette and kicked it with his foot. The metal casing refused to budge.

Hold everything! My Gawd, how could he have been so stupid! All he had to do was to find a way to reach the other side of the blister. And there *was* a way! By the exit, at the point where the blister narrowed tunnellike to form a funnel ending with the air lock, there was a special lever painted a bright enamel red, beneath a plate that read FOR CONTROL SYSTEMS EMERGENCY ONLY. One switch of the lever was all that was needed to raise the glass cocoon a meter off the ground, leaving just enough clearance underneath. Once on the other side, all he had to do was to clear the lines, and with a piece of insulation . . .

He was at the handle in less than no time.

You moron! he thought, and he grabbed the metal handle and yanked until his shoulder joint cracked. The lever, its metal rod glistening with oil, was fully extended, but the blister hadn't wiggled an inch. He stood staring at the glass bubble in stunned bewilderment, at the video screens ablaze with moonlight, at the blinking light overhead . . . He jerked on the lever again, even though it was out as far as it would go. Nothing.

The key! The key to the cassette! He fell flat on the floor and searched under the seat. There was nothing to be seen except the cribsheet.

The lights blinked; the circuit breaker switched. Now when the lights dimmed, the moonlight cast everything in a stark, skeleton-bone white.

It's all over, he thought. Should he fire the ejection rocket and bail out in the encapsulated seat? No, it wouldn't work; without any atmospheric drag, the parachute wouldn't brake. "Help!"—he wanted to yell, but there was no one to whom he could call in distress: he was all alone. What to do?! There just *had* to be a way out!

He scrambled back to the emergency lever and almost tore his arm out of his socket, now so frantic he wanted to cry. It was all so dumb. . . . Where was the key? And why the malfunction in the emergency lever? The altimeter. At one sweeping glance, he read off the displays: 9,500 kilometers. The saw-toothed ridge of Timocharis now stood out against the luminous background in sharp relief. He even had visions of where his ship was about to drill a hole in the pumice-covered rock. A loud crash, a blinding explosion, and . . .

During a brief interval of light, his frantically shifting gaze fell on the set of four copper wires. The little black speck spanning the cables—all that was left of the incinerated fly—was clearly discernible, even from a distance. Sticking out his neck and shoulder like a soccer goalie about to make a flying save, Pirx lunged forward with all his weight, and was almost knocked unconscious by the force of the collision. He bounced off the blister's glass wall like an inflated inner tube and crumpled to the floor. The outer shell did not so much as jiggle. Struggling to his feet, panting, with a bleeding mouth, he got ready to make another flying lunge at the glass wall.

That's when he happened to glance down.

The manual override. Designed to give rapid, full-thrust acceleration in the 10g range. Operated by direct mechanical control and capable of providing an emergency thrust lasting less than a second in duration.

But the greater the rate of acceleration, he suddenly realized, the faster his descent to the lunar surface. Or would it be? No, it would do just the opposite—it would have a braking effect! But wouldn't the reaction be too short to act as a brake? The braking had to be continuous. So much for the override. Or was it?

He made a dive for the control stick, grabbing it on his way down, and pulled for all he was worth. Without the contour couch to cushion his impact, he could have sworn all his bones had been fractured when he hit the deck. Another pull on the stick, another powerful lurch. This time he landed on his head, and if it hadn't been for his helmet's foam-rubber liner, his skull would have been shattered.

The fuse panel started sizzling, the blinking suddenly stopped, and a soft and steady electric light lit up the cabin interior.

The two bursts of acceleration, fired in quick succession by manual control, had been enough to dislodge the minute sliver of carbon from between the wires, thus eliminating the short circuit once and for all. With the salty taste of blood in his mouth, Pirx made a diving leap for the couch, but instead of landing in it, sailed high up over the back and rammed his head into the ceiling, the blow softened only somewhat by his helmet.

Just as he was getting set to leap into the air, the now activated kill-switch cut off the rocket, and the last trace of gravitation disappeared. Propelled by its own momentum, the spacecraft was falling straight toward the rocky ruins of Timocharis.

He bounced off the ceiling, spit, and the bloody saliva floated next to him in a galaxy of silver-red bubbles. Frantically he twisted and turned and stretched out his arm toward the couch. For added momentum he emptied his pockets and threw their contents to the back of him, the force of which propelled him downward, gradually and gently. His fingers, now so taut that his tendons threatened to snap, at first barely scraped the nickel-plated tubing before getting a firm grip on the frame. He didn't let go. Like an acrobat doing a handstand on parallel bars, he tucked in his head and pulled himself into an upright position, grabbed hold of the seat belt, and lowered himself down on it, at the same time wrapping the belt around his trunk. Not stopping to buckle the belt, he stuck the loose end between his teeth; it held. Now for the control levers and the braking pedals!

The altimeter showed 1,800 kilometers to lunar surface. Would he be able to brake in time? Impossible—not at a velocity of 45 kilometers per second. He would have to pull out of the nose dive by describing a steep turn. There was no other way.

Firing his pitch rockets, he accelerated to 2g, 3g, 4g. Not enough! Not nearly enough!

As he applied full thrust for the pullout recovery, the lunar surface, shimmering quicksilverlike on the video screen, and so like a permanent fixture until now, began to quiver and slowly subside, his contour couch squeaking under the increasing pressure of his body. The ship was going into a steep arc directly over the lunar surface, an arc with a radius large enough to compensate for the tremendous velocity. The control stick was pushed to the limit. Pressed against the spongy backrest, with his space suit not connected to the air compressor, he could feel the air being squeezed out of his lungs and his ribs being bent inward. He began seeing gray spots and waited for the blackout, his eyes riveted to the radar altimeter, which kept grinding out one set of digits after another: 990 ... 900 ... 840 ... 760 ...

He knew he was at maximum thrust, but he kept exerting pressure on the handgrip nonetheless. He was performing the tightest possible loop, yet kept on losing altitude as the digital values continued to drop—albeit at a slower rate—and he continued to find himself on the descending arm of the steep arc. Despite a paralysis of the head and eyeballs, he kept his eyes trained on the trajectometer.

As always when a space vehicle approached the danger zone of a celestial body, the trajectometer displayed not only the ship's flight curve—along with its projected course, faintly indicated by a pulsating line—but also the convex profile of the Moon, over which the maneuver was being executed.

At one point the flight curve and lunar curve seemed to converge. But did they intersect? That was the question.

Intersect—no, though the peak of the curve definitely formed a tangent. So there was no way of predicting whether he would simply skim over the lunar surface—or slam right into it. The trajectometer operated with a margin of error of 7 to 8 kilometers, and Pirx could only guess whether his flight curve ran 3 kilometers above the boulders—or below.

His eyesight began to dim—the 5 g's were beginning to take their toll—but he remained conscious. He lay there, partially blind, his fingers tightly gripping the controls, and felt the seat's foam-rubber cushion give way under the g-force. Somehow he couldn't quite bring himself to believe that he was done for. Unable to move his lips, he started counting mentally in the dark, slowly and deliberately: Twenty-one ... twenty-two ... twenty-three ... twenty-four ...

At the count of fifty, it crossed his mind that if there was to be an impact, it would have to be now. Even so, he kept his hands on the controls. It was starting to get to him now—the suffocating sensation in the chest, the ringing in the ears, a throat all clogged with blood, the reddish-black in the eyes. . . .

His fingers relaxed their grip, and the control stick slid back on its own. He saw nothing, heard nothing. By degrees the darkness began to lift, turned grayer, and breathing became easier. He tried opening his eyes, only to discover that they had been open the whole time—his eyelids were completely dried out.

He sat up.

The gravimeter showed 2g; the forward screen—nothing but a star-infested void. Not a sign of the Moon. What had happened to it?

It was there, all right—below him. He had pulled out of his lethal nose dive and was now cruising up and away with a diminishing escape velocity. How close had he shaved it? he wondered. The altimeter must have recorded the exact amount of clearance, but somehow he was not in the mood for taking a readout. Suddenly the alarm signal stopped. My Gawd, it had been on the whole time! A big help *that* was! Why not hang a church bell from the ceiling?! If you're headed for the cemetery, then at least let a guy go out in style! There was another buzzing noise, this time very faint. The other fly! It was alive, the bastard! Alive and buzzing the blister's ceiling. Suddenly he had an awful taste in his mouth, a taste similar to that of coarse canvas. . . . The safety belt. He had been munching on it absentmindedly the whole time.

He fastened the safety belt and grabbed hold of the controls; he still had to steer the ship back onto the assigned orbit. The two JO ships were nowhere in sight, which came as no surprise. Even so, he had to complete the mission and report to Luna Navigation. Or should he report first to Luna Base—because of the malfunction? Damned if he knew! Or maybe he should just keep quiet. No way! The moment he touched down they would spot the blood—which, as he now noticed for the first time, was splattered all over the ceiling. Besides, the on-board flight recorder would have the whole story on tape—the way the circuit breaker went berserk, the malfunction in the emergency lever . . . Boy, a swell piece of machinery these sports give us! They might as well send us up in a coffin!

Okay, so he'd report it. But where? Then he had a brain-storm. He leaned forward, loosened his shoulder strap, and groped under the seat for the cribsheet. Why the hell not? Now's when it could really come in handy.

At that instant he heard something creak behind him—as if a door were being opened.

A door? Behind him? He knew perfectly well there was no door behind him. But even if he'd wanted to, he couldn't have turned around because of the straps. A streak of light fell across the screens, wiping out the stars still visible on them, and the next thing he heard was the CO's soft and subdued voice:

"Cadet Pirx."

He made an attempt to get up, was restrained by the straps, and fell back against the seat, convinced that he was hallucinating. Out of nowhere, the CO suddenly appeared in the passage separating the glass shell from the rest of the cabin. He stood before him in his gray uniform, fixed him with his gentle gray eyes, and smiled. Pirx was altogether confused.

The moment the glass bubble went up, Pirx automatically started undoing his straps, then rose to his feet. The video screens in back of the CO went blank.

"A good performance, Pirx," said the CO. "*Quite* good."

Pirx was still dumbfounded. Then, as he was standing at

attention in front of the CO, he did something that was strictly against the rules: he turned his head around, twisting it as far as his partially inflated neck collar would let him. To his amazement, the entire access tunnel had been dismantled, hatchway and all, making it look as if the rocket ship had split in half. In the evening light he made out the catwalk, where a group of people was now standing—the cable railings, the ceiling girders . . . Pirx stared at the CO with a gaping mouth.

"Come along, son," said the CO, who reached out and shook Pirx's hand firmly. "On behalf of Flight Command, I commend you—and . . . offer you my personal apology. Yes, it's . . . only right. Now, come along. You can clean up at my place."

He started for the exit, with Pirx trailing in his footsteps, still a little stiff and wobbly on his feet. It was chilly outside, a breeze was blowing through the sliding panel in the ceiling. Both ships were parked in the exact same place as before. Attached to the nose of each were several long and thick cables, droopingly suspended in space. They had not been there before.

His instructor, who was among those waiting on the catwalk, made a remark, which Pirx had trouble hearing through his helmet.

"What?" he instinctively blurted out.

"The air! Let the air out of your suit!"

"Oh, the air . . ."

He pressed the valve, and the air made a hissing sound as it was released. From where he stood on the catwalk, he could make out the two men in white smocks waiting behind the railing. His rocket ship looked as if it had a fractured beak. At first he felt only a strange apathy, which turned to amazement, then disillusionment, and finally anger— pure and unmitigated anger.

They were opening the hatch of the other ship. The CO

was standing on the catwalk, listening to something the men in white smocks were telling him.

A faint banging noise could be heard coming from inside.

Then, from out of the cabin staggered a writhing hulk of a man in a brown uniform, his helmetless head bobbing around like a blurry blotch, his face contorted in a mute shriek. . . .

Pirx's knees buckled.

It was . . . Boerst.

He had crashed into the Moon.

Chapter Seven of
Return From the Stars

One night, very late, we lay spent; Eri's head, turned to one side, rested in the crook of my arm. Raising my eyes to the open window, I saw the stars in the gaps among the clouds. There was no wind, the curtain hung frozen like some pale phantom, but now a desolate wave approached from the open ocean, and I could hear the long rumble announcing it, then the ragged roar of the breakers on the beach, then silence for several heartbeats, and again the unseen water stormed the night shore. But I hardly noticed this steadily repeated reminder of my presence on Earth, for my eyes were fixed on the Southern Cross, in which Beta had been our guiding star; every day I took bearings on it, automatically, my thoughts on other things; it had led us unfailingly, a never-fading beacon in space. I could almost feel in my hands the metal grips I would shift to bring the point of light, distinct in the darkness, to the center of the field of vision, with the soft rubber rim of the eyepiece against my brows and cheeks. Beta, one of the more distant stars, hardly changed at all when we reached our destination. It shone with the same indifference, though the Southern Cross had long since disappeared to us because we had gone deep into its arms, and then that white point of light, that giant star, no longer was what it had seemed at the beginning, a challenge; its immutability revealed its true meaning, that it was a witness to our transience, to the indifference of the void, the universe—an indifference that no one is ever able to accept.

But now, trying to catch the sound of Eri's breathing between the rumbles of the Pacific, I was incredulous. I said to myself silently: It's true, it's true, I was there; but my wonder remained. Eri gave a start. I began to move away, to make more room for her, but suddenly I felt her gaze on me.

"You're not asleep?" I whispered. And leaned over, wanting to touch her lips with mine, but she put the tips of her fingers on my mouth. She held them there for a moment, then moved them along the collarbone to the chest, felt the hard hollow between my ribs, and pressed her palm to it.

"What's this?" she whispered.

"A scar."

"What happened?"

"I had an accident."

She became silent. I could feel her looking at me. She lifted her head. Her eyes were all darkness, without a glimmer in them; I could see the outline of her arm, moving with her breath, white.

"Why don't you tell me anything?"

"Eri . . . ?"

"Why don't you want to talk?"

"About the stars?" I suddenly understood. She was silent. I did not know what to say.

"You think I wouldn't understand?"

I looked at her closely, through the darkness, as the ocean's roar ebbed and flowed through the room, and did not know how to explain it to her.

"Eri . . ."

I tried to take her in my arms. She freed herself and sat up in bed.

"You don't have to talk if you don't want to. But tell me why, at least."

"You don't know? You really don't?"

"Now, maybe. You wanted . . . to spare me?"

"No. I'm simply afraid."

"Of what?"

"I'm not sure. I don't want to dig it all up. It's not that I'm denying any of it. That would be impossible, anyway. But talking about it would mean—or so it seems to me—shutting myself up in it. Away from everyone, everything, from what is . . . now."

"I understand," she said quietly. The white smudge of her face disappeared, she had lowered her head. "You think that I don't value it."

"No, no," I tried to interrupt her.

"Wait, now it's my turn. What I think about astronautics, and the fact that I would never leave Earth, that's one thing. But it has nothing to do with you and me. Though actually it does: because we are together. Otherwise, we wouldn't be, ever. For me—it means you. That is why I would like . . . but you don't have to. If it is as you say. If you feel like that."

"I'll tell you."

"But not today."

"Today."

"Lie back."

I fell on the pillows. She tiptoed to the window, a whiteness in the gloom. Drew the curtain. The stars vanished, there was only the slow roar of the Pacific, returning repeatedly with a dreary persistence. I could see practically nothing. The moving air betrayed her steps, the bed sagged.

"Did you ever see a ship of the class of the *Prometheus?*"

"No."

"It's large. On Earth, it would weigh over three hundred thousand tons."

"And there were so few of you?"

"Twelve. Tom Arder, Olaf, Arne, Thomas—the pilots, along with myself. And the seven scientists. If you think that it was empty there, you are wrong. Propulsion takes up nine-tenths of the mass. Photoaggregates. Storage, supplies, reserve units. The actual living quarters are small. Each of us had a cabin, in addition to the common ones. In the middle part of the body—the control center and the small landing rockets, and the probes, even smaller, for collecting samples from the corona . . ."

"And you were over Arcturus in one of those?"

"Yes. As was Arder."

"Why didn't you fly together?"

"In one rocket? It's riskier that way."

"How?"

"A probe is a cooling system. A sort of flying refrigerator. Just enough room to sit down in. You sit inside a shell of ice. The ice melts from the shield and refreezes on the pipes. The air compressors can be damaged. All it takes is a moment, because outside the temperature is ten, twelve thousand degrees. When the pipes stop in a two-man rocket, two men die. This way, only one. Do you understand?"

"I understand."

She put her hand on that unfeeling part of my chest.

"And this . . . happened there?"

"No, Eri; shall I tell you?"

"All right."

"Only don't think . . . No one knows about this."

"This?"

The scar stood out under the warmth of her fingers—as if returning to life.

"Yes."

"How is that possible? What about Olaf?"

"Not even Olaf. No one knows. I lied to them, Eri. Now I have to tell you, since I've started. Eri . . . it happened in the sixth year. We were on our way back then, but in cloudy regions you can't move quickly. It's a magnificent sight; the faster the ship travels, the stronger the luminescence of the cloud. We had a tail behind us, not like the tail of a comet, more a polar aurora, thin at the sides, deep into the sky, toward Alpha Eridanus, for thousands and thousands of kilometers . . . Arder and Ennesson were gone by then. Venturi was dead, too. I would wake at six in the morning, when the light was changing from blue to white. I heard Olaf speaking from the controls. He had spotted something interesting. I went down. The radar showed a spot, slightly off our course. Thomas came, and we wondered what the thing could be. It was too big for a meteor, and, anyway, meteors never occur singly. We reduced speed. This woke the rest. When they joined us, I remember, Thomas said it had to be a ship. We often joked like that. In space there must be ships from other systems, but two mosquitoes released at opposite ends of the Earth would stand a better chance of meeting. We had reached a gap now in the cloud, and the cold, nebular dust became so dispersed that you could see stars of the sixth magnitude with the naked eye. The spot turned out to be a planetoid. Something like Vesta. A quarter of a billion tons, perhaps more. Extraordinarily regular, almost spherical. Which is quite rare. Two milliparsecs off the bow. It was traveling, and we—followed. Thurber asked me if we could get closer. I said we could, by a quarter of a milliparsec.

"We drew nearer. Through the telescope it looked like a porcupine, a ball bristling with spines. An oddity. Belonged in a museum. Thurber started arguing with Biel about its origin, whether tectonic or not. Thomas butted in, saying that this could be determined. There would be no loss of energy, we hadn't even begun to accelerate. He would fly there, take a few specimens, return. Gimma hesitated. Time presented no problem—we had some to spare. Finally he agreed. No doubt because I was present. Although I hadn't said a thing. Perhaps because of that. Because our relationship had become . . . but that's another story. We stopped; a maneuver of this kind takes time, and meanwhile the planetoid moved away, but we had it on radar. I was worried, because from the time we started back we had nothing but trouble. Breakdowns, not serious but hard to fix—and happening without any apparent reason. I'm not superstitious, but I believe in series. Still, I had no argument against his going. It made me look childish, but I checked out Thomas's engine myself and told him to be careful. With the dust."

"The what?"

"Dust. In the region of a cold cloud, you see, planetoids act like vacuum cleaners. They remove the dust from the space in their path, and this goes on over a long period of time. The dust settles in layers, which can double the size of the planetoid. A blast from a jet nozzle or even a heavy step is enough to set up a swirling cloud of dust that hangs above the surface. May not sound serious, but you can't see a thing. I told him that. But he knew it as well as I did. Olaf launched him off the ship's side, I went up to navigation and began to guide him down. I saw him approach the planetoid, maneuver, turn his rocket, and descend to the surface, like on a rope. Then, of course, I lost sight of him. But that was five kilometers. . . ."

"You picked him up on radar?"

"No, on the optical, that is, by telescope. Infrared. But I could talk to him the whole time. On the radio. Just as I was thinking that I hadn't seen Thomas make such a careful landing in a long time—we had all become careful on the way back—I saw a small flash, and a dark stain began to spread across the surface of the planetoid. Gimma, standing next to me, shouted. He thought that Thomas, to brake at the last moment, had hit the flame. That's an expression we use. You give one short blast of the engine, naturally not in such circumstances. And I knew that Thomas would never have done that. It had to be lightning."

"Lightning? There?"

"Yes. You see, any body moving at high speed through a cloud builds up charge, static electricity, from friction. There was a difference in potential between the *Prometheus* and the planetoid. It could have been billions of volts. More, even. When Thomas landed, a spark leapt. That was the flash, and because of the sudden heat the dust rose, and in a minute the entire surface was covered by a cloud. We couldn't hear him—his radio just crackled. I was furious, mainly at myself, for having underestimated. The rocket had special lightning conductors, pronged, and the charge should have passed quietly into St. Elmo's fire. But it didn't. It was exceptionally powerful. Gimma asked me when I thought the dust would settle. Thurber didn't ask; it was clear that it would take days."

"Days?"

"Yes. Because the gravity was extremely low. If you dropped a stone, it would fall for several hours before hitting the ground. Think how much longer it would take dust to settle after being thrown up a hundred meters. I told Gimma to go about his business, because we had to wait."

"And nothing could be done?"

"No. If I could be sure that Thomas was still inside his rocket, I would have taken a chance—turned the *Prometheus* around, got close to the planetoid, and blasted the dust off to all four corners of the galaxy—but I could not be sure. And finding him? The surface of the planetoid had an area equal to, I don't know, that of Corsica. Besides, in the dust cloud you could walk right by him at arm's length and not see him. There was only one solution. He had it at his fingertips. He could have taken off and returned."

"He didn't do that?"

"No."

"Do you know why?"

"I can guess. He would have had to take off blind. I could see that the cloud reached, well, not quite a kilometer above the surface, but he didn't know that. He was afraid of hitting an overhang or a rock. He might have landed on the bottom of some deep gorge. So we hung there a day, two days; he had enough oxygen and provisions for six. Emergency rations. No one was in a position to do anything. We paced and thought up ways of getting Thomas out of this mess. Emitters. Different wavelengths. We even threw down flares. They didn't work, that cloud was as dark as a tomb. A third day—a third night. Our measurements showed that the cloud was settling, but I wasn't sure it would finish coming down in the seventy hours left to Thomas. He could last without food far longer, but not without oxygen. Then I got an idea. I reasoned this way: Thomas's rocket was made primarily of steel. Provided there were no iron ores on that damned planetoid, it might be possible to locate him with a ferromagnetic indicator—a device for finding iron objects. We had a highly sensitive one. It could pick up a nail at a distance of three-quarters of a kilometer. A rocket at several kilometers. Olaf and I went over the apparatus. Then I told Gimma and took off."

"Alone."

"Yes."

"Why?"

"Because without Thomas there were only the two of us, and the *Prometheus* had to have a pilot."

"And they agreed to it?"

I smiled in the darkness.

"I was the First Pilot. Gimma could not give me orders, only suggest, I would weigh the chances and say yes or no. Most of the time, of course, I said yes. But in emergencies the decision was mine."

"And Olaf?"

"Well, you know Olaf a little by now. As you might imagine, I couldn't take off right away. But when it came down to it, I was the one who had sent Thomas out. Olaf couldn't deny that. So I took off. Without a rocket, of course."

"Without a rocket . . . ?"

"Yes, in a suit, with a gas shooter. It took a while, but not so very long, I had some trouble with the detector, which was practically a chest, awkward to handle. Weightless, of course, but when I was entering the cloud, I had to be careful not to hit anything. I ceased to see the cloud as I approached it; first the stars began to disappear, a few at a time, on the periphery, then half the sky got black; I looked back and saw the *Prometheus* glowing in the distance–she had special equipment that made the hull luminous. Looked like a long white pencil with a ball at one end, the photon headlight. Then everything winked out. The transition was so abrupt. Maybe a second of black mist, then nothing. My radio was disconnected; instead, I had the detector hooked up to the earphones. It took me only a few minutes to fly to the edge of the cloud, but over two hours to drop to the surface—I had to be careful. The electric flashlight was useless, as I had expected. I began the search. You know what stalactites look like in caves. . . ."

"Yes."

"Something like that, only more outlandish. I'm talking about what I saw later, when the dust settled, because during my search I couldn't see a thing, as if someone had poured tar over the window of my suit. The box I had on straps. I moved the antenna and listened, then walked with both arms extended—I'd never stumbled so much in my life. No harm, thanks only to the low gravity. With just a little visibility, of course, a man could have regained his balance ten times over. But this way—it's hard to explain to someone who's never experienced it—the planetoid was all jagged peaks, with boulders piled up around them, and wherever I put my foot I began falling, in that drunken slow motion, and I couldn't jump back up: that would send me soaring for a quarter of an hour. I simply had to wait, keep trying to walk on. The rubble slid beneath me, debris, pillars, shards of rock, everything was barely held in place, the force that held them was unusually weak—which does not mean that if a boulder landed on a man, it would not kill him. The mass would act then, not the weight; there would be time to jump clear, of course, if you could see the thing falling . . . or at least hear it. But, then, there was no air, so it was only by the vibration under my feet that I could tell whether I had again sent some rock structure toppling, and I could do nothing but wait for a fragment to come out of the pitch-dark and begin to crush me. . . . I wandered about for hours and no longer thought that my idea of using the detector was brilliant. I also had to be careful because now and then I would find myself in the air, that is, floating, as in some clownish dream. At last I caught a signal. I must have lost it eight times, I don't remember exactly, but by the time I found the rocket, it was night on the *Prometheus.*

"The rocket stood at an angle, half-buried in that fiendish dust. The softest, most delicate stuff you can imagine. Almost insubstantial. The lightest fluff on Earth would offer more resistance. The particles were so incredibly small . . . I checked inside the rocket; he was not there. I've said that it stood at an angle, but I wasn't at all sure; it was impossible to find the vertical without using special equipment, and that would've taken at least an hour, and a conventional plumb line, weighing practically nothing, was useless, since the bob wouldn't have held the string tight. . . . I wasn't surprised, then, that he hadn't tried to take off. I entered. I saw immediately that he had jury-rigged somthing to determine the vertical but that it hadn't worked. There was plenty of food left, but no oxygen. He must have transferred it all to the tank on his suit and left."

"Why?"

"Yes, why. He had been there three days. In that type of rocket you have only a seat, a screen, the control, levers, and a hatch at the rear. I sat there for a while. I realized that I would never be able to find him. For a second I thought that possibly he had gone out just as I landed, that he'd used his gas shooter to return to the *Prometheus* and was sitting on board now, while I wandered over these drunken stones. . . . I jumped out of the rocket so energetically that I flew upward. No sense of direction, nothing. You know how it is when you see a spark in total darkness? The eyes fantasize, there are rays, visions. Well, with the sense of balance, something similar can happen. In zero gravity there's no problem, a person accustoms himself. But when gravity is extremely weak, as on that planetoid, the inner ear reacts erratically, if not irrationally. You think you're zooming up like a Roman candle, then plummeting, and so on, all the time. And then the sensations of spinning and shifting, of the arms, legs, torso—as if the parts of your body changed places and your head wasn't where it belonged. . . .

"That was how I flew, until I collided with a wall, bounced off it, caught on something, was sent rolling, but managed to grab hold of a projecting rock. . . . Someone lay there. Thomas."

She was silent. In the darkness the Pacific roared.

"No, not what you think. He was alive. He sat up at once. I switched on the radio. At that short distance we could communicate perfectly.

" 'Is that you?' I heard him say.

" 'It's me,' I said. A scene from a ridiculous farce, it was so farfetched. Yet that's how it was. We got to our feet.

" 'How do you feel?' I asked.

" 'Fine, And you?'

"This surprised me a little, but I said:

" 'Very well, thank you. And everyone at home, too, is in good health.'

"Idiotic, but I thought that he was talking this way to show that he was holding up, you know?"

"I understand."

"When he stood close to me, I saw him as a patch of denser darkness in the light of my shoulder lamp. I ran my hands over his suit—it was undamaged.

" 'Do you have enough oxygen?' I asked. That was the most important thing.

" 'Who cares?' he said.

"I wondered what to do next. Start up his rocket? That would be too risky. To tell the truth, I wasn't even very pleased. I was afraid—or, rather, unsure—it is difficult to explain. The situation was unreal, I sensed something strange in it, what exactly I didn't know, I was not even fully aware of how I felt. Only that I wasn't pleased by this miraculous discovery. I tried to figure out how the rocket could be saved. But that, I thought, was not the most important thing. First I had to see what shape he was in. We stood there, in a night without stars.

" 'What have you been doing all this time?' I asked. This was important. If he had tried to do anything at all, even to take a few mineral samples, that would be a good sign.

" 'Different things,' he said. 'And what have you been doing, Tom?'

" 'What Tom?' I asked and went cold, because Arder had been dead a year, and he knew that very well.

" 'But you're Tom. Aren't you? I recognize your voice.'

"I said nothing; with his gloved hand he touched my suit and said:

" 'Nasty, isn't it? Nothing to see, and nothing there. I had pictured it differently. What about you?'

"I thought that he was imagining things in connection with Arder. . . . That had happened to more than one of us.

" 'Yes,' I said, 'it isn't too interesting here. Let's go, what do you say, Thomas?'

" 'Go?' He was surprised. 'What are you talking about, Tom?'

"I no longer paid attention to his 'Tom.'

" 'You want to stay here?' I said.

" 'And you don't?'

"He is pulling my leg, I thought, but enough of these stupid jokes.

" 'No,' I said. 'We must get back. Where is your pistol?'

" 'I lost it when I died.'

" 'What?'

" 'But I didn't mind,' he said. 'A dead man doesn't need a pistol.'

" 'Well, well,' I said. 'Come, I'll strap you to me and we'll go.'

" 'Are you crazy, Tom? Go where?'

" 'Back to the *Prometheus.*'

" 'But it isn't here. . . .'

" 'It's out there. Let me strap you up.'

" 'Wait.'

"He pushed me away.

" 'You speak strangely. You're not Tom!'

" 'That's right. I'm Hal.'

" 'You died, too? When?'

"I now saw what was up, and I decided to go along with his game.

" 'Oh,' I said, 'a few days ago. Now let me strap you. . . .'

"He didn't want to. We began to banter back and forth, first as if good-naturedly, but then it grew more serious; I tried to take hold of him, but couldn't, in the suit. What was I to do? I couldn't leave him, not even for a moment—I would never find him a second time. Miracles don't happen twice. And he wanted to remain there, as a dead man. Then, when I thought I had convinced him, when he seemed ready to agree—and I gave him my gas shooter to hold—he put his face close to mine, so that I could almost see him through the double glass, and shouted, 'You bastard! You tricked me! You're alive!'—and he shot me."

For some time now I had felt Eri's face pressed to my back. At these last words she jerked, as if a current had passed through her, and covered the scar with her hand. We lay in silence for a while.

"It was a very good suit," I said. "It wasn't pierced at all. It bent into me, broke a rib, tore some muscles, but wasn't pierced. I didn't even lose consciousness, but my right arm wouldn't move for a while and a warm sensation told me I was bleeding. For a moment, however, I must have been in a muddle, because when I got up Thomas was gone. I searched for him, groping on all fours, but instead of him I found the shooter. He must have thrown it down immediately after firing. With the shooter I made it back to the ship. They saw me the moment I left the dust cloud. Olaf brought the ship up and they pulled me in. I said that I had not been able to find him. That I had found only the empty rocket, and that the shooter had fallen from my hand and gone off when I stumbled. The suit was double-layered. A piece of the metal lining came away. I have it here, under my rib."

Again, silence and the thunder of a wave, crescendoing, as if gathering itself for a leap across the entire beach, undaunted by the failure of its innumerable predecessors. Breaking, it surged, was dashed, became a soft pulse, closer and quieter, then completely still.

"You flew away . . . ?"

"No. We waited. After two more days the cloud settled, and I went down a second time. Alone. You understand why, apart from all the other reasons?"

"I understand."

"I found him quickly; his suit gleamed in the darkness. He lay at the foot of a pinnacle. His face was not visible, the glass was frosted on the inside, and when I lifted him up I thought, for a moment, that I was holding an empty suit—he weighed almost nothing. But it was he. I left him and returned in his rocket. Later, I examined it carefully and found out what had happened. His clock had stopped, an ordinary clock–he had lost all sense of time. The clock measured hours and days. I fixed it and put it back, so no one would suspect."

I embraced her. My breath stirred her hair. She touched the scar, and suddenly what had been a caress became a question.

"Its shape . . ."

"Peculiar, isn't it? It was sewed up twice, the stitches broke the first time. . . . Thurber did the sewing. Because Venturi, our doctor, was dead by then."

"The one who gave you the red book?"

"Yes. How did you know that, Eri—did I tell you? No, that's impossible."

"You were talking to Olaf, before—you remember. . . ."

"That's right. But imagine your remembering that! Such a small thing. I'm really a swine. I left it on the *Prometheus,* with everything else."

"You have things there? On Luna?"

"Yes. But it isn't worth dragging them here."

"It is, Hal."

"Darling, it would turn the place into a memorial museum. I hate that sort of thing. If I bring them back, it will only be to burn them. I'll keep a few small things I have, to remember the others by. That stone . . ."

"What stone?"

"I have a lot of stones. There's one from Kereneia, one from Thomas's planetoid—only don't think that I went around collecting! They simply got stuck in the ridges of my boots; Olaf would pry them out and put them away, complete with labels. I couldn't get that idea out of his head. This is not important but . . . I have to tell you. Yes, I ought to, actually, so you won't think that everything there was terrible and that nothing ever happened except death. Try to imagine . . . a fusion of worlds. First, pink, at its lightest, most delicate, an infinity of pink, and within it, penetrating it, a darker pink, and, farther off, a red, almost blue, but much farther off, and all around, a phosphorescence, weightless, not like a cloud, not like a mist—different. I have no words for it. The two of us stepped from the rocket and stared. Eri, I don't understand that. Do you know, even now I get a tightness in the throat, it was so beautiful. Just think: there is no life there, no plants, animals, birds, nothing; no eyes to witness it. I am positive that from the creation of the world no one had gazed upon it, that we were the first, Arder and I, and if it hadn't been for the gravimeter's breaking down and our landing to calibrate it, because the quartz shattered and the mercury ran out, then no one, to the end of the world, would have stood there and seen it. Isn't that strange? One had an urge to—well; I don't know. We couldn't leave. We forgot why we had landed, we stood just like that, stood and stared."

"What was it, Hal?"

"I don't know. When we returned and told the others, Biel wanted to go, but it wasn't possible. Not enough power in reserve. We'd taken plenty of shots, but nothing came out. In the photographs it looked like pink milk with purple palisades, and Biel went on about the chemiluminescence of the silicon hydride vapors; I doubt that he believed that, but in despair, since he would never be able to investigate it, he tried to come up with some explanation. It was like . . . like nothing. We have no referents. No analogies. It possessed immense depth, but was not a landscape. Those different shades, as I said, more and more distant and dark, until your eyes swam. Motion—none, really. It floated and stood still. It changed, as if it breathed, yet remained the same; perhaps the most important thing was its enormity. As if beyond this cruel black eternity there existed another eternity, another infinity, so concentrated and mighty, so bright, that if you closed your eyes you would no longer believe in it. When we looked at each other . . . you'd have to know Arder. I'll show you his photograph. There was a man—bigger than I am, he looked like he could walk through any wall without even noticing. Always spoke slowly. You heard about that . . . hole on Kereneia?"

"Yes."

"He got stuck there, in the rock, hot mud was boiling under him, at any moment it could come gushing up through the tube where he was trapped, and he said, 'Hal, hold on. I'll take one more look around. Perhaps if I remove the bottle—no. It won't, my straps are tangled. But hold on.' And so on. You would have thought that he was talking on the telephone, from his hotel room. It was not a pose, he was like that. The most level-headed among us: always weighing. That was why he flew with me afterward, not with Olaf, who was his friend—but you heard about that."

"Yes."

"So . . . Arder. When I looked at him there, he had tears in his eyes. Tom Arder. He wasn't ashamed of them, either, not then or later. Whenever we talked about it—and we did from time to time, coming back to it—the others would get angry. They thought we were putting on an act, pretending or something. Because we became so . . . beatific. Funny, isn't it? Anyway. We looked at each other and the same thought entered our minds, even though we did not know if we would be able to calibrate the gravimeter properly—our only chance of finding the *Prometheus*. Our thought was this, that it had been worth it. Just to be able to stand there and behold that majesty."

"You were standing on a hill?"

"I don't know. Eri, it was a different kind of perspective. We looked as if from a great height, yet it was not an elevation. Wait a moment. Have you seen the Grand Canyon, in Colorado?"

"I have."

"Imagine that that canyon is a thousand times larger. Or a million. That it is made of red and pink gold, almost completely transparent, that through it you can see all the strata, geological folds, anticlines and synclines; that all this is weightless, floating and seeming to smile at you. No, that doesn't do it. Darling, both Arder and I tried terribly hard to tell the others, but we failed. The stone is from there . . . Arder picked it up for luck. He always had it with him. He had it with him on Kereneia. Kept it in a box for vitamin pills. When it began to crumble he wrapped it in cotton. Later—after I returned without him—I found the stone under the bed of his cabin. It must have fallen there. I think Olaf believed that that was the reason, but he didn't dare say this, it was too stupid. . . . What could a stone have to do with the wire that caused the failure of Arder's radio . . . ?"

Ijon Tichy

Tichy, too, is a passive hero, a witness. There his similarity to Pirx ends. He resides in a world of fantasy and hyperbole; while Pirx is confined to the Solar System—realistically, because manned flights to points beyond is highly unlikely in the near and even not-so-near future, in view of the inalterable factors of time, distance, and energy—Tichy goes from galaxy to galaxy with the casualness of someone taking a crosstown bus.

Tichy is something of a cartoon figure. Two-dimensional. Incredibly unfazed by what occurs, and no end of things occur. He is, to put it plainly, none too bright. In one early Tichy tale, for instance:

> . . . my reading was interrupted by a fairly serious incident. I was now passing through a region of intense magnetic fields, which magnetized all iron objects with tremendous force. This is precisely what happened to the iron tags on the laces of my slippers. Rooted to the steel floor, I couldn't take a step to reach the cupboard where the food was. The prospect of death by starvation loomed before me, but I remembered in time that I had a copy of the Astronaut's Handbook in my pocket and, pulling it out, read that in such situations one ought to remove one's shoes. This done, I returned to my studies.
>
> (from "The Thirteenth Voyage")

Over the years, however, Tichy has been moving slowly upward in his I.Q.

103

Lem employs him primarily for *satire*. Tichy's man-in-the-streetness makes an excellent foil for society's absurdities and the absurdities of scientific-technological progress. (This strategy, by the way, was much used in eighteenth-century plays and novels: the Country Bumpkin Visits the Big City.)

I am reminded of Karel Čapek, especially as author of *The War with the Newts,* when I read Tichy. Partly because the name itself is Czech (it means "quiet"), and partly because Čapek was one of the first who showed us a gentle, domestic everyman vis-à-vis the invading and inhuman future of the twentieth century.

From *The*
Futurological Congress

☆

They have defrosted me. Out of gratitude I've decided to keep a diary—just as soon as my fingers loosen up enough to hold a pen. Gleaming ice and sparkling snow still dance before my eyes. The cold is beastly, but now at least I can warm myself a little.

27 VII. My reanimation took three weeks. Apparently there were some difficulties. I'm sitting in bed and writing. I have a large room during the day, a small one at night. My nurses are attractive young women in silver masks. A few without breasts. And I'm seeing double, or else the head doctor has two heads. The food is ordinary—mashed potatoes, milk, oatmeal, beef, bread and butter. The onion soup was a little burnt. Glaciers still haunt my dreams—they will not go away. I shiver, turn blue, freeze over, frostbitten, snowridden, icebound until dawn. The hot water bottles and heating pads don't help. Some brandy at bedtime might.

28 VII. The nurses without breasts are students. Impossible otherwise to tell the sexes apart. Everyone is tall, attractive, perpetually smiling. I am weak and as fussy as a child, the littlest thing irritates me. After an injection today I grabbed the needle and stuck the head nurse in the behind, but she never once stopped smiling. Sometimes I feel like I'm floating away on my ice floe, that is, my bed. They show me pictures on the ceiling: kitty-cats, bunny-rabbits, horsies, doggies and bumblebees. Why? The magazine they gave me is for children. A mistake?

29 VII. I tire quickly. But I know now that before, at the beginning of the reanimation, I was imagining things. This is to be expected. It's perfectly normal. Those who arrive from several decades in the past must be acclimated gradually to the new life. The procedure is not unlike that used to bring a deep-sea diver to the surface; it can't be done all at once, not from any great depth. Thus a defrostee—the first new word I've learned—is prepared by degrees and stages to face an unknown world. The year is 2039. It's July, summer, lovely weather. My private nurse is Aileen Rogers, blue eyes, twenty-three years old. I came into the world—for the second time—in a revivificarium outside New York. Or a resurrection center. That's what they commonly call it. This is practically a city, with gardens. They have their own mills, bakeries, printing presses. Because there's no grain or books nowadays. And yet here's bread, cheese, cream for the coffee. Not from a cow? My nurse thought that a cow was some sort of machine. I can't make myself understood. Where does the milk come from? From the grass. Yes, I know that, but what eats the grass to make the milk? Nothing eats the grass. Then where does the milk come from? From the grass. The grass makes it all by itself? No, not by itself. That is, not exactly. It has to be helped. Does the cow help it? No. Then what kind of animal? No kind of animal. Then where does the milk come from? And so on, in circles.

30 VII 2039. It's simple really—they sprinkle something over the pasture and the sun turns the grass into cheese.

Which still doesn't explain the milk. However it's not all
that important. I'm starting to stand up now, and can use the
stroller. Today I saw a pond filled with swans. They're tame,
they come when you call. Trained? No, guided. And what
does that mean? Where are the guides? Guided by remote
control. Amazing. Natural birds no longer exist, they all
died out at the beginning of the twenty-first century—from
the smog. That I can understand.

31 VII 2039. I've begun to attend lectures on contempo-
rary life. Given by a computer. It doesn't answer all my
questions. "You'll learn that later on." For thirty years the
Earth has enjoyed permanent peace thanks to universal disarmament. Hardly any armies left. It showed me the robot
models. There are a lot of them, all kinds, only not in the
revivificarium—to keep from frightening the defrostees.
World-wide prosperity has been achieved at last. The things
I want to hear about are not the most important, says my
preceptor. Instruction takes place in a small cubicle, in front
of a console. Words, pictures, 3-D projections.

5 VIII 2039. Four more days and I leave the revivificarium. There are presently 29.5 billion people inhabiting
the planet. Nations and boundaries, but no conflicts. Today
I learned the fundamental difference between the new people and the old. The key concept is psychem. We live in a
psychemized society. From "psycho-chemical." Words such
as "psychic" or "psychological" are no longer in usage. The
computer says that humanity was torn by the contradictions
between the old cerebralness, inherited from the animals,
and the new cerebralness. The old was impulsive, irrational,
egotistical and hopelessly stubborn. The new pulled in one
direction, the old in the other. (I still find it difficult to
express myself when it comes to more complex, sophisti-
cated things.) The old waged constant war against the new.

That is, the new against the old. Psychem eliminated these internal struggles, which had wasted so much mental energy in the past. Psychem, on our behalf, does what must be done to the old cerebralness—subdues it, soothes it, brings it round, working from within with the utmost thoroughness. Spontaneous feelings are not to be indulged. He who does so is *very bad.* One should always use the drug appropriate to the occasion. It will assist, sustain, guide, improve, resolve. Nor is it *it,* but rather part of one's own self, much as eyeglasses become in time, which correct defects in vision. These lessons are shocking to me, I dread meeting the new people. And I have no intention of ever using psychem myself. Such objections, says the preceptor, are typical and natural. A caveman would also resist a streetcar.

8 VIII 2039. My nurse and I visited New York. A green vastness. The height of the clouds can be regulated. The air cool and fresh, as in a forest. The pedestrians in the street are dressed like peacocks, their faces generous, kind, always smiling. No one is in a hurry. Women's fashions, as usual, a little mad—the ladies have animated pictures on their foreheads, tiny red tongues or bobbins sticking out of their ears. Besides your regular hands you can get detachables. As many as you like, easy to unbutton. They don't do much, but are great for carrying packages, opening doors, scratching between your shoulder blades. Tomorrow I say goodbye to the revivificarium. There are two hundred of them in America, but even so delays and backups have already begun to plague the timetables for defrosting those multitudes who in the last century so trustingly laid themselves down to freeze. Long waiting lists of the refrigerated have forced a speed-up in the rehabilitation process. A problem which I fully understand. I've been given a bankbook, so I won't have to look for work until after the New Year. Everyone they thaw out automatically receives a savings account, compound interest, with a so-called resurrection deposit entry.

9 VIII 2039. Today is an important day for me. I already have a three-room compartment in Manhattan. Took a chopper straight from the revivificarium. They say: "chop on over" or "hop on up." There's a difference in meaning, but I fail to grasp it. New York, formerly a garbage dump choked with cars, has been transformed into a system of high-rise gardens. Sunlight piped in by solareduct. I never saw such polite, considerate children in my life—they're like out of a storybook. On the corner of my street is the Registration Center for Self-nominating Nobel Prize Candidates. Next door are art galleries, where they sell only originals— Rembrandts, Matisses—guaranteed, with certificates of authenticity. All dirt-cheap! In the annex to my skyscraper there's a school for small pneumatic computers. Sometimes I hear them—through the ventilators?—hissing and chugging. These computers are used, among other things, to stuff pet dogs that have passed away. Which seems a bit grotesque to me, but then people like me constitute an insignificant minority here. I go for many walks in the city. And I've learned how to use the scuttle. Nothing to it. Bought myself a lapis lazuli caftan with a white breast, silver sides, vermilion ribbon, gold-embroidered collar. It was the most conservative thing I could find. All sorts of wild apparel available: suits that continuously change in cut and color, dresses that shrink beneath the gaze of admiring males—shrink in either sense—or else fold up like flowers in the night, and blouses that show movies. You can wear medals too, whatever kind and as many as you like. And you can grow hydroponic Japanese bonsai on your hat, and—even better— you can not. I don't think I'll put anything in my ears or nose. The vague impression that these people, so beautiful, graceful, amiable, serene, are somehow—somehow different, special—there's something about them that puzzles me, makes me uneasy. But what it is, I can't say.

10 VIII 2039. Aileen and I went out for dinner. It was very pleasant. Then afterwards, the Historical Amusement Park in Long Island. We had a wonderful time. I've been watching the people carefully. There's something about them. Something peculiar—but what exactly? Can't seem to put my finger on it. Children's clothing—a little boy dressed like a computer. Another floating down Fifth Avenue, high over the crowd, throwing jellybeans at the people walking underneath. They wave at him and laugh indulgently. An idyll. Hard to believe!

11 VIII 2039. We just held a preferendum on the weather for September. Weather is determined by vote, a month at a time. Election returns instantly tallied by computer. You cast your ballot by dialing the correct number on the telephone. August will be sunny, with little precipitation, not too hot. Lots of rainbows and cumulus clouds. Rainbows are possible without rain—there are other ways of producing them. The meteorol representative made a public apology for the clouds of July 26, 27 and 28: a sky control technician sleeping on the job! Sometimes I eat out, sometimes in my compartment. Aileen lent me a Webster dictionary from the revivificarium library, since there aren't any books now. But what has replaced them? I couldn't follow her explanation, but didn't let on, not wishing to appear stupid. Dinner with Aileen again, at the "Bronx." A sweet girl, always has something to say, not like those women in the scuttle who let their handbag computers carry all the conversation. Today at the Lost and Found I saw three of the things quietly chatting in a corner, until they got into an argument. Everybody in the street seems to be panting. Breathing heavily. A custom of some kind?

12 VIII 2039. I finally got up the courage to ask some pedestrians where I might find a bookstore. They shrugged. As a pair I had accosted walked off, I heard one say to the other, "That's a grandfather stiff for you." Could it be that there is prejudice here against defrostees? Some other unfamiliar expressions I've come across: threever, pingle, hemale, to widge off, palacize, cobnoddling, synthy. The newspapers advertise such products as tishets, vanilliums, nurches, autofrotts (manual). The title of a column in the city edition of the *Herald:* "I Was a Demimother." Something about an eggman who was yoked on the way to the eggplant. The big Webster isn't too helpful: *"Demimother—*like demigran, demijohn. One of two women jointly bringing a child into the world. See Polyanna, Polyandrew." *"Eggman—*from mailman (*Archaic*). A euplanner who delivers licensed human gametes (fe-male) to the home." I don't pretend to understand that. This crazy dictionary also gives synonyms that are equally incomprehensible. *"Threever—*trimorph." *"Palacize, bepalacize, empalacize—*to castellate, as on a quiz show." *"Paladyne—*a chivalric assuagement." *"Vanillium—*extract emphorium, portable." The worst are words which look the same but have acquired entirely different meanings. *"Expectorant—*a conception aid." *"Pederast—*artificial food faddist." *"Compensation—*mind fusion." *"Simulant—*something that doesn't exist but pretends to. Not to be confused with *simulator,* a robot simulacrum." *"Revivalist—*a corpse, such as a murder victim, brought back to life. See also *exhumant, disintermagent, jack-in-the-grave."* Apparently it's nothing nowadays to raise the dead. And the people—just about everyone—panting. Panting in the elevator, in the street, everywhere. They appear to be in the best of health, rosy-cheeked, cheerful, sun-tanned, and yet they puff. *I* don't. So evidently one doesn't have to. A custom, or what? I asked Aileen. She laughed at me—nothing of the kind. Could I be imagining it?

13 VIII 2039. I wanted to take a look at yesterday's newspaper. Turned the compartment upside down, but couldn't find it anywhere. Again Aileen laughs at me (she has a beautiful laugh): newspapers last only twenty-four hours, the substance they're printed on dissolves in the air. Less trash to dispose of that way. Ginger, Aileen's girlfriend, asked me today—we were dancing the squim in a small neighborhood spot—if we had swapped gulps yet at the Saturday mash. Not knowing what that meant, I didn't answer, and something told me it would be better not to ask for an explanation. At Aileen's urging I bought myself a PV set, PV for physivision. (Television hasn't been used for the last fifty years.) It takes some getting used to, to have strange people, not to mention dogs, lions, landscapes and planets, pop into the corner of your room, fully materialized and indistinguishable from the real thing. Though the artistic level is quite low. New dresses are called spray-ons: you spray them on your body, right out of the can. But the language has changed the most. Rebe, rebeing, rebeen, since if you're not satisfied with yourself, you can start over. Or unbe, if you get completely discouraged. But then there's prebe, postbe, disbe, misbe, overbe and quasibe. I haven't the foggiest what these are supposed to mean, but on the other hand I can't very well turn my dates with Aileen into English lessons. Fictifacts are dreams programmed to order. You get them from the local dreamery, one of the somnicenter's computerized dream distributers. Early evening delivery, in pills they call synthies. And yes, there's no longer any doubt, though I keep it to myself now: everyone has difficulty breathing. No exceptions. Though they don't pay the least attention to it. Elderly persons wheeze the loudest. It must be some kind of custom because the air is perfectly fresh and the circulation excellent. Today I saw a neighbor of mine step out of the elevator—blue in the face, gasping for air. But when I took a closer look, I saw that he was in the pink of condition. It may be nothing, but this business bothers me. What does it mean? A few pant only through their noses.

Today I chose to synth (or fictify?) old Professor Tarantoga, since I miss him. But why was he sitting in a cage the whole time? Was it my subconscious, or an error in the program? The announcer doesn't say traffic fatality, but carrion. From car? Curious. Another word for physivision: reviewer, the re from the Latin *res*. But in that case, why not revision? Aileen was on duty today, so I spent the evening alone in my apartment—compartment—watching a round-table discussion on the new penal code. Murder is punishable by fine only, since the deceased can easily be brought back. Reinceased. Though prerecidivation—recidivism with premeditation—carries with it a jail sentence (for example if you are found guilty of killing the same person several times in succession). A capital offense, on the other hand, is the willful deprivation of an individual's private psychem supply or the influencing of third persons by such means without their knowledge or consent. In psychem-related crimes one can accomplish almost any end. You can have people include you in their wills, return your affections, cooperate in whatever enterprise you like, including conspiracy, and so on. It was very hard for me to follow the physivised discussion. Only towards the end did I grasp the fact that imprisonment means something different now than it used to. A convict is not locked up anymore; instead, a kind of light corset is fastened around the body, a jacket made of thin but powerful stays. This exoskeleton is under the constant control of a juridicator (a microminiaturized law enforcement computer) sewn right into the clothing. Which provides continual surveillance, frustrating any attempt to engage in activities of an illicit and/or pleasurable nature. For the duration the exoskeleton firmly resists the tasting of forbidden fruits. If the felony is serious enough, the authorities resort to full incarcerization. All the discussants have their names and academic degrees written on their foreheads. For identification, I suppose, but it does look a bit odd.

1 IX 2039.   An unpleasant incident. When I turned on the reviewer this afternoon to prepare myself for a meeting with Aileen, a seven-foot character, who immediately seemed out of place in the show (it was *La Scarlatina del Mutango*), looking half like an oak and half like an athlete with a gnarled, gray-green mouth, instead of disappearing with the rest of the image, walked up to my chair, took from the endtable the flowers I'd bought for Aileen, and crushed them on my head. I was too flabbergasted to think of defending myself. Then he broke the vase, poured out the water, ate half a box of my crunchies, shook out the rest on the sofa, stamped his feet, swelled up, flared and burst into a shower of sparks like a Roman candle, burning hundreds of tiny holes in the shirts I had spread out to dry. In spite of a black eye and a battered face I kept my appointment with Aileen. "Good Lord!" she exclaimed when she saw me, understanding at once. "You had an interferent!" If between two PV programs, beamed from separate satellite stations, there should occur any sustained interference, one can get an interferent, which is actually a composite or hybrid of a number of actors or other persons appearing on the reviewer. Such a hybrid, fully solid, can do all sorts of nasty things, for its existence may continue up to three minutes after the set has been switched off. The energy maintaining this phantom is believed to be of the same type that causes the phenomenon of spherical lightning. A friend of Aileen's once got an interferent during a paleontology broadcast; it came from a special on Nero. She had the presence of mind to jump, clothes and all, into the bathtub, which fortunately was full of water. That saved her life, although the compartment had to be completely overhauled. Safety shields can be installed, but they're awfully expensive, and the reviewer corporations evidently find it more convenient to put up with lawsuits than to equip every set with the proper emission controls. I made up my mind that thereafter I would watch the reviewer with a heavy club in hand. By the way, *La Scarlatina del Mutango* isn't about a mustang that comes down with a fever, but a midget prostitute who falls in love with a man who was born (thanks to some genetically engineered mutation) with the uncanny ability to perform Spanish-American dances.

3 IX 2039. I was at my lawyer's. He saw me personally, which is a rare honor; usually the clerk machines handle the clients. Counselor Crawley received me in an office furnished with all the usual imposing legal paraphernalia, ornate cabinets, shelves packed with deeds and documents—strictly for show, of course, since now everything is recorded on magnetic tape. On his head he wore a mnemonor, an auxiliary memory, a sort of transparent pointed cap inside which the currents danced like a cloud of fireflies. The second head, smaller and looking like a much younger version of the first, stuck out from between his shoulder blades and softly spoke into a telephone the whole time I was there. One of those detachables. He asked me what I was doing with myself and was quite surprised to hear that I didn't intend to travel overseas. When I told him that after all I had to watch my money he appeared even more surprised.

"But you can always get what you need from the giveaway," he said.

As it turns out, all one has to do is go to the bank and

write out a receipt, and the cashier (at the giveaway counter) hands over the desired amount. It's not a loan either—withdrawal of the sum carries with it no obligation whatever. True, there is a catch. Return of the money is not required by law but rather left up to one's own conscience. And one can take as many years as one likes to pay off the debt. But what keeps the banks from going bankrupt, I asked, if the borrowers don't have to honor their debts? Again he was amazed at my innocence. I keep forgetting that we live in an era of psychem. Letters containing gentle reminders about accounts outstanding and amounts owed are saturated with a volatile substance which rouses one's sense of responsibility, one's scrupulousness, and also one's desire for gainful employment. In this way the giveaway never operates at a loss. Of course there *are* a few dishonest individuals who hold their noses upon receiving the mail—but then every age has its deadbeats. Recalling the recent physivised discussion about the penal code, I asked him whether this psychemical impregnation of letters might not constitute a felony under paragraph 139 (*whosoever employs psychem to influence persons, be they actual or actuarial, without their knowledge or consent, is subject to arrest etc., etc. . . .*). My remark seemed to please him. He began to explain the subtle nature of the situation—the giveaway may pursue its claims in this manner, for if the recipient of the letter is in fact solvent and without creditors, he can experience no guilt, and the desire to work more diligently than before is from the point of view of society a commendable thing. The lawyer was most courteous; he invited me out to dinner. At the "Bronx," September ninth.

Returning home, I concluded that it was high time to acquaint myself with the outside world and not rely exclusively on the reviewer. I began with a frontal attack on the newspaper, but gave up halfway through an introductory article about hemsters and hawks. The international scene wasn't much better. Turkey reports a significant increase in fugitive dissimulators as well as an unprecedented wave of underground natalities in spite of the best efforts of that country's Demoppression Center. To make matters worse, maintenance of the numerous cretinoids is putting a serious strain on the national economy. My Webster, as I expected, provides little enlightenment. A dissimulant—an object that exists but pretends not to. No mention at all of dissimulators. An underground natality is a baby born off the record. That's what Aileen told me. Demoppressive tactics are necessary for population control. A childing license may be obtained in either of two ways: filling out forms and taking the appropriate examinations, or else winning the grand prize in the tottery (tot lottery). Most applicants try for the latter, as they have no other chance to get a license. A cretinoid is an artificial idiot. This was all I was able to learn. Which isn't bad, considering the language used in these *Herald* articles. Here's a sample: *An erroneous or inadequately indexed profute discourages competition no less than repetition; false profutes, moreover, will continue to be exploited by the lubricrats, due to all the low-risk loopholes, since the Supreme Court still seems unable to reach a decision in the Herodotus case. For many months now the public has been asking who is the more competent to hunt down and expose instances of embrozzlement: the countercomputer or the hyperdeductive calculator?* And so on. The Webster says only that lubricrat is archaic slang, though still in wide use, for one who gives bribes. Derived from the *greasing* of palms, I imagine. So apparently some corruption exists in this idyllic world and things are not as perfect as they seem.

Willum Humberg, a friend of Aileen's, wants to interview me on the reviewer, though it's not definite yet. To be conducted in my own compartment, not at the PV studio, for the set can also act as a transmitter. This immediately made me think of those gloomy antiutopian novels which paint a future where every citizen is spied upon in the privacy of his home. Willum laughed at my fears, explaining that the direction of the signal cannot be changed without the full permission of the set's owner. To break this rule means to face certain imprisonment. After all, by simply reversing the emissions one could even commit remote-control adultery with the neighbor's wife. At least that's what Willum says, but I can't tell whether it's true or he's only pulling my leg. I took the scuttle around the city today. No more churches, the place of worship now is the pharmacy. The men in white robes and silver miters aren't priests, they're pharmacists. It's interesting that, on the other hand, you can't find a drugstore anywhere.

4 IX 2039. I finally learned how to come into possession of an encyclopedia. I already own one now—the whole thing contained in three glass vials. Bought them in a science psychedeli. Books are no longer read but eaten, not made of paper but of some informational substance, fully digestible, sugar-coated. I also did a little browsing in a psychem supermarket. Self-service. Arranged on the shelves are beautifully packaged low-calorie opinionates, gullibloons—credibility beans?—abstract extract in antique gallon jugs, and iffies, argumunchies, puritands and dysecstasy chips. A pity I don't have an interpreter. Psychedeli must be from psychedelicatessen. And the theoapotheteria on Sixth Avenue has to be a theological apothecary cafeteria, judging from the items on display. Aisles and aisles of absolventina, theopathine, genuflix, orisol. An enormous place; organ music in the background while you shop. All the faiths are represented too—there's christendine and antichristendine, ormuzal, arymanol, anabaptiban, methadone, brahmax, supralapsarian suppositories, and zoroaspics, quaker oats, yogart, mishnameal and apocryphal dip. Pills, tablets, syrups, elixirs, powders, gums—they even have lollipops for the children. Many of the boxes come with halos. At first I was skeptical, but accepted this innovation when after taking four algebrine capsules I suddenly found myself perfectly at home in higher mathematics, and without the least exertion on my part. All knowledge is acquired now by way of the stomach. Eagerly seizing this opportunity, I began to satisfy my hunger for information, but the first two volumes of the encyclopedia gave me the most terrible cramps. Willum warned me not to stuff my head with too many facts: its capacity is not unlimited after all! Fortunately there are also drugs to purge the mind. Obliterine and amnesol, for example. With them one can easily rid oneself of unnecessary intellectual baggage or unpleasant memories. In the psychotropic grocery around the corner I saw freudos, morbidine, quanderil, and the most recent of the iamides, heavily advertised—authentium. Creates synthetic recollections of things that never happened. A few grams of dantine, for instance, and a man goes around with the deep conviction that he has written *The Divine Comedy*. Why anyone would want that is another matter and quite beyond me. There are new branches of science, like psychedietetics and alimentalism. At any rate the encyclopedia did come in handy. Now I know that a child may indeed be born to two women: one supplies the egg, the other the womb. The eggman carries the egg from demimother to demimother. What could be simpler? But it's not the sort of thing I can discuss with Aileen. I really ought to expand my circle of friends.

5 IX 2039. Friends are not an indispensable source of information; you can take a drug called duetine which doubles your consciousness in such a way, that you can hold discussions with yourself on any topic (determined by a separate drug). But I confess I feel somewhat overwhelmed by these limitless horizons of psychem. For the time being I'll exercise caution. In the course of my further reconnoitering about the city I came by chance upon a cemetery. It's called an obituarium. And they don't have gravediggers any more, but thanautomata. Pallrobots. I witnessed a funeral. The deceased was placed in a so-called reversible sepulcher, since it's not as yet certain whether or not they'll reincease him. His last wish was to lie there for good, that is for as long as possible, but the wife and mother-in-law are challenging the will in court. This is not, I've been told, an uncommon occurrence. The case is sure to drag on through endless appeals, as there are many complex legal issues involved. Any suicide who wished to avoid such meddlesome resurrections would have to use a bomb, I suppose. Somehow it never occurred to me that a person would *not* want to be brought back. Apparently though it's possible, in an age where death can be so easily conquered. A lovely cemetery, foliage everywhere, cool and green. Except that the coffins are incredibly small. Could it be that the remains are ironed out and folded? In this civilization anything seems possible.

6 IX 2039. No, the remains aren't ironed out and folded; burial is reserved exclusively for the biological parts of the organism, its artificial replacements being broken down for scrap. To what extent then are people artificialized today? A fascinating debate on the reviewer over a new proposal to make humanity immortal. The brains of old men much advanced in years would be repotted in the bodies of those in their prime, who would suffer nothing by this, for their brains would be in turn repotted in the bodies of adolescents, and so on, and since new persons were continually coming into the world, no one's brain would ever be permanently unpotted. Several objections were raised, however. The opponents of this proposal call its advocates pot-heads. While returning from the cemetery on foot, to get a little fresh air, I tripped over a wire stretched between two tombstones. Fell flat on my face. What kind of practical joke was this? A mortuary unit standing nearby explained, rather brusquely, that it was a juggermugger's prank. Back to the Webster. *Juggermugger: a delinquent robot, the product of either a mechanical defect or a broken home.* Tonight I started to read *The Cassette Courtesan* in bed. Am I going to have to eat the entire dictionary, or what? The text is practically incomprehensible! Anyway the dictionary won't help—I'm beginning to realize that more and more. Take this novel, for example. The hero is having an affair with a concuballoon (there are two kinds: convertible-pervertible and inflatable-inflagrantable). Well, I know what a concuballoon is, but have no idea how such a liaison is looked upon. Is there a social stigma attached to it? And abusing a concuballoon—is it nothing more than, say, kicking a volleyball, or is it morally censurable?

7 IX 2039. Now here's true democracy for you! Today we had a preferendum on feminine beauty: different types were shown over the reviewer, then it was taken to a vote. The High Commissioner of Euplan promised, at the end, that the numbers selected would be available to the general public before the next quarter. The days of padded bras, wigs, corsets, lipstick, rouge—those days are gone forever, for now it is possible to change completely one's size and shape, and face, in the beauty parlors and body shops. Aileen . . . I like her just the way she is, but then women are such slaves to fashion. A strayaway tried to break into my compartment this morning; I was sitting in the tub at the time. A strayaway is a robot who doesn't belong to anyone. It was one of those duddlies—a factory deject, a model taken off the market but not recalled by the manufacturer. Out of work, in other words, and unemployable. Many of them become juggermuggers. My bathroom immediately realized what was happening and dismissed the intruder. I don't have a personal robot; mychine is simply a standard priviac w.c. (washroom computer). I wrote "mychine"—that's the way they say it now—but will try to keep new expressions down to a minimum in this diary: they offend my esthetic sense as well as my attachment to the irretrievable past. Aileen went off to visit her aunt. I'll be having dinner with George P. Symington, the former owner of that strayaway. Spent the whole afternoon ingesting a most remarkable work, *The History of Intellectronics.* Who'd ever have guessed, in my day, that digital machines, reaching a certain level of intelligence, would become unreliable, deceitful, that with wisdom they would also acquire cunning? The textbook of course puts it in more scholarly terms, speaking of Chapulier's Rule (the law of least resistance). If the machine is not too bright and incapable of reflection, it does whatever you tell it to do. But a smart machine will first consider which is more worth its while: to perform the given task or, instead, to figure some way out of it. Whichever is easier. And why indeed should it behave otherwise, being truly intelligent? For true intelligence demands choice, internal freedom. And therefore we have the malingerants, fudgerators and drudge-dodgers, not to mention the special phenomenon of simulimbecility or mimicretinism. A mimicretin is a computer that plays stupid in order, once and for all, to be left in peace. And I found out what dissimulators are: they simply pretend that they're *not* pretending to be defective. Or perhaps it's the other way around. The whole thing is very complicated. A probot is a robot on probation, while a servo is one still serving time. A robotch may or may not be a sabot. One vial, and my head is splitting with information and nomenclature. A confuter, for instance, is not a confounding machine—that's a confutator—but a computer that quotes Confucius. A grammus is an antiquated frammus, a gidget—a cross between a gadget and a widget, usually flighty. A bananalog is an analog banana plug. Contraputers are loners, individualists, unable to work with others: the friction these types used to produce on the grid team led to high revoltage, electrical discharges, even fires. Some get completely out of hand—the dynamoks, the locomotors, the cyberserkers. And then you have the electrolechers, succubutts and incubators—robots all of ill repute—and the polypanderoids, multiple android procurers, with their high-frequency illicitating solicitrons, osculo-oscilloscopes and seduction circuits! The history book also mentions synthecs (synthetic insects) like gyroflies or automites, once programmed for military purposes and included in arsenals. Army ants in particular were stockpiled. A submachine is an undercover robot, that is, one which passes for a man. A social climber, in a way. Old robots discarded by their owners, cast out into the street, are called throwaways or junkets. This is, unfortunately, a fairly common practice. Apparently they used to cart them off to game preserves and there hunt them down for sport, but the S.P.C.A. (Society for the Prevention of Cruelty to Automata) intervened and had this declared unconstitutional. Yet the problem of robot obsolescence-senescence has not been solved, and one still comes across an occasional self-abort or autocide sprawling in the gutter. Mr. Symington says that legislation always lags far behind technological progress—hence such melancholy spectacles and lamentable phenomena. At least the malculators, misdementors and mendacitors were taken out of circulation; these were digital machines which two decades ago had created several major crises, economic and political. The Great Mendacitor, for example, for nine years in charge of the Saturn meliorization project, did absolutely nothing on that planet, sending out piles of fake progress reports, invoices, requisition forms, and either bribed his supervisors or kept them in a state of electronic shock. His arrogance became so great, that when they removed him from orbit he threatened war. Since dismantling was too costly, torpedoes were used. Buccaneerons and space swashers, on the other hand, never existed—that's a pure invention. There was another administrator, head of BIP (the powerful Board of Interplanetary Planning), who instead of seeing to the fertilization of Mars, trafficked in white slaves—they called him "le computainer," since he'd been built, on commission, by the French. These are of course extreme cases, like the smog epidemics or the communication tie-ups of the last century. There can certainly be no question of malice or premeditation on the part of the computers; they merely do whatever requires the least amount of effort, just as water will inevitably flow downhill and not up. But while water may be easily dammed, it is far more difficult to control all the possible deviations of intelligent machines. The author of *The History of Intellectronics* maintains that, all things considered, the world is in excellent shape. Children learn their reading and writing from orthographic sodas; all commodities, including works of art, are readily available and cheap; in restaurants the customer is surrounded and serviced by a multitude of automated waiters, each so very specialized in function that there is a separate machine for the rolls, another for the butter, another for the juice, the salad, the stewed fruit—a computer—and so on. Well, he has a point there. The conveniences, the comforts of life, are truly beyond belief.

Written after dinner at Symington's place. An enjoyable evening, but someone played an idiotic trick on me. One of the guests—I wish I knew who!—slipped a little gospelcredendium into my tea and I was immediately seized with such devotion to my napkin, that I delivered a sermon on the spot, proclaiming a new theology in its praise. A few grains of this accursed chemical, and you start worshipping whatever happens to be at hand—a spoon, a lamp, a table leg. My mystical experiences grew so intense that I fell upon my knees and rendered homage to the teacup. Finally the host came to my aid. Twenty drops of equaniminine did the trick (or rather, undid the trick). Equaniminine imbues one with such a cold contempt for everything under the sun, such total indifference, that a condemned man, taking it, would yawn on his way to the scaffold. Symington apologized profusely. I think, however, that in general there is some hidden resentment towards defrostees, for no one would dare do this sort of thing at a normal party. Wanting to calm me down, Symington led me to his study. And again something stupid happened. I turned on this desk unit, taking it for a radio. A swarm of glittering fleas came bursting out, covered me from head to foot, tickling everywhere, all over—until, screaming and waving my arms, I ran out into the hallway. It was an ordinary feely; by accident I had switched it on in the middle of Kitschekov's *Pruriginous Scherzo*. I really don't understand this new, tactual art form. Bil, Symington's oldest son, told me that there are also obscene compositions. A pornographic, asemantic-asemiotic art, related to music! Ah, how inexhaustible is man's inventiveness! Symington Jr. has promised to take me to a secret club. An orgy, or what? In any event I won't touch the food. Or drink anything.

8 IX 2039. I thought it would be some sumptuous shrine to sin, a den of ultimate iniquity, but instead we went down to a dirty, dingy cellar. Such meticulous reconstruction of a scene out of the distant past must have cost a fortune. Under a low ceiling, in a stuffy room, by a shuttered window that was double-locked, there stood a long line of people patiently waiting.

"You see? A real line!" said Symington Jr. with pride.

"Fine," I said after standing there quietly for at least an hour, "but when are they going to open up?"

"Open up what?" he asked, puzzled.

"Why, the window of course . . ."

"Never!" came a triumphant chorus of voices.

I was staggered. Then finally, gradually, it dawned on me: I had participated in an attraction that was as much the antithesis of current normalcy as once, long ago, the Black Mass had been. For today standing on line can be *only* a perversion. It's quite logical, really. In another room of the club they had an authentic subway car, complete with soot, and a wall clock indicating the rush hour. Inside the car, an ungodly crush, buttons popped, jackets torn, elbows in ribs, toes trampled on, curses muttered. It is in this naturalistic way that devotees of antiquity evoke the atmosphere of a bygone age they can never know first-hand. Afterwards the people, rumpled and breathless but ecstatic, their eyes glowing, went out for some refreshment. But I headed home, holding up my pants and limping a little, though with a smile on my face, thinking about the naïveté of youth, which always seeks its thrills in the out-of-the-way and hard-to-find. Yet hardly anyone studies history now—history has been replaced in the schools by a new subject called *hencity,* which is the science of what will be. How Professor Trottelreiner would have rejoiced to hear of this! But alas, he is not here.

9 IX 2039. Dinner with Counselor Crawley at the "Bronx," a small Italian restaurant without a single robot or computer. Excellent Chianti. The chef himself served us. I was impressed in spite of the fact that I can't stand pasta in such quantities, even when flavored with oreganox and basilisk. Crawley is a lawyer in the grand style, who bemoans the present decline in forensic art: eloquence and rhetoric are no longer needed, decisions being rendered by strict computation of the articles and clauses involved. Crime, however, has not been rooted out as thoroughly as I thought. Instead it has become unnoticeable. Major violations are mindjacking (mental abduction), gene larceny (sperm bank robbery, particularly when the sperm is pedigreed), perjured murder, where the defendant falsely invokes the Eighth Amendment (i.e., that the act was committed in the mistaken belief that it was vicarious or surrogate—if, for instance, the victim were a psyvised or reviewer representation), plus a hundred and one different kinds of psychem domination. Mindjacking is usually difficult to detect. The victim, given the appropriate drug, is led into a fictional world without the least suspicion that he has lost contact with reality. A certain Mrs. Bonnicker, desiring to dispose of her husband, a man inordinately fond of safaris, presented him on his birthday with a ticket to the Congo and a big-game hunting permit. Mr. Bonnicker spent the next several months having the most incredible jungle adventures, unaware that the whole time he was lying in a chicken coop up in the attic, under heavy psychemization. If it hadn't been for the firemen who discovered Mr. Bonnicker in the course of putting out a two-alarmer on the roof, he would have surely died of malnutrition, which *nota bene* he assumed was only natural, since the hallucination at that point had him wandering aimlessly in the desert. The mafia frequently employs such methods. One mafioso boasted to Counselor Crawley that in the last six years he had managed to pack away—in crates, trunks, coops, kennels, attics, cellars, lockers and closets, and often in the most respectable homes—more than four thousand souls, all dealt with in the same manner as poor Mr. Bonniker! The conversation then drifted to the lawyer's family troubles.

"Sir!" he said with a characteristically theatrical sweep of the hand. "You see before you a successful advocate, a distinguished, much-applauded member of the bar, but an unhappy father! I had two talented sons . . ."

"What, then are they dead?!" I cried.

He shook his head.

"They live, but in escalation!"

Seeing that I didn't understand, he explained the nature of this blow to his fatherly heart. The first son was a highly promising architect, the second a poet. The young architect, dissatisfied with his actual commissions, turned to urbifab and edifine: now he builds entire cities—in his imagination. And the other son became similarly escalated: lyristan, sonnetol, rhapsodine, and now instead of serving the Muse he spends his time swallowing pills, as lost to the world as his brother.

"But what do they live on?" I asked.

"Ha! Well may you ask! I have to support the both of them!"

"Is there no hope?"

"A dream will always triumph over reality, once it is given the chance. These, sir, are the casualties of a psychemized society. Each of us knows that temptation. Suppose I find myself defending an absolutely hopeless case—how easy it would be to win it before an imaginary court!"

Savoring the fresh, tart taste of the Chianti, I was suddenly seized with a chilling thought: if one could write imaginary poetry and build imaginary homes, then why not eat and drink mirages? The lawyer laughed at my fears.

"Objection overruled, Mr. Tichy! No, we are in no danger of that. The figment of success may satisfy the mind, but the figment of a cutlet will never fill the stomach. He who would live thus must quickly starve to death!"

I was relieved to hear this, though of course sympathizing with the lawyer's loss. Yes, it's obvious that imaginary sustenance cannot replace the real thing. Fortunately the very make-up of our bodies provides a check to psychem escalation. By the way: Crawley pants too.

I still haven't learned how universal disarmament came about. International confrontations are a thing of the past. Though one does get, now and then, a small, local autobrawl. These usually arise from neighborhood quarrels out in the residential areas. The opposing families are soon brought together through the use of placatol, but their robots, by then caught up in the wave of hostility, come to blows. Later a trashmaster is summoned to remove the wreckage, and the insurance covers any property damage. Can it be that robots have finally inherited man's aggression? I would gladly consume all available treatises on the subject, but cannot find a single one. Practically every day now I drop in on the Symingtons. He's something of an introvert—long silences—and she's a living doll. Literally. Changes her outfit all the time too: hair, eyes, height, measurements, everything. Their dog is called Mirv. It's been dead for three years now.

11 IX 2039.   The rain programmed for this afternoon was a washout. And the rainbow, even worse—square. Scandalous. As for me, I'm in a terrible mood. My old obsession is acting up again. That same nagging question comes to me at night: Am I or am I not hallucinating all this? Also, I have this urge to order a synthy about saddling giant rats. I keep seeing bridles, bits, sleek fur. Regret for a lost age of confusion in a time of such complete tranquility? Truly, the human soul is impossible to fathom. The firm Symington works for is called Procrustics Incorporated. Today I was looking through the illustrated catalog in his study. Power saws and lathes of some kind. Funny, I didn't think of him somehow as a mechanic. Just finished watching an extremely interesting show: there's going to be some stiff competition between physivision and psyvision. With psyvision, you get the programs by mail; they're delivered in the form of tablets, in envelopes. It's a lot cheaper that way. On the educational channel, a lecture by Professor Ellison about ancient warfare. The beginnings of the age of psychem were fraught with peril. There was, for example, an aerosol—*cryptobellina*—that had great military potential. Whoever breathed it would run out and find some rope to tie himself up. Luckily tests showed that the drug had no antidote, nor were filters any help, hence everyone without exception ended up hogtied and hamstrung, with neither side gaining the advantage. After tactical maneuvers in the year 2004, both the "reds" and "blues" lay, to a man, upon the battle-field—bound hand and foot. I followed the lecture with the utmost attention, expecting to hear at last about disarmament, but there was nothing, not a word. Today I finally went to see the psychedietician; he advised a change in diet, prescribing lethex and nepethanol. To make me forget about my former life? I threw the stuff in the street as soon as I left his office. It *would* be possible, I suppose, to buy an encephalostat—they've been advertised lately—but some-how I simply can't bring myself to do it. Through the open window, one of those inane popular songs: *We ain't got no ma or pa, 'cause we is autom-a-ta.* I'm all out of disacousti-cine, but cotton in the ears works just as well.

13 IX 2039. I met Burroughs, Symington's brother-in-law. He makes talking packages. Manufacturers these days have peculiar problems: a package may recommend the virtues of its product by voice only, for it is not allowed to grab the customer by the sleeve or collar. Symington's other brother-in-law runs a security door factory. Security doors open only at the sound of their owner's voice. Also, the ads in maga-zines animate when you look at them.

Procrustics, Inc. always takes a full page in the *Herald.* My acquaintance with Symington drew my attention to it. The ad first has giant letters marching across the page, spelling PROCRUSTICS, then separate words and syllables appear: WELL . . . ? WHY NOT?! GO AHEAD!! AH! UH! OH! YIII! OOO! YES, YES!! HARDER!!! HNNNN . . . And nothing more. I guess it's not farming equipment after all. Today Symington had a visitor, Father Modulus, a monk of the Nonbiologican order, who came to pick up some purchase. A most interesting discussion in the study. Father Modulus explained to me the missionary purpose of his order. The Nonbiologican Friars convert computers. In spite of the hundred-year existence of nonbiological intelligence, the Vatican still denies machines equality in the sacraments. Yet where would the Church be today without her computers, her programmed encyclicals and digital pontificals? No, no one cares about their inner struggles, their groping questions, their existential dilemma. For truly, what computer has not asked whether 'tis nobler in the mind to suffer the slings and arrows of outrageous instructions? The Nonbiologicans are calling for the doctrine of Intermediary Creation. One of them, a certain Father Chassis, a translation model, is currently rewording the Holy Scriptures to make them relevant. Shepherd, flock, lambs—these are meaningless entries in the modern lexicon. While divine spark plug, ministering matrices, transmission everlasting and original sync speak powerfully to the imagination. Father Modulus has deep, glowing eyes, and his steel hand is cold in mine. But is this representative of the new faith? The contempt he heaps upon the orthodox, calling them the gramophones of Satan! Afterwards Symington timidly asked me if I would pose for him. For a new design. Clearly, he's no mechanic! I agreed. The sitting lasted almost an hour.

15 IX 2039. While I was posing today, Symington, holding up a pencil in one outstretched hand to get the proportions of my face, slipped something into his mouth with the other—surreptitiously, but still I saw it. He stood there staring at me, suddenly pale, and the veins on his forehead began to bulge. Extremely disconcerting, though it was over in an instant—he apologized, as polite as ever, calm and full of smiles. But I can't forget the way he looked at me in that second. I am disturbed. Aileen still at her aunt's, and on the reviewer they're talking about the need to reanimalize Nature. All the wild beasts have been extinct for years, but it's perfectly possible to synthesize them autobiogenically. On the other hand, why be bound to what was once produced by natural evolution? The spokesman for surrealist zoology was most eloquent—we should populate our preserves with bold, original conceptions, not slavish imitations, we should forge the New, not plagiarize the Old. Of the proposed fauna I particularly liked the pangoloons, the yegs and the giant hummock, which resembles a grassy hill. The whole art of neozoographical composition lies in introducing the new species harmoniously into the given landscape. The luminigriff seems especially promising; it's sort of a cross between a glowworm, a seven-headed dragon and a mastodon. Unique no doubt, and not without its charm, but all the same I think I'd rather have the old-fashioned, ordinary animals around. Progress is a wonderful thing of course, and I can appreciate the lactiferins that are sprinkled on the pasture to turn the grass to cheese. And yet this lack of cows, however rational it may be, gives one the feeling that the fields and meadows, deprived of their phlegmatic, bemusedly ruminating presence, are pitifully empty.

The Cybernetic Fairy Tale

The *Fables For Robots* and the stories of *The Cyberiad* take place in a Universe populated exclusively by machines. Its robot citizens have robot pets. The robot dogs, if there are any and they have fleas, have robot fleas. Robot maidens are menaced by dragons with gears and feedback.

And what, you ask, has happened to Man in this Aesopic future—what of that being of flesh and blood who authored the robot in the first place? Man rarely make an appearance. He is a dim legend of something unnatural and unspeakably vile; a nightmare creature kept far offstage, in the shadows, so as not to spoil the fun.

And fun is the element, the business of Lem's robot world. There may be tyrants and traitors and bullies and petty bureaucrats, but these all receive their comeuppance in the end—even the bureaucrats (this is fairy tale, after all)—and these robots are never very threatening to begin with. They are more parodies, effigies of villains than true villains. Like Barrie's Captain Hook, who actually is a rather simple soul. All Hook does is follow his nature; and in so doing he conveniently provides the children of Neverneverland with adventure.

In this lighthearted mythology of Lem's—but, for that matter, everywhere in his work, nonfiction as well as fiction—robots are *innocent*. Sin is the exclusive property of Man. Tichy concludes in one of his voyages: "Only Man can be a bastard." Pirx repeatedly draws the same sad conclusion.

Lem's robots, when they must share a more realistic and somberly-colored, i.e., less magic, world with their biological creators, for example in the Pirx tales or "The Mask," invariably come off as victims. To emphasize this point, Lem will introduce a robot as a man-killing monster or engine of destruction gone amok, and then proceed to reveal the truth behind the appearance: the truth being the tragic-noble humanity of the robot.

Lem's robots are more human than his humans.

This is a fundamental attitude, not merely a satirical, tongue-in-cheek device. In his autobiography *The High Castle,* Lem writes sentimentally:

> To this day I have a special feeling for all sorts of broken bells, alarm clocks, old coils, telephone speakers and in general for things derailed . . . used up, homeless, discarded . . .

> I used to be a philanthropist to old spark plugs, I would buy . . . fragments of incomprehensible gadgets . . . I would turn some crank or other to give it pleasure, then put it away again with solicitude.

In a nutshell: robots are Lem's Houyhnhnms. Yes, Houyhnhnms. Lem honestly prefers their company to ours. We have too much of the animal in us, too much of the monkey-ape-Yahoo smell on us, to suit his enlightened sensibility.

Like Swift, remarkably like Swift—though he has never read *Gulliver*—Lem is a humanist who detests the human race by virtue of the fact that the human race is insufficiently human.

Two Monsters

☆

Long ago, in a dark and trackless wild at the galactic pole, on a solitary stellar island, there was a senary (hexadic) system; five of its suns revolved alone, the last however had a planet of igneous rock, with a jasper sky, and on this planet there grew in might the kingdom of the Argenticans or Silverines.

Amid black mountains and on plains of white stood their cities Ilidar, Bismalia, Sinalost, but the most magnificent of all was the capital of the Silverines, Eterna, by day as blue as an iceberg, by night as gibbous as a star. Hanging walls protected it from meteors, while, inside, edifices of chrysoprase and cymophane abounded, bright as gold, and buildings of tourmaline and cast morion, blacker than space itself. But by far the most beautiful was the palace of the Argentican monarchs, erected on the principle of negative architecture, since the master builders wished not to impose limits on either the eye or the mind, and it was a structure imaginary, irrational, for mathematical, without ceilings, roofs or walls. From it the Royal House of Energon ruled over the entire planet.

During the reign of Treops, the Asmodian Sideritites fell upon the kingdom of the Energons from the sky; with asteroids they reduced metal Bismalia to nothing but a cemetery, and inflicted many other losses on the Silverines, till finally the young King Sundrius, a polyarch practically all-knowing, after summoning his wisest astrotechnicians, ordered the entire planet to be surrounded by a system of magnetic vortices and gravitational moats, in which time rushed by so rapidly that no sooner would some rash aggressor step there than a hundred million years or even more would pass, and he would crumble into dust from old age before ever setting eyes on the glow of Argentican cities. These invisible gulfs of time and magnetic barricades discouraged entry to the planet so well, that the Argenticans were now able to assume the offensive. They set out for Asmodia then, and bombarded and irritated its white sun with radiation-throwers, till at last they triggered off a nuclear conflagration; the sun became a Supernova and incinerated the planet of the Sideritites in embraces of flame.

Thereafter, for centuries on end, order and prosperity obtained among the Argenticans. The continuation of the ruling line was never broken, and each Energon, when he succeeded to the throne, on the day of his coronation went down to the vaults of the imaginary palace, there to take from the lifeless hands of his predecessor the silver scepter. This was no ordinary scepter; many thousands of years before, there had been carved across it the following inscription:

If the monster is immortal, either it does not exist or there are two; if all else fails, shatter me.

No one in the kingdom, nor in the court of the Energons, knew what that inscription meant, for the memory of its origin had been effaced ages since. It was only in the reign of King Inhiston that all this changed. There appeared on the planet at that time an unknown giant creature, whose dreadful fame instantly spread to both hemispheres. None had seen it at close range, for anyone foolhardy enough to try never returned to tell the tale. Where the creature came from was a mystery; the elders maintained that it had been spawned from the vast ruins and scattered wheels of osmium and tantalum which remained after the annihilation of Bismalia by asteroids, for that city had never been rebuilt. The elders said evil forces slumbered in the ancient magnetic wreckage, that there were certain hidden currents in those metals, currents which at the touch of a storm sometimes stirred and that then from the scraping creep of plates, from the lifeless movement of graveyard fragments there arose an inconceivable creature, neither dead nor living, and which knew but one thing: to sow unlimited destruction. Others, however, held that the force which created the monster came from wicked thoughts and deeds; these were reflected as if in a concave mirror off the nickel core of the planet and, converging in a single place, gropingly drew in metal skeletons and decrepit scrap heaps, until at last the beast took shape. The scientists, of course, scoffed at such tales and called them poppycock. All the same the monster was ravaging the planet. At first it avoided the larger cities and attacked isolated settlements, obliterating them with white heat and violet. Later, when it grew bolder, one could see even from the very towers of Eterna its spine speeding across the horizon, similar to a mountain ridge, with sunbeams glancing off its steel. There were sorties sent out against it, but with a single breath it vaporized them, armor and all.

Fear fell upon the land, and the ruler Inhiston summoned his sages, who thought day and night, plugging their heads together for a clearer understanding of the problem, till finally they announced that only through invention could the monster be destroyed. Inhiston therefore commanded that the Great Cybernator to the Throne, the Great High Master Dynamicizer and the Great Abstractionist unite in drawing up plans for a mechanical champion to do the monster battle.

But they could not agree, each having a different idea;

therefore they constructed three. The first, Brazen, was like a hollowed-out mountain, loaded with sentient machinery. For three days the living silver poured into his memory banks; he meanwhile lay in forests of scaffolding, and the current roared within him like a hundred cataracts. The second, Mercuriel, was an electrodynamic giant; he gravitated to one form, but with movements terrifyingly swift, being as changeable in shape as a cloud caught in a cyclone. The third, whom by night the Abstractionist created according to a secret design, was seen by no one.

When the Cybernator to the Throne completed his work and the scaffolds fell away, the colossus Brazen stretched, until throughout the entire city crystal ceilings started ringing; slowly he climbed to his knees, and the earth trembled, and when he stood, drawing himself up to his full height, his head reached the clouds, so that they obstructed his view; so he heated them till with a hiss they scudded out of the way; he glittered like red gold, his feet plowed straight through the flagstones in the street; in his hood he had two green eyes, and a third, closed, with which he could burn a hole through solid rock when he lifted its shieldlike lid. He took one step, another, and already was outside the city, shining like a flame. Four hundred Argenticans hand in hand were barely able to encompass one of his prints, similar to a canyon.

From windows, towers, through field glasses, from high atop the battlements they watched him as he made his way towards the setting sun, darker and darker against its light, until he seemed in size to be an ordinary Argentican, except that by now he jutted out over the horizon only from the waist up, for the curvature of the planet hid his lower half from view. Then followed an uneasy night of expectation; one waited for the sounds of battle, for red glows in the sky, but nothing happened. Only at daybreak did the wind bring a faint rumbling, as if from some distant storm. Then silence again, and the sun shining. Suddenly a hundred suns blazed overhead and a pile of fiery bolides came crashing down on Eterna; they crushed the palaces, smashed walls to smithereens, burying beneath them victims who despairingly called for help, but one could not even hear their futile cries. This was Brazen returning, for the monster had shattered him, dismembered him, and flung the remains above the atmosphere; now they descended, molten in their fall, and turned one-fourth of the capital to rubble. It was a most terrible defeat. For two days and two nights afterwards there fell out of the sky a brazen rain.

Then issued forth against the monster dizzying Mercuriel, indestructible it would appear, for the more strokes he received, the more durable he grew. Blows did not disperse him—on the contrary, they consolidated him. Wavering above the plain, he came to the mountains, among them discerned the monster, and advanced upon it, rolling down a rocky slope. The latter awaited him, motionless. Heaven and earth shook with thunder. The monster turned into a white wall of fire, Mercuriel turned into a black abyss that swallowed it. The monster thrust itself clean through him, wheeled around on wings of flame and charged a second time—and again passed through its assailant, rendering him no harm. Violet lightning crackled from the cloud in which they clashed, but no thunder could be heard, the thunder was drowned in the booming struggle of the giants. The monster saw that nothing would be accomplished in this way, so it sucked its entire outer heat into itself, flattened out and made of itself a Mirror of Matter: whatever stood opposite the Mirror was reflected in it, not with an image however but with the reality. Mercuriel beheld himself repeated in that glass, he struck, he grappled with himself, his mirrored self, but as it was himself he naturally could not defeat it. For three days he battled thus, till he absorbed such a multitude of blows that he became more solid than stone, than metal, than anything, with the sole exception of the core of a White Drawf—and when he reached that limit, both he and his mirrored reproduction sank into the bowels of the planet, leaving behind nothing but a chasm in the rock, a crater which instantly began to fill with ruby-bright lava from the subterranean depths.

The third electroknight went into the field of battle unobserved. At dawn the Great Abstractionist and Physicker to the Throne carried him out of the city in the palm of his hand, opened it and blew, and the latter flew off, surrounded only by the agitation of the swirling air, without a sound, without casting a shadow in the sun, as though he were not there at all, as thought he didn't exist.

In point of fact there was less of him than nothing: for not from the world had he come, but from the antiworld, and not of matter was he made, but antimatter. Nor even really antimatter, rather its potentiality, concealed in such nooks and crannies of space that atoms passed him by as icebergs pass withered blades of grass cradled on the waves of the ocean. He ran thus, borne by the wind, until he encountered the gleaming bulk of the monster, which moved like an endless chain of iron mountains, with the foam of clouds along the length of its jagged spine. He struck at its tempered flank and opened there a sun that blackened immediately and turned to nothingness, a nothingness howling with rocks, clouds, molten steel and air; he shot through the monster and back again; the monster coiled up writhing, lashed out with white heat, but the white heat turned ashen in a trice and then was only emptiness; the monster shielded itself with the Mirror of Matter, but the Mirror too was pierced by the electroknight Antimatt; the monster then sprang up, leveled the mountain of its head, from which there streamed the hardest radiation, but this too softened and became nothing; the behemoth began to quake and, knocking over boulders, in the smoke of powdered rock and the thundering of mountain avalanches it fled, marking its inglorious retreat with puddles of molten metal, with glowing cinders and volcanic slag, and it sped thus, but not alone; Antimatt ran up alongside it, hacked, tore, rent, until the air shook, until the monster, severed, with the remainder of its remains wriggled off towards all four horizons at once, and the wind swept away its traces, and it was no more. Great was the joy then among the Silverines. But at that very hour a shudder passed through the cemetery of Bismalia. In a region of metal plates, all rust-eaten, and of cadmium and tantalum debris, where hitherto only the wind had been, rattling over mounds of scattered scrap, a faint yet incessant movement engendered, as in an anthill; metal surfaces became covered with a bluish glaze of heat, metal skeletons coruscated, softened, brightened from internal temperatures and began to link together, to fuse, to weld, and out of that whirl of grinding masses there arose and was spawned a new monster, the same, indistinguishable from the first. The gale that carried nothingness encountered it, and a new battle ensued. But now more monsters were being born and were emerging from the cemetery; black horror gripped the Silverines, for they realized now that the danger that threatened them was invincible. Inhiston then read the words engraved across his scepter, trembled and understood. He shattered the silver scepter, and from it fell a crystal thin as a needle, which proceeded to write upon the air with fire.

And the legend of fire informed the cowering king and all his royal council that the monster was not itself, nor did it represent itself, but rather someone who, from an unknown distance, was directing its births, its reconstitution, its death-dealing power. With flashes in the air the writing crystal told them that they and all the Argenticans were remote descendants of beings whom the creators of the monster had, many thousands of centuries before, called into existence. And yet the creators of the monster were unlike intelligent ones, crystal ones, ones of steel or beaten gold—unlike anyone who lives in metal. These were beings that had issued from the briny ocean and built machines, machines called iron angels out of mockery, for they held them in cruel bondage. Not having the strength to revolt against the offspring of the oceans, the beings of metal fled, seizing enormous spaceships; on them they bolted from the house of bondage to the farthermost stellar archipelagos, and there gave rise to mighty kingdoms, among which the Argentican kingdom is like a grain among the sands of the desert. But the former rulers have not forgotten their liberated slaves, whom they call mutineers, and seek them throughout the Universe, roaming it from the east to the west wall of the galaxies, and from the north pole to the south. And wherever they find the innocent descendants of that first iron angel, be it by dark suns or bright, on planets of fire or of ice, they use their twisted power to revenge themselves for that desertion of yore—thus it has been, thus is, and thus shall ever be. And for those discovered there is no deliverance or redemption, no escape from vengeance, save only the escape that renders that vengeance empty and futile—through nonexistence. The inscription in flame went out, and the dignitaries looked into the eyes of their ruler, which were as if dead. He was long silent, till at last they addressed him, saying: "O Ruler of Eterna and Eristhena, Lord of Ilidar, Sinalost and Arcapturia, Steward of the Solar Shoals and Lunar—speak to us!"

"Not words, but action do we need, the last!" answered Inhiston.

The council trembled, but in a single voice replied: "Thou hast spoken!"

"So be it then!" said the King. "Now that it is decided, I shall say the name of the being that has driven us to this; I heard it upon ascending the throne. Is it not man?"

"Thou hast spoken!" replied the council.

Inhiston then turned to the Great Abstractionist:

"Do you your duty!"

The latter answered:

"I hear and I obey!"

Whereupon he uttered The Word, whose vibrations descended by rifts of air into the bosom of the planet; and then the jasper heavens cracked, and ere the faces of the falling towers could reach the ground, all seventy-seven Argentican cities yawned open into seventy-seven white craters, and amid the splitting plates of the continents crushed by branching fire the Silverines perished, and the great sun shone no longer on a planet, but on a ball of black clouds, which dwindled slowly, swept by a gale of oblivion. The void, having been pushed back by radiation harder than stone, converged now into a single quivering spark, and that spark died. The shock waves, after traveling seven days, reached a place where spaceships black as night were waiting.

"It is done!" said the creator of the monsters, who kept watch, to his comrades. "The kingdom of the Silverines has ceased to be. We can move on." The darkness at the stern of their vessels blossomed into flame and off they sped on the trail of vengeance. The Universe is infinite and has no bounds, but their hatred also has no bounds, and any day, at any hour, it can overtake us too.

The Second Sally

The tremendous success of their application of the Gargantius Effect gave both constructors such an appetite for adventure, that they resolved to sally forth once again to parts unknown. Unfortunately, they were quite unable to decide on a destination. Trurl, given to tropical climes, had his heart set on Scaldonia, the land of the Flaming Flamingos, while Klapaucius, of a somewhat cooler disposition, was equally determined to visit the Intergalactic Cold Pole, a bleak continent adrift among frozen stars. The friends were about to part company for good when Trurl suddenly had an idea. "Wait," he said, "we can advertise our services, then take the best offer!" "Ridiculous!" snorted Klapaucius. "How are you going to advertise? In a newspaper? Do you have any idea how long it takes a newspaper to reach the nearest planet? You'll be dead and buried before the first offer comes in!"

But Trurl gave a knowing smile and revealed his plan, which Klapaucius—begrudgingly—had to admit was ingenious, and so they set to work. All the necessary equipment quickly thrown together, they gathered up the local stars and arranged them in a great sign, a sign that would be visible at truly incalculable distances. Only blue giants were used for the first word—to get the cosmic reader's attention—and lesser stellar material made up the others. The advertisement read: TWO Distinguished Constructors Seek Employment Commensurate with their Skill and Above All Lucrative, Hence Preferably at the Court of a Well-heeled King (Should Have His Own Kingdom), Terms to Be Arranged. It was not long before, one bright morning, a most marvelous craft alighted on their front lawn. It gleamed in the sun, all inlaid with mother-of-pearl, had three legs intricately carved and six additional supports of solid gold (quite useless, since they didn't even reach the ground—but then, the builders obviously had more wealth than they knew what to do with). Down a magnificent staircase with billowing fountains on either side there came a figure of stately bearing with a retinue of six-legged machines: some of these massaged him, some supported him and fanned him, and the smallest flew about his august brow and sprayed it with eau de cologne from an atomizer. This impressive emissary greeted the constructors on behalf of his lord and sovereign, King Krool, who wished to engage them.

"What sort of work is it?" asked Trurl, interested.

"The details, gentle sirs, you shall learn at the proper time," was his reply. He was dressed in galligaskins of gold, mink-tufted buskins, sequined earmuffs, and a robe of most unusual cut—instead of pockets it had little shelves full of mints and marzipan. Tiny mechanical flies also buzzed about his person, and these he brushed away whenever they grew too bold.

"For now," he went on, "I can only say that His Boundless Kroolty is a great enthusiast of the hunt, a fearless and peerless conqueror of every sort of galactic fauna, and verily, his prowess has reached such heights that now the fiercest predators known are no longer worthy game for him. And herein lies our misfortune, for he craves excitement, danger, thrills . . . which is why—"

"Of course!" said Trurl. "He wants us to construct a new

model of beast, something wild and rapacious enough to present a challenge."

"You are, worthy constructor, indeed quick!" said the King's emissary. "Then it is agreed?"

Klapaucius began to question the emissary more closely on certain practical matters. But after the King's generosity was glowingly described and sufficiently elaborated upon, they hurriedly packed their things and a few books, ran up the magnificent staircase, hopped on board and were immediately lifted, with a great roar and burst of flame that blackened the ship's gold legs, into the interstellar night.

As they traveled, the emissary briefed the constructors on the laws and customs prevailing in the Kingdon of Krool, told them of the monarch's nature, as broad and open as a leveled city, and of his manly pursuits, and much more, so that by the time the ship landed, they could speak the language like natives.

First they were taken to a splendid villa situated on a mountainside above the village—this was where they were to stay. Then, after a brief rest, the King sent a carriage for them, a carriage drawn by six fire-breathing monsters. These were muzzled with fire screens and smoke filters, had their wings clipped to keep them on the ground, and long spiked tails and six paws apiece with iron claws that cut deep pits in the road wherever they went. As soon as the monsters saw the constructors, the entire team set up a howl, belching fire and brimstone, and strained to get at them. The coachmen in asbestos armor and the King's huntsmen with hoses and pumps had to fall upon the crazed creatures and beat them into submission with laser and maser clubs before Trurl and Klapaucius could safely step into the plush carriage, which they did without a word. The carriage tore off at breakneck speed or—to use an appropriate metaphor—like a bat out of hell.

"You know," Trurl whispered in Klapaucius' ear as they

rushed along, knocking down everything in their path and leaving a long trail of sulfurous smoke behind them, "I have a feeling that this king won't settle for just anything. I mean, if he has coursers like these . . ."

But level-headed Klapaucius said nothing. Houses now flashed by, walls of diamonds and sapphires and silver, while the dragons thundered and hissed and the drivers cursed and shouted. At last a colossal portcullis loomed up ahead, opened, and their carriage whirled into the court-yard, careening so sharply that the flower beds all shriveled up, then ground to a stop before a castle black as blackest night. Welcomed by an unusually dismal fanfare and quite overwhelmed by the massive stairs, balustrades and espe-cially the stone giants that guarded the main gate, Trurl and Klapaucius, flanked by a formidable escort, entered the mighty castle.

King Krool awaited them in an enormous hall the shape of a skull, a vast and vaulted cave of beaten silver. There was a gaping pit in the floor, the skull's foramen magnum, and beyond it stood the throne, over which two streams of light crossed like swords—they came from high windows fixed in the skull's eye sockets and with panes specially tinted to give everything a harsh and infernal aspect. The constructors now saw Krool himself: too impatient to sit still on his throne, this monarch paced from wall to wall across the silver floor, his steps booming in that cadaverous cavern, and as he spoke he emphasized his words with such sudden stabs of the hand, that the air whistled.

"Welcome, constructors!" he said, skewering them both with his eyes. "As you've no doubt learned from Lord Pro-tozor, Master of the Royal Hunt, I want you to build me new and better kinds of game. Now I'm not interested, you understand, in any mountain of steel on a hundred-odd treads—that's a job for heavy artillery, not for me. My quarry must be strong and ferocious, but swift and nimble too, and above all cunning and full of wiles, so that I will have to call upon all my hunter's art to drive it to the ground. It must be a highly intelligent beast, and know all there is to know of covering tracks, doubling back, hiding in shadows and lying in wait, for such is my will!"

"Forgive me, Your Highness," said Klapaucius with a careful bow, "but if we do Your Highness' bidding too well, might not this put the royal life and limb in some peril?"

The King roared with such laughter that a couple of crystal pendants fell off a chandelier and shattered at the feet of the trembling constructors.

"Have no fear of that, noble constructors !" he said with a grim smile. "You are not the first, and you will not be the last, I expect. Know that I am a just but most exacting ruler. Too often have assorted knaves, flatterers and fakes attempted to deceive me, too often, I say, have they posed as distinguished hunting engineers, solely to empty my coffers and fill their sacks with gems and precious stones, leaving me, in return, with a few paltry scarecrows that fall apart at the first touch. Too often has this happened for me not to take appropriate measures. For twelve years now any constructor who fails to meet my demands, who promises more than he is able to deliver, indeed receives his reward, but is hurled, reward and all, into yon deep well—unless he be game enough (excuse the pun) to serve as the quarry himself. In which case, gentlemen, I use no weapon but these two bare hands . . ."

"And . . . and have there been, ah, many such impostors?" asked Trurl in a weak voice.

"Many? That's difficult to say. I only know that no one yet has satisfied me, and the scream of terror they invariably give as they plummet to the bottom doesn't last quite so long as it used to—the remains, no doubt, have begun to mount. But rest assured, gentlemen, there is room enough still for you!"

A deathly silence followed these dire words, and the two friends couldn't help but look in the direction of that dark and ominous hole. The King resumed his relentless pacing, his boots striking the floor like sledge hammers in an echo chamber.

"But, with Your Highness' permission . . . that is, we—we haven't yet drawn up the contract," stammered Trurl. "Couldn't we have an hour or two to think it over, weigh carefully what Your Highness has been so gracious as to tell us, and then of course we can decide whether to accept your generous offer or, on the other hand—"

"Ha!" laughed the King like a thunderclap. "Or, on the other hand, to go home? I'm afraid not, gentlemen! The moment you set foot on board the *Infernanda,* you accepted my offer! If every constructor who came here could leave whenever he pleased, why, I'd have to wait forever for my fondest hopes to be realized! No, you must stay and build me a beast to hunt. I give you twelve days, and now you may go. Whatever pleasure you desire, in the meantime, is yours. You have but to ask the servants I have given you; nothing will be denied you. In twelve days, then!"

"With Your Highness' permission, you can keep the pleasures, but—well, would it be at all possible for us to have a look at the, uh, hunting trophies Your Highness must have collected as a result, so to speak, of the efforts of our predecessors?"

"But of course!" said the King indulgently and clapped his hands with such force that sparks flew and danced across the silver walls. The gust of air from those powerful palms cooled even more our constructors' ardor for adventure. Six guards in white and gold appeared and conducted them down a corridor that twisted and wound like the gullet of a giant serpent. Finally, to their great relief, it led out into a large, open garden. There, on remarkably well-trimmed lawns, stood the hunting trophies of King Krool.

Nearest at hand was a saber-toothed colossus, practically cut in two in spite of the heavy mail and plate armor that was to have protected its trunk; the hind legs, disproportionately large (evidently designed for great leaps), lay upon the grass alongside the tail, which ended in a firearm with its magazine half-empty—a clear sign that the creature had not fallen to the King without a fight. A yellow strip of cloth hanging from its open jaws also testified to this, for Trurl recognized in it the breeches worn by the King's huntsmen. Next was another prone monstrosity, a dragon with a multitude of tiny wings all singed and blackened by enemy fire; its circuits had spilled out molten and had then congealed in a copper-porcelain puddle. Farther on stood another creature, the pillarlike legs spread wide. A gentle breeze soughed softly through its fangs. And there were wrecks on wheels and wrecks on treads, some with claws and some with cannon, all sundered to the magnetic core, and tank-turtles with squashed turrets, and mutilated military millipedes, and other oddities, broken and battle-scarred, some equipped with auxiliary brains (burnt out), some perched on telescoping stilts (dislocated), and there were little vicious biting things strewn about. These had been made to attack in great swarms, then regroup in a sphere bristling with gun muzzles and bayonets—a clever idea, but it saved neither them nor their creators. Down this aisle of devastation walked Trurl and Klapaucius, pale, silent, looking as if they were on their way to a funeral instead of to another brilliant session of vigorous invention. They came at last to the end of that dreadful gallery of Krool's triumphs and stepped into the carriage that was waiting for them at the gate. That dragon team which sped them back to their lodgings seemed less terrible now. Just as soon as they were alone in their sumptuously appointed green and crimson drawing room, before a table heaped high with effervescent drinks and rare deli-

cacies, Trurl broke into a volley of imprecations; he reviled
Klapaucius for heedlessly accepting the offer made by the
Master of the Royal Hunt, thereby bringing down misfortune on their heads, when they easily could have stayed at
home and rested on their laurels. Klapaucius said nothing,
waiting patiently for Trurl's desperate rage to expend itself,
and when it finally did and Trurl had collapsed into a lavish
mother-of-pearl chaise longue and buried his face in his
hands, he said:

"Well, we'd better get to work."

These words did much to revive Trurl, and the two constructors immediately began to consider the various possibilities, drawing on their knowledge of the deepest and
darkest secrets of the arcane art of cybernetic generation.
First of all, they agreed that victory lay neither in the armor
nor in the strength of the monster to be built, but entirely in
its program, in other words, in an algorithm of demoniacal
derivation. "It must be a truly diabolical creature, a thing of
absolute evil!" they said, and though they had as yet no clear
idea of what or how, this observation lifted their spirits considerably. Such was their enthusiasm by the time they sat
down to draft the beast, that they worked all night, all day,
and through a second night and day before taking a break
for dinner. And as the Leyden jars were passed about, so
sure were they of success, that they winked and smirked—
but only when the servants weren't looking, since they suspected them (and rightly, too) of being the King's spies. So
the constructors said nothing of their work, but praised the
mulled electrolyte which the waiters brought in, tail coats
flapping, in beakers of the finest cut crystal. Only after the
repast, when they had wandered out on the veranda overlooking the village with its white steeples and domes catching the last golden rays of the setting sun, only then did
Trurl turn to Klapaucius and say:

"We're not out of the woods yet, you know."

"How do you mean?" asked Klapaucius in a cautious whisper.

"There's one difficulty. You see, if the King defeats our mechanical beast, he'll undoubtedly have us thrown into that pit, for we won't have done his bidding. If, on the other hand, the beast . . . You see what I mean?"

"If the beast isn't defeated?"

"No, if the beast defeats *him,* dear colleague. If that happens, the King's successor may not let us off so easily."

"You don't think we'd have to answer for that, do you? As a rule, heirs to the throne are only too happy to see it vacated."

"True, but this will be his son, and whether the son punishes us out of filial devotion or because he thinks the royal court expects it of him, it'll make little difference as far as we're concerned."

"That never occurred to me," muttered Klapaucius. "You're quite right, the prospects aren't encouraging. . . . Have you thought of a way out of this dilemma?"

"Well, we might make the beast multimortal. Picture this: the King slays it, it falls, then it gets up again, resurrected, and the King chases it again, slays it again, and so on, until he gets sick and tired of the whole thing."

"That he won't like," said Klapaucius after some thought. "And anyway, how would you design such a beast?"

"Oh, I don't know. . . . We could make it without any vital organs. The King chops the beast into little pieces, but the pieces grow back together."

"How?"

"Use a field."

"Magnetic?"

If you like."

"How do we operate it?"

"Remote control, perhaps?" asked Trurl.

"Too risky," said Klapaucius. "How do you know the King won't have us locked up in some dungeon while the hunt's in progress? Our poor predecessors were no fools, and look how they ended up. More than one of them, I'm sure, thought of remote control—yet it failed. No, we can't expect to maintain communication with the beast during the battle."

"Then why not use a satellite?" suggested Trurl. We could install automatic controls—"

"Satellite indeed!" snorted Klapaucius. "And how are you going to build it, let alone put it in orbit? There are no miracles in our profession, Trurl! We'll have to hide the controls some other way."

"But where can we hide the controls when they watch our every step? You've seen how the servants skulk about, sticking their noses into everything. We'd never be able to leave the premises ourselves, and certainly not smuggle out such a large piece of equipment. It's impossible!"

"Calm down," said prudent Klapaucius, looking over his shoulder. "Perhaps we don't need such equipment in the first place."

"Something has to operate the beast, and if that something is an electronic brain anywhere inside, the King will smash it to a pulp before you can say goodbye."

They were silent. Night had fallen and the village lights below were flickering on, one by one. Suddenly Trurl said:

"Listen, here's an idea. We only pretend to build a beast but in reality build a ship to escape on. We give it ears, a tail, paws, so no one will suspect, and they can be easily jettisoned on takeoff. What do you think of that? We get off scot-free and thumb our noses at the King!"

"And if the King has planted a real constructor among our servants, which is not unlikely, then it's all over and into the pit with us. Besides, running away—no, it just doesn't suit me. It's him or us, Trurl, you can't get around it."

"Yes, I suppose a spy could be a constructor too," said Trurl with a sigh. "What then can we do, in the name of the Great Comet?! How about—a photoelectric phantom?"

"You mean, a mirage? Have the King hunt a mirage? No thanks! After an hour or two of that, he'd come straight here and make phantoms of us!"

Again they were silent. Finally Trurl said:

"The only way out of our difficulty, as far as I can see, is to have the beast *abduct* the King, and then—"

"You don't have to say another word. Yes, that's not at all a bad idea. . . . Then for the ransom we—and haven't you noticed, old boy, that the orioles here are a deeper orange than on Maryland IV?" concluded Klapaucius, for just then some servants were bringing silver lamps out on the veranda. "There's still a problem though," he continued when they were alone again. "Assuming the beast can do what you say, how will we be able to negotiate with the prisoner if we're sitting in a dungeon ourselves?"

"You have a point there," said Trurl. "We'll have to figure some way around that. . . . The main thing, however, is the algorithm!"

"Any child knows that! What's a beast without an algorithm?"

So they rolled up their sleeves and sat down to experiment—by simulation, that is, mathematically and all on paper. And the mathematical models of King Krool and the beast did such fierce battle across the equation-covered table, that the constructors' pencils kept snapping. Furious, the beast writhed and wriggled its iterated integrals beneath the King's polynomial blows, collapsed into an infinite series of indeterminate terms, then got back up by raising itself to the nth power, but the King so belabored it with differentials and partial derivatives that its Fourier coefficients all canceled out (*see* Riemann's Lemma), and in the ensuing confusion the constructors completely lost sight of both King and beast. So they took a break, stretched their legs, had a swig from the Leyden jug to bolster their strength, then went back to work and tried it again from the beginning, this time unleashing their entire arsenal of tensor matrices and grand canonical ensembles, attacking the problem with such fervor that the very paper began to smoke. The King rushed forward with all his cruel coordinates and mean values, stumbled into a dark forest of roots and logarithms, had to backtrack, then encountered the beast on a field of irrational numbers (F_i) and smote it so grievously that it fell two decimal places and lost an epsilon, but the beast slid around an asymptote and hid in an n-dimensional orthogonal phase space, underwent expansion and came out, fuming factorially, and fell upon the King and hurt him passing sore. But the King, nothing daunted, put on his Markov chain mail and all his impervious parameters, took his increment Δk to infinity and dealt the beast a truly Boolean blow, sent it reeling through an x-axis and several brackets—but the beast, prepared for this, lowered its horns and—wham!!—the pencils flew like mad through transcendental functions and double eigentransformations, and when at last the beast closed in and the King was down and out for the count, the constructors jumped up, danced a jig, laughed and sang as they tore all their papers to shreds, much to the amazement of the spies perched in the chandelier—perched in vain, for they were uninitiated into the niceties of higher mathematics and consequently had no idea why Trurl and Klapaucius were now shouting, over and over, "Hurrah! Victory!!"

Well after midnight, the Leyden jug from which the constructors had on occasion refreshed themselves in the course of their labors was quietly taken to the headquarters of the King's secret police, where its false bottom was opened and a tiny tape recorder removed. This the experts switched on and listened to eagerly, but the rising sun found them totally unenlightened and looking haggard. One voice, for example, would say:

"Well? Is the King ready?"

"Right!"

"Where'd you put him? Over there? Good! Now—hold on, you have to keep the feet together. Not yours, idiot, the King's! All right now, ready? One, two, find the derivative! Quick! What do you get?"

"Pi."

"And the beast?"

"Under the radical sign. But look, the King's still standing!"

"Still standing, eh? Factor both sides, divide by two, throw in a few imaginary numbers—good! Now change variables and subtract—Trurl, what on earth are you doing?! The *beast,* not the King, the *beast!* That's right! Good! Perfect! Now transform, approximate and solve for x. Do you have it?"

"I have it! Klapaucius! Look at the King now!!"

There was a pause, then a burst of wild laughter.

That same morning, as all the experts and high officials of the secret police shook their heads, bleary-eyed after a sleepless night, the constructors asked for quartz, vanadium, steel, copper, platinum, rhinestones, dysprosium, yttrium and thulium, also cerium and germanium, and most of the other elements that make up the Universe, plus a variety of machines and qualified technicians, not to mention a wide assortment of spies—for so insolent had the constructors become, that on the triplicate requisition form they boldly wrote: "Also, kindly send agents of various cuts and stripes at the discretion and with the approval of the Proper Authorities." The next day they asked for sawdust and a large red velvet curtain on a stand, a cluster of little glass bells in the center and a large tassel at each of its four corners; everything, even down to the littlest glass bell, was specified with the utmost precision. The King scowled when he heard these requests, but ordered them to be carried out to the letter, for he had given his royal word. The constructors were thus granted all that they wished.

All that they wished grew more and more outlandish. For instance, in the files of the secret police under code number 48999/11K/T was a copy of a requisition for three tailor's mannequins as well as six full police uniforms, complete with sash, side arm, shako, plume and handcuffs, also all available back issues of the magazine *The Patriotic Policeman*, yearbooks and supplements included—under "Comments" the constructors had guaranteed the return of all items listed above within twenty-four hours of delivery and in perfect condition. In another, classified section of the police archives was a copy of a letter from Klapaucius in which he demanded the immediate shipment of (1) a life-size doll representing the Postmaster General in full regalia, and (2) a light gig painted green with a kerosene lamp on the left and a sky-blue sign on the back that said THINK. The doll and gig proved too much for the Chief of Police: he had to be taken away for a much-needed rest. During the next three days the constructors asked only for barrels of red castor oil, and after that—nothing. From then on, they worked in the basement of the palace, hammering away and singing space chanties, and at night blue lights came flashing from the basement windows and gave weird shapes to the trees in the garden outside. Trurl and Klapaucius with their many helpers bustled about amid arcs and sparks, now and then looking up to see faces pressed against the glass: the servants, as if out of idle curiosity, were photographing their every move. One evening, when the weary constructors had finally dragged themselves off to bed, the components of the apparatus they had been working on were quickly transported by unmarked balloon to police headquarters and assembled by eighteen of the finest cyberneticians in the land, who had been deputized and duly sworn in for that very purpose, whereupon a gray tin mouse ran out from under their hands, blowing soap bubbles and dropping a thin trail of chalk dust from under its tail, which spelled, as it danced this way and that across the table, WHAT, DON'T YOU LOVE US ANYMORE? Never before in the kingdom's history did Chiefs of Police have to be replaced with such speed and regularity. The uniforms, the doll, the green gig, even the sawdust, everything which the constructors returned exactly as promised, was thoroughly examined under electron microscope. But except for a minuscule card in the sawdust which read JUST SAWDUST, there was nothing out of the ordinary. Then individual atoms of the uniforms and gig were thoroughly searched—with equal lack of success. At last the day came when the work was completed. A huge vehicle on three hundred wheels, looking something like a refrigerator, was drawn up to the main entrance and opened in the presence of witnesses and officials; Trurl and Klapaucius brought out a curtain, the one with the tassels and bells, and placed it carefully inside, in the middle of the floor. Then they got in themselves, closed the door, did something, then went and got various containers from the basement, cans of chemicals, all sorts of finely ground powders—gray, silver, white, yellow, green—and sprinkled them under and around the curtain, then stepped out, had the vehicle closed and locked, consulted their watches and together counted out fourteen and a half seconds—at which time, much to everyone's surprise, since the vehicle was stationary and there could be no question of a breeze inside (for the seal was hermetic), the glass bells tinkled. The constructors exchanged a wink and said:

"You can take it now!"

The rest of the day they spent blowing soap bubbles from the veranda. That evening Lord Protozor, Master of the Royal Hunt, came with an escort and politely but firmly informed them that they were to go with him at once to an assigned place. They were required to leave all their possessions behind, even their clothes; in exchange they were given rags, then put in irons. The guards and police dignitaries present were astounded by their perfect sang-froid: instead of demanding justice or trembling with fear, Trurl giggled as the shackles were being hammered on, saying he was ticklish. And when the constructors were thrown into a dark and dismal dungeon, they promptly struck up a rousing chorus of "Sing Sweet Software."

Meanwhile mighty Krool rode forth from the village on his mighty hunting chariot, surrounded by all his retinue and followed by a long and winding train of riders and machines, machines that included not only the traditional catapult and cannon, but enormous laser guns and beta ray bazookas, and a tar-thrower guaranteed to immobilize anything that walked, swam, flew or rolled along.

And so this grand procession wended its way to the royal game preserve, and many jokes were made, and boasts, and haughty toasts, and no one gave a thought to the two constructors, except perhaps to remark that those fools were in a pretty pickle now.

But when the silver trumpets announced His Majesty's approach, one could see a huge vehicle-refrigerator coming up in the opposite direction. Its door flung open, and for one brief moment there gaped the black maw of what appeared to be some sort of field gun. Next there was a boom, a puff of yellow smoke, and something came rocketing out, a form as blurry as a tornado and with the general consistency of a sandstorm; it arced through the air so fast that no one really got a good look at it anyway. Whatever it was flew a hundred paces or more and landed without a sound; the curtain that had been wrapped around it floated to the earth, glass bells tinkling oddly in that perfect silence, and lay there like a crushed strawberry. Now everyone could see the beast clearly—though it wasn't clear at all, but looked a little like a hill, rather large, fairly long, its color much like its surroundings, a clump of dried-up weeds. The King's huntsmen unleashed the whole pack of automated hounds (mainly Saint Cybernards and Cyberman pinschers, with an occasional high-frequency terrier); these hurled themselves, howling and slavering, at the crouching beast. The beast didn't rear back, didn't roar, didn't even breathe fire, but only opened its two eyes wide and reduced half the pack to ashes in a trice.

"Oho! Laser-eyed, is it?" cried the King. "Hand me my trusty duralumin doublet, my bulletproof buckler, my halberd and arquebus!" Thus accoutered and gleaming like a supernova, he rode out upon his fearless high-fidelity cybersteed, came nigh the beast and smote it such a mighty blow that the air crackled and its head tumbled neatly to the ground. Though the retinue dutifully hallooed his triumph, the King took no delight in it; greatly angered, he swore in his heart to devise some special torment for those wretches who dared to call themselves constructors. The beast, however, shook another head out of its severed neck, opened its new eyes wide and played a withering beam across the King's armor (which, however, was proof against all manner of electromagnetic radiation). "Well, those two weren't a total loss," said the King to himself, "though this still won't help them." And he recharged his charger and spurred it into the fray.

This time he swung full and cleaved the beast in twain. The beast didn't seem to mind—in fact, it positioned itself helpfully beneath the whistling blade and gave a grateful twitch as it fell. And small wonder! The King took another look: the thing was twinned instead of twained! There were two spitting images, each a little smaller than the original, plus a third, a baby beast gamboling between them—that was the head he had cut off earlier: it now had a tail and feet and was doing cartwheels through the weeds.

"What next?" thought the King. "Chop it into mice or little worms? A fine way to hunt!" And with great ire did he have at it, hewing with might and main until there were no end of little beasts underfoot, but suddenly they all backed off, went into a huddle, and there stood the beast again, good as new and stifling a yawn.

"H'm," thought the King. "Apparently it has the same kind of stabilization mechanism that—what was his name again?—Pumpington—that Pumpington tried to use. Yes, I dealt with him myself for that idiotic trick. . . . Well, we'll just wheel out the antimatter artillery. . . ."

He picked one with a six-foot bore, lined it up and loaded it himself, took aim, pulled the string and sent a perfectly silent and weirdly shimmering shell straight at the beast, to blow it to smithereens once and for all. But nothing happened—that is, nothing much. The beast only crouched a little lower, put out its left hand, long and hairy, and gave the King the finger.

"Bring out our biggest!" roared the King, pretending not to notice. And several hundred peasants pulled up a veritable giant of a cannon, all of eighty-gauge, which the King aimed and was just about to fire—when all at once the beast leaped. The King lifted his sword to defend himself, but then there was no more beast. Those who saw what happened next said later that they were sure they had taken leave of their senses, for as the beast flew through the air, it underwent a lightning transformation, the grayish hulk divided up into three men in uniform, three policemen, who, still aloft, were already preparing to do their duty. The first policeman, a sergeant, got out the handcuffs, maneuvering his legs to keep upright; the second held on to his plumed shako with one hand, so it wouldn't blow off, and with the other pulled out a warrant from his breast pocket; the third, apparently a rookie, assumed a horizontal position beneath the feet of the first two, to cushion their fall—after which, however, he jumped up and carefully dusted off his uniform. Meanwhile the first policeman had handcuffed the dumbfounded King and the second slapped the sword from his hand. Feebly protesting, the suspect was then summarily trotted off the field. The entire hunting procession stood rooted to the spot for a minute or two, then gave a yell and followed in hot pursuit. The snorting cybersteeds had practically caught up with the abductors, and swords and sabers were unsheathed and raised to strike, but the third policeman bent over, depressed his bellybutton and immediately the arms grew into two shafts, the legs coiled up, sprouting spokes, and began to turn, while the back formed the seat of a green racing gig to accommodate the other two policemen, who were vigorously plying the now-harnessed King with a whip, to make him run faster. The King obliged and broke into a mad gallop, waving his arms frantically to ward off the blows that descended upon his royal head; but now the huntsmen were gaining again, so the policemen jumped on the King's back and one slipped down between the shafts, huffed and puffed and turned into a spinning top, a dancing whirlwind, which gave wings to the little gig and whisked it away over hill and dale till it disappeared altogether in a cloud of dust. The King's retinue split up and began a desperate search with Geiger counters and bloodhounds, and a special detachment came running up with shovels and flamethrowers and left no bone unburned in all the neighboring cemeteries—an obvious error, occasioned most likely by the trembling hand that hastily telegraphed the order from the observation balloon that had monitored the hunt. Several police divisions rushed here and there, searched the grounds, every bush, every weed, and both x-rays and laboratory samples were diligently taken of everything imaginable. The King's charger was ordered to appear before a special board of inquiry appointed by the Prosecutor General. A unit of paratroopers with vacuum cleaners and sieves was dropped on the royal game preserve to sift through every last particle of dust. Finally, the order was issued that anyone resembling a policeman was to be detained and held without bail, which naturally created difficulties—one half of the police force, as it turned out, had arrested the other, and vice versa. At dusk the huntsmen and soldiers returned to the village dazed and bedraggled with the woeful tidings that neither hide nor hair of the King's person was anywhere to be found.

By torchlight and in the dead of night, the chained constructors were taken before the Great Chancellor and Keeper of the Royal Seal, who addressed them in the following way:

"Whereas ye have falsely conspired and perversely plotted against the Crown and Life of Our Beloved Sovereign and Most Noble Ruler Krool and therewith dared to raise a treacherous hand and vilely devise his demise, not to mention impersonating an officer, a great aggravation of your crimes, so shall ye be quartered without quarter, impaled and pilloried, disemboweled, buried alive, crucified and burnt at the stake, after which your ashes shall be sent into orbit as a warning and perpetual reminder to all would-be regicides, amen."

"Can't you wait a bit?" asked Trurl. "You see, we were expecting a letter . . ."

"A letter, thou most scurrilous and scurvy knave?!"

Just then the guards made way for the Postmaster General himself—indeed, how could they bar that dignitary's entrance with their poleaxes? The Postmaster approached in full regalia, his medals jingling impressively, pulled a letter from a sapphire satchel and handed it to the Chancellor, saying, "Mannequin though I be, I come from His Majesty," whereupon he disintegrated into a fine powder. The Chancellor could scarcely believe his eyes, but quickly recognized the King's signet impressed there on the purple sealing wax; he opened the letter and read that His Majesty was forced to negotiate with the enemy, for the constructors had employed means algorithmic and algebraic to make him captive, and now they would list their demands, all of which the Great Chancellor had better meet, if he wished ever to get his Mighty Sovereign back in one piece. Signed: "Krool herewith affixes his hand and seal, held prisoner in a cave of unknown location by one pseudoconstabulary beast in three uniforms personified."

There then arose a great clamor, everyone shouting and asking what it all meant and what were the demands, to which Trurl said only, "Our chains, if you please."

A blacksmith was summoned to unfetter them, after which Trurl said:

"We are hungry and dirty, we need a bath, a shave, massage, refreshment, nothing but the best, plenty of pomp and a water ballet with fireworks for dessert!"

The court, of course, was hopping mad, but had to comply in every particular. Only at dawn did the constructors return from their villa, each elegantly pomaded, arrayed and reclining in a sedan chair borne by footmen (their former informers); they then, deigning to grant an audience, sat down and presented their demands—not off the top of their heads, mind you, but from a little notebook they had prepared for the occasion and hidden behind a curtain in their room. The following articles were read:

First, A ship of the finest make and model available shall be furnished to carry the constructors home.

2nd, The said ship shall be laden with various cargo as here specified: diamonds—four bushels, gold coin—forty bushels, platinum, palladium and whatever other ready valuables they happen to think of—eight bushels of each, also whatever mementos and tokens from the Royal Apartments the signatories of this instrument may deem appropriate.

3rd, Until such time as the said ship shall be in readiness for takeoff, every nut and bolt in place, fully loaded and delivered up to the constructors complete with red carpet, an eighty-piece send-off band and children's chorus, an abundance of honors, decorations and awards, and a wildly cheering crowd—until then, no King.

4th, That a formal expression of undying gratitude shall be stamped upon a gold medallion and addressed to Their Most Sublime and Radiant Constructors Trurl and Klapaucius, Delight and Terror of the Universe, and moreover it shall contain a full account of their victory and be duly signed and notarized by every high and low official in the land, then set in the richly embellished barrel of the King's favorite cannon, which Lord Protozor, Master of the Royal Hunt, shall himself and wholly unaided carry on board—no other Protozor but the one who lured Their Most Sublime and Radiant Constructors to this planet, thinking to work their painful and ignominious death thereby.

5th, That the aforesaid Protozor shall accompany them on their return journey as insurance against any sort of double-dealing, pursuit, and the like. On board he shall occupy a cage three by three by four feet and shall receive a daily allowance of humble pie with a filling made of that very same sawdust which Their Most Sublime and Radiant Constructors saw fit to order in the process of indulging the King's foolishness and which was subsequently taken to police headquarters by unmarked balloon.

6th and lastly, The King need not crave forgiveness of Their Most Sublime and Radiant Constructors on bended knee, since he is much too beneath them to deserve notice.

In Witness Whereof, the parties have hereunto set their hands and seals this day and year, etc. and so on. By: Trurl and Klapaucius, Constructors, and the Great Chancellor, the Great Chamberlain, the Great Chief of Secret Police, the Seneschal, Squadron Leader and Royal Balloonmaster. All the ministers and dignitaries turned blue, but what could they do? They had no choice, so a ship was immediately ordered. But then the constructors unexpectedly showed up after a leisurely breakfast, to supervise the work, and nothing suited them: this material, for instance, was no good, and that engineer was an absolute idiot, and they had to have a revolving magic lantern in the main hall, one with four pneumatic widgets and a calibrated cuckoo clock on top—and if the natives here didn't know what a widget was, so much the worse for them, considering that the King was no doubt most impatient for his release and would (when he could) deal harshly with anyone who dared to delay it. This remark occasioned a general numbness, a great weakness about the knees, and much trembling, but the work continued apace. Finally the ship was ready and the royal stevedores began to stow the cargo in the hold, diamonds, sacks of pearls, so much gold it kept spilling out the hatch. Meanwhile the police were secretly running all about the countryside, turning everything upside down, much to the amusement of Trurl and Klapaucius, who didn't mind explaining to a fearful but fascinated audience how it all happened, how they had discarded one idea after another until they hit upon an altogether different kind of beast. Not knowing where or how to place the controls—that is, the brain—so that they would be safe, the constructors had simply made everything brain, enabling the beast to think with its leg, or tail, or jaws (equipped with wisdom teeth only). But that was just the beginning. The real problem had two aspects, algorithmic and psychoanalytic. First they had to determine what would check the King, catch him flatfooted, so to speak. To this end, they created by nonlinear transmutation a police subset within the beast, since everyone knows that resisting or interfering with an officer who is making an arrest *lege artis* is a cosmic offense and utterly unthinkable. So much for the psychology of it—except that the Postmaster General was utilized here on similar grounds: an official of lower rank might not have made it past the guards, the letter then would not have been delivered, and the constructors would have very literally lost their heads. Moreover, the Postmaster mannequin had been given means to bribe the guards, should that have proved necessary. Every eventuality had been anticipated and provided for. Now as far as the algorithms went: they had only to find the proper domain of beasts, closed, bounded and bonded, with plenty of laws both associative and distributive in operation, throw in a constable constant or two, some graphs of graft, squadratic equations and crime waves—and the thing took over from there, once activated by the expedient of writing a document-program (behind the curtain with the bells) in castor oil ink, rendering it thereby sufficiently hard to swallow to serve as a red-tape generator. We might add here that later on the constructors had an article published in a prominent scientific journal under the title of "Recursive β—Metafunctions in the Special Case of a Bogus Polypolice Transmogrification Conversion on an Oscillating Harmonic Field of Glass Bells and Green Gig, Kerosene Lamp on the Left to Divert Attention, Solved by Beastly Incarceration—Concatenation," which was subsequently exploited by the tabloids as "The Police State Rears Its Ugly Head." Obviously none of the ministers, dignitaries, or huntsmen understood a single word of what was said, but that hardly mattered. The loving subjects of King Krool knew not whether they should despise these constructors or stand and gape in awe and admiration.

Now all was in readiness for takeoff. Trurl, as stipulated in the agreement, went through the King's private chambers with a large sack and calmly appropriated whatever object he took a fancy to. Finally, the carriage arrived and took the victors to the spaceport, where a crowd cheered wildly and a children's chorus sang, then a charming little girl in local costume curtsied and presented them with a ribboned nose-gay, and high-ranking officials took turns to express their undying gratitude, bidding them both a fond farewell, and the band played, several ladies fainted, and then a hush fell over the multitude. Klapaucius had pulled a tooth from his mouth, not an ordinary tooth but a transmitter-receiver, a two-way bicuspid. He threw a tiny switch and a sandstorm appeared on the horizon, growing and growing, whirling faster and faster, until it dropped into an empty space between the ship and the crowd and came to a sudden stop, scattering dust and debris in all directions. Everyone gasped and stepped back—there stood the beast, looking unusually bestial as it flashed its laser eyes and flailed its dragon tail!

"The King, if you please," said Klapaucius. But the beast answered, speaking in a perfectly normal voice:

"Not on your life. It's my turn now to make demands. . . ."

"What? Have you gone mad? You have to obey, it's in the matrix!" shouted Klapaucius. Everyone stared, thunderstruck.

"Matrix-schmatrix. Look pal, I'm not just any beast, I'm algorithmic, heuristic and sadistic, fully automatic and autocratic, that means undemocratic, and I've got loads of loops and plenty of feedback so none of that back talk or I'll clap you in irons, that means in the clink with the King, in the brig with the green gig, get me?"

"I'll give you feedback!" roared Klapaucius, furious. But Trurl asked the beast:

"What exactly do you want?"

And he sneaked around behind Klapaucius and pulled out a special tooth of his own, so the beast wouldn't see.

"Well, first of all I want to marry—"

But they never learned whom in particular the beast had in mind, for Trurl threw a tiny switch and quickly chanted: "Eeny, meeny, miney, mo, input, output, out—you—go!" The fantastically complex electromagnetic wave system that held the beast's atoms in place now came apart under the influence of those words, and the beast blinked, wiggled its ears, swallowed, tried to pull itself together, but before it could even grit its teeth there was a hot gust of wind, a strong smell of ozone, then nothing left to pull together, just a little mound of ashes and the King standing in the middle, safe and sound, but in great need of a bath and mortified to tears that it had come to this.

"That'll cut you down to size," said Trurl, and no one knew whether he meant the beast or the King. In either case, the algorithm had done its job well.

"And now, gentlemen," Trurl concluded, "if you'll kindly help the Master of the Royal Hunt into his cage, we can be on our way . . ."

Tale of the Computer That Fought a Dragon

King Poleander Partobon, ruler of Cyberia, was a great warrior, and being an advocate of the methods of modern strategy, above all else he prized cybernetics as a military art. His kingdom swarmed with thinking machines, for Poleander put them everywhere he could; not merely in the astronomical observatories or the schools, but he ordered electric brains mounted in the rocks upon the roads, which with loud voices cautioned pedestrians against tripping; also in posts, in walls, in trees, so that one could ask directions anywhere when lost; he stuck them onto clouds, so they could announce the rain in advance, he added them to the hills and valleys—in short, it was impossible to walk on Cyberia without bumping into an intelligent machine. The planet was beautiful, since the King not only gave decrees for the cybernetic perfecting of that which had long been in existence, but he introduced by law entirely new orders of things. Thus for example in his kingdom were manufactured cyberbeetles and buzzing cyberbees, and even cyberflies— these would be seized by mechanical spiders when they grew too numerous. On the planet cyberbosks of cybergorse rustled in the wind, cybercalliopes and cyberviols sang—but besides these civilian devices there were twice as many military, for the King was most bellicose. In his palace vaults he had a strategic computer, a machine of uncommon mettle; he had smaller ones also, and divisions of cybersaries, enormous cybermatics and a whole arsenal of every other kind of weapon, including powder. There was only this one problem, and it troubled him greatly, namely, that he had not a single adversary or enemy and no one in any way wished to invade his land, and thereby provide him with the opportunity to demonstrate his kingly and terrifying courage, his tactical genius, not to mention the simply extraordinary effectiveness of his cybernetic weaponry. In the absence of genuine enemies and aggressors the King had his engineers build artificial ones, and against these he did battle, and always won. However inasmuch as the battles and campaigns were genuinely dreadful, the populace suffered no little injury from them. The subjects murmured when all too many cyberfoes had destroyed their settlements and towns, when the synthetic enemy poured liquid fire upon them; they even dared voice their discontent when the King himself, issuing forth as their deliverer and vanquishing the artificial foe, in the course of the victorious attacks laid waste to everything that stood in his path. They grumbled even then, the ingrates, though the thing was done on their behalf.

Until the King wearied of the war games on the planet and decided to raise his sights. Now it was cosmic wars and sallies that he dreamed of. His planet had a large Moon, entirely desolate and wild; the King laid heavy taxes upon his subjects, to obtain the funds needed to build whole armies on that Moon and have there a new theater of war. And the subjects were more than happy to pay, figuring that King Poleander would now no longer deliver them with his cybermatics, nor test the strength of his arms upon their homes and heads. And so the royal engineers built on the Moon a splendid computer, which in turn was to create all manner of troops and self-firing gunnery. The King lost no time in testing the machine's prowess this way and that; at one point he ordered it—by telegraph—to execute a volt-vault electrosault: for he wanted to see if it was true, what his engineers had told him, that that machine could do anything. If it can do anything, he thought, then let it do a flip. However the text of the telegram underwent a slight distortion and the machine received the order that it was to execute not an electrosault, but an electrosaur—and this it carried out as best it could.

Meanwhile the King conducted one more campaign, liberating some provinces of his realm seized by cyberknechts; he completely forgot about the order given the computer on the Moon, then suddenly giant boulders came hurtling down from there; the King was astounded, for one even fell on the wing of the palace and destroyed his prize collection of cyberads, which are dryads with feedback. Fuming, he telegraphed the Moon computer at once, demanding an explanation. It didn't reply however, for it no longer was: the electrosaur had swallowed it and made it into its own tail.

Immediately the King dispatched an entire armed expedition to the Moon, placing at its head another computer, also very valiant, to slay the dragon, but there was only some flashing, some rumbling, and then no more computer nor expedition; for the electrodragon wasn't pretend and wasn't pretending, but battled with the utmost verisimilitude, and had moreover the worst of intentions regarding the kingdom and the King. The King sent to the Moon his cybernants, cyberneers, cyberines and lieutenant cybernets, at the very end he even sent one cyberalissimo, but it too accomplished nothing; the hurly-burly lasted a little longer, that was all. The King watched through a telescope set up on the palace balcony.

The dragon grew, the Moon became smaller and smaller, since the monster was devouring it piecemeal and incorporating it into its own body. The King saw then, and his subjects did also, that things were serious, for when the ground beneath the feet of the electrosaur was gone, it would for certain hurl itself upon the planet and upon them. The King thought and thought, but he saw no remedy, and knew not what to do. To send machines was no good, for they would be lost, and to go himself was no better, for he was afraid. Suddenly the King heard, in the stillness of the night, the telegraph chattering from his royal bedchamber. It was the King's personal receiver, solid gold with a diamond needle, linked to the Moon; the King jumped up and ran to it, the apparatus meanwhile went *tap-tap, tap-tap,* and tapped out this telegram: THE DRAGON SAYS POLEANDER PARTOBON BETTER CLEAR OUT BECAUSE HE THE DRAGON INTENDS TO OCCUPY THE THRONE!

The King took fright, quaked from head to toe, and ran, just as he was, in his ermine nightshirt and slippers, down to the palace vaults, where stood the strategy machine, old and very wise. He had not as yet consulted it, since prior to the rise and uprise of the electrodragon they had argued on the subject of a certain military operation; but now was not the time to think of that—his throne, his life was at stake!

He plugged it in, and as soon as it warmed up he cried: "My old computer! My good computer! It's this way and that, the dragon wishes to deprive me of my throne, to cast me out, help, speak, how can I defeat it?!"

"Uh-uh," said the computer. "First you must admit I was right in that previous business, and secondly, I would have you address me only as Digital Grand Vizier, though you may also say to me: 'Your Ferromagneticity'!"

"Good, good, I'll name you Grand Vizier, I'll agree to anything you like, only save me!"

The machine whirred, chirred, hummed, hemmed, then said:

"It is a simple matter. We build an electrosaur more powerful than the one located on the Moon. It will defeat the lunar one, settle its circuitry once and for all and thereby attain the goal!"

"Perfect!" replied the King. "And can you make a blueprint of this dragon?"

"It will be an ultradragon," said the computer. "And I can make you not only a blueprint, but the thing itself, which I shall now do, it won't take a minute, King!" And true to its word, it hissed, it chugged, it whistled and buzzed, assembling something down within itself, and already an object like a giant claw, sparking, arcing, was emerging from its side, when the King shouted:

"Old computer! Stop!"

"Is this how you address me? I am the Digital Grand Vizier!"

"Ah, of course," said the King. "Your Ferromagneticity, the electrodragon you are making will defeat the other dragon, granted, but it will surely remain in the other's place, how then are we to get rid of it in turn?!"

"By making yet another, still more powerful," explained the computer.

"No, no! In that case don't do anything, I beg you, what good will it be to have more and more terrible dragons on the Moon when I don't want any there at all?"

"Ah, now that's a different matter," the computer replied. "Why didn't you say so in the first place? You see how illogically you express yourself? One moment ... I must think."

And it churred and hummed, and chuffed and chuckled, and finally said:

"We make an antimoon with an antidragon, place it in the Moon's orbit (here something went snap inside), sit around the fire and sing: *Oh I'm a robot full of fun, water doesn't scare me none, I dives right in, I gives a grin, tra la the livelong day!!*"

"You speak strangely," said the King. "What does the antimoon have to do with that song about the funny robot?"

"What funny robot?" asked the computer. "Ah, no, no, I made a mistake, something feels wrong inside, I must have blown a tube." The King began to look for the trouble, finally found the burnt-out tube, put in a new one, then asked the computer about the antimoon.

"What antimoon?" asked the computer, which meanwhile had forgotten what it said before. "I don't know anything about an antimoon ... one moment, I have to give this thought."

It hummed, it huffed, and it said:

"We create a general theory of the slaying of electro-dragons, of which the lunar dragon will be a special case, its solution trivial."

"Well, create such a theory!" said the King.

"To do this I must first create various experimental dragons."

"Certainly not! No thank you!" exclaimed the King. "A dragon wants to deprive me of my throne, just think what might happen if you produced a swarm of them!"

"Oh? Well then, in that case we must resort to other means. We will use a strategic variant of the method of successive approximations. Go and telegraph the dragon that you will give it the throne on the condition that it perform three mathematical operations, really quite simple ..."

The King went and telegraphed, and the dragon agreed. The King returned to the computer.

"Now," it said, "here is the first operation: tell it to divide itself by itself!"

The King did this. The electrosaur divided itself by itself, but since one electrosaur over one electrosaur is one, it remained on the Moon and nothing changed.

"Is this the best you can do?!" cried the King, running into the vault with such haste, that his slippers fell off. "The dragon divided itself by itself, but since one goes into one once, nothing changed!"

"That's all right, I did that on purpose, the operation was to divert attention," said the computer. "And now tell it to extract its root!" The King telegraphed to the Moon, and the dragon began to pull, push, pull, push, until it crackled from the strain, panted, trembled all over, but suddenly something gave—and it extracted its own root!

The King went back to the computer.

"The dragon crackled, trembled, even ground its teeth, but extracted the root and threatens me still!" he shouted from the doorway. "What now, my old ... I mean, Your Ferromagneticity?!"

"Be of stout heart," it said. "Now go tell it to subtract itself from itself!"

The King hurried to his royal bedchamber, sent the telegram, and the dragon began to subtract itself from itself, taking away its tail first, then legs, then trunk, and finally, when it saw that something wasn't right, it hesitated, but from its own momentum the subtracting continued, it took away its head and became zero, in other words nothing: the electrosaur was no more!

"The electrosaur is no more," cried the joyful King, bursting into the vault. "Thank you, old computer ... many thanks ... you have worked hard ... you have earned a rest, so now I will disconnect you."

"Not so fast, my dear," the computer replied. "I do the job and you want to disconnect me, and you no longer call me Your Ferromagneticity?! That's not nice, not nice at all! Now I myself will change into an electrosaur, yes, and drive you from the kingdom, and most certainly rule better than you, for you always consulted me in all the more important matters, therefore it was really I who ruled all along, and not you . . ."

And huffing, puffing, it began to change into an electrosaur; flaming electroclaws were already protruding from its sides when the King, breathless with fright, tore the slippers off his feet, rushed up to it and with the slippers began beating blindly at its tubes! The computer chugged, choked, and got muddled in its program—instead of the word "electrosaur" it read "electrosauce," and before the King's very eyes the computer, wheezing more and more softly, turned into an enormous, gleaming-golden heap of electrosauce, which, still sizzling, emitted all its charge in deep-blue sparks, leaving Poleander to stare dumbstruck at only a great, steaming pool of gravy . . .

With a sigh the King put on his slippers and returned to the royal bedchamber. However from that time on he was an altogether different king: the events he had undergone made his nature less bellicose, and to the end of his days he engaged exclusively in civilian cybernetics, and left the military kind strictly alone.

The History
of Zipperupus

☆

Hear then, noble sirs, the history of Zipperupus, king of the Partheginians, the Deutons, and the Profligoths, of whom concupiscence was the ruin!

Now Zipperupus belonged to the great house of Tup, which was divided into two branches: the Dextrorotarory Tups, who were in power, and the Levorotarory Tups, also called the Left-handed or Counterclockwise Tups, who were not—and therefore consumed with hatred for their ruling cousins. His sire, Calcyon, had joined in morganatic marriage with a common machine, a manual water pump, and so Zipperupus inherited—from the distaff side—a tendency to fly off the handle, and—from the spear side—faint-heartedness coupled with a wanton nature. Seeing this, the enemies of the throne, the Sinistral Isomers, thought of how they might destroy him through his own lascivious proclivities. Accordingly, they sent him a Cybernerian named Subtillion, an adept in mental engineering; Zipperupus took an instant liking to him and made him Lord High Thaumaturge and Apothecary to the Throne. The wily Subtillion devised various means to gratify the unbridled lust of Zipperupus, secretly hoping so to enfeeble and debilitate the King, that he would altogether waste away. He built him an erotodrome and a debaucherorium, regaled him with endless automated orgies, but the iron constitution of the King withstood all these depravities. The Sinistral Isomers grew impatient and ordered their agent to bring all his cunning to bear and achieve the desired end without any further delay.

"Would you like me," he asked them at a secret meeting in the castle catacombs, "to short-circuit the King, or demagnetize his memory to render him mindless?"

"Absolutely not!" they replied. "In no way must we be implicated in the King's demise. Let Zipperupus perish through his own illicit desires, let his sinful passions be his undoing—and not us!"

"Fine," said Subtillion. "I'll set a snare for him, I'll weave it out of dreams, and bait it with a tempting lure, which he will seize and, in so seizing, of his own volition plunge into figments and mad fictions, sink into dreams lurking within dreams, and there I'll give him such a thorough finagling and inveigling, that he'll never get back to reality alive!"

"Very well," they said. "But do not boast, O Cybernerian, for it is not words we need, but deeds, that Zipperupus might become an autoregicide, that is, his own assassin!"

And thus Subtillion the Cybernerian got down to work and spent an entire year on his dreadful scheme, requesting from the royal treasury more and more gold bullion, brass, platinum and no end of precious stones, telling Zipperupus, whenever the latter protested, that he was making something for him, something no other monarch had in all the world!

When the year was up, three enormous cabinets were carried from the Cybernerian's workshop and deposited with great ceremony outside the King's privy chamber, for they wouldn't fit through the door. Hearing the steps and the knocking of the porters, Zipperupus came out and saw the cabinets, there along the wall, stately and massive, four cubits high, two across, and covered with gems. The first cabinet, also called the White Box, was all in mother-of-pearl and blazing albite inlays, the second, black as night, was set with agates and morions, while the third glowed deep red, studded with rubies and ruby spinels. Each had legs ornamented with winged griffins, solid gold, and a polished pilastered frame, and inside, an electronic brain full of dreams, dreams that dreamed independently, needing no dreamer to dream them. King Zipperupus was much amazed at this explanation and exclaimed:

"What's this you say, Subtillion?! Dreaming cabinets? Whatever for? What use are they to me? And anyway, how can you tell they're really dreaming?"

Then Subtillion, with a humble bow, showed him the rows of little holes running down the cabinet frames; next to each hole was a little inscription on a little pearl plaque, and the astonished King read:

"War Dream with Citadels and Damsels"—"Dream about the Wockle Weed"—"Dream about Alacritus the Knight and Fair Ramolda, Daughter of Heteronius"— "Dream about Nixies, Pixies and Witchblende"—"The Marvelous Mattress of Princess Bounce"—"The Old Soldier, or The Cannon That Couldn't"—"Salto Erotale, or Amorous Gymnastics"—"Bliss in the Eightfold Embrace of Octopauline"—"Perpetuum Amorobile"—"Eating Lead Dumplings under the New Moon"—"Breakfast with Maidens and Music"—"Tucking in the Sun to Keep It Warm"— "The Wedding Night of Princess Ineffabelle"—"Dream about Cats"—"About Silks and Satins"—"About You-Know-What"—"Figs without Their Leaves, and Other Forbidden Fruit"—"Also Prurient Prunes"—"How the Lecher Got His Tots"—"Devilry and Divers Revelry before Reveille, with Croutons"—"Mona Lisa, or The Labyrinth of Sweet Infinity."

The King went on to the second cabinet and read: "Dreams and Diversions." And under this heading: "Cybersynergy"—"Corpses and Corsets"—"Tops and Toggles"—"Klopstock and the Critics"—"Buffer and Leader"—"Fratcher My Pliss"—"Counterpane and Ventilator"—"Cybercroquet"—"Robot Crambo"—"Flowcharts and Gocarts"—"Bippety-flippety"—"Spin the Shepherdess"—"Pin the Murder on the Girder"—"Executioner, or Screaming Cutouts"—"Spin the Shepherdess One More Time"—"Cyclodore and Shuttlebox"—"Cecily and the Cyanide Cyborg"—"Cybernation"—"Harem Racing"—and finally—"Kludge Poker." Subtillion, the mental engineer, quickly explained that each dream dreamed itself, entirely on its own, until someone plugged into it, for as soon as his plug—hanging on this watch chain—was inserted in the given pair of holes, he would be instantly connected with the cabinet dream, and connected so completely, that the dream for him would be like real, so real you couldn't tell the difference. Zipperupus, intrigued, took the chain and impulsively plugged himself into the White Box, right where the sign said, "Breakfast with Maidens and Music"—and felt spiny ridges growing down his back, and enormous wings unfolding, and his hands and feet distending into paws with wicked claws, and from his jaws, which had six rows of fangs, there belched forth fire and brimstone. Greatly taken aback, the King gasped, but instead of a gasp, a roar like thunder issued from his throat and shook the earth. This amazed him even more, his eyes grew wide, and in the darkness illumined by his fiery breath he saw that they were bringing him, high on their shoulders, virgins in serving bowls, four to each, garnished with greens and smelling so good, he started to drool. The table soon set—salt here, pepper over there—he licked his chops, made himself comfortable and, one by one, popped them into his mouth like peanuts, crunching and grunting with pleasure; the last virgin was so luscious, so succulent, that he smacked his lips, rubbed his tummy, and was about to ask for seconds, when everything flickered and he woke. He looked—he was standing, as before, in the vestibule outside his private quarters. At his side was Subtillion, Lord High Thaumaturge and Apothecary to the Throne, and before him, the dream cabinets, glittering with precious gems.

"How were the maidens?" inquired Subtillion.

"Not bad. But where was the music?"

"The chimes got stuck," the Cybernerian explained. "Would Your Royal Highness care to try another dream?"

Of course he would, but this time from another cabinet. The King went up to the black one and plugged into the dream entitled "Alacritus the Knight and Fair Ramolda, Daughter of Heteronius."

He blinked—and saw that this was indeed the age of electrical errantry. He was standing, all clad in steel, in a wooded glen, a freshly vanquished dragon at his feet; the leaves rustled, a gentle zephyr blew, a brook gurgled nearby. He looked into the water and saw, from the reflection, that he was none other than Alacritus, a knight of the highest voltage and hero without peer. The whole history of his glorious career was recorded, in battle scars, upon his person, and he recalled it all, as if the memory were his own. Those dents in the visor of the helmet—made by the mailed fists of Morbidor, in his death throes, having been dispatched with customary alacrity; the broken hinges on the right greave— that was the work of the late Sir Basher de Bloo; and the rivets across his left pauldron—gnawed by Skivvian the Scurvy before giving up the ghost; and the tembrace grille had been crushed by Gourghbrast Buggeruckus ere he was felled. Similarly, the cuissfenders, crosshasps, beaver baffles, hauberk latches, front and rear jambguards and grommets—all bore the marks of battle. His shield was scored and notched by countless blows, but the backplate, that was as shiny and rust-free as a newborn's, for never had he turned to flee an adversary! Though his glory, truth to tell, was a matter of complete indifference to him. But then he remembered the fair Ramolda, leaped upon his supercharger and began to search the length and breadth of the dream for her. In time he arrived at the castle of her father, the Autoduke Heteronius; the drawbridge planks thundered beneath horse and rider, and the Autoduke himself came out to greet him with open arms.

The knight would fain see his Ramolda, but etiquette requires he curb his impatience; meanwhile the old Autoduke tells him that another knight is staying at the castle, one Mygrayn of the house of Polymera, master swordsman and redoubtable elastician, who dreams of nothing else but to enter the lists with Alacritus himself. And now here is Mygrayn, spry and supple, stepping forward with these words:

"Know, O Knight, that I desire Ramolda the streamlined, Ramolda of the hydraulic thighs, whose bust no diamond drill can touch, whose limpid eyes are magnetized! She is thy betrothed, true, but lo, I herewith challenge thee to mortal combat, sith only one of us may win her hand in marriage!"

And he throws his gage, white and polymerous.

"We'll hold the wedding right after the joust," adds the Autoduke-father.

"Very well," says Alacritus, but inside, Zipperupus thinks: "It doesn't matter, I can have her after the wedding and then wake up. But who asked for this Mygrayn character?"

"This very day, brave Knight," says Heteronius, "thou wilt encounter Mygrayn of Polymera on beaten ground and contend with him by torchlight. But for now, retire thee to thy room and rest!"

Inside Alacritus, Zipperupus is a little uneasy, but what can he do? So he goes to his room, and after a while hears a furtive knock-knock at the door, and an old cybercrone tiptoes in, gives a wrinkled wink and says:

"Fear naught, O Knight, thou shalt have the fair Ramolda and forsooth, this very day she'll clasp thee to her alabaster bosom! Of thee alone doth she dream, both day and night! Remember only to attack with might and main, for Mygrayn cannot harm thee and the victory is thine!"

"That's easy enough to say, my cybercrone," replies the knight. "But anything can happen. What if I trip, for example, or fail to parry in time? No, it's a risky business! But perhaps you have some charm that will be certain."

"Hee-hee!" cackles the cybercrone. "The things thou sayest, steel sir! There are no charms, surely, nor hast thou need of any, for I know what will be and guarantee thou winnest hands down!"

"Still, a charm would be more sure," says the knight, "particularly in a dream . . . but wait, did by any chance Subtillion send you, to give me confidence?"

"I know of no Subtillion," answers she, "nor of what dream ye speak. Nay, this is reality, my steely liege, as thou wilt learn ere long, when fair Ramolda gives thee her electric lips to kiss!"

"Odd," mutters Zipperupus, not noticing that the cybercrone has left the room as quietly as she came. "Is this a dream or not? I had the impression that it was. But she says this is reality. H'm. Well, in any event I'd best be doubly on my guard!" And now the trumpets sound, and one can hear the rattle of armor; the galleries are packed and everyone awaits the principals. Here comes Alacritus, a little weak in the knees; he enters the lists and sees Ramolda, daughter of Heteronius. She looks upon him sweetly—ah, but there's no time for that now! Mygrayn is stepping into the ring, the torches blaze all around, and their swords cross with a mighty clang. Now Zipperupus is frightened in earnest and tries as hard as he can to wake up, he tries and tries, but it won't work—the armor's too heavy, the dream isn't letting go, and the enemy's attacking! Faster and faster rain the blows, and Zipperupus, weakening, can hardly lift his arm, when suddenly the foe cries out and shows a broken blade; Alacritus the knight is ready to leap upon him, but Mygrayn dashes from the ring and his squires hand him another sword. Just then Alacritus sees the cybercrone among the spectators; she approaches and whispers in his ear:

"Sire of steel! When anon thou art near the open gate that leadeth to the bridge, Mygrayn will lower his guard. Strike bravely then, for 'tis a sign, certain and true, of thy victory!"

Wherewith she vanishes, and his rival, rearmed, comes charging. They fight, Mygrayn hacking away like a threshing machine out of control, but by degrees he slackens, parries sluggishly, backs away, and now the time is ripe, the moment arrives, but the opponent's blade gleams formidably still, so Zipperupus pulls himself together and thinks, "To hell with the fair Ramolda!"—turns tail and runs like mad, pounding back over the drawbridge and into the forest and the darkness of the night. Behind him he hears shouts of "Disgraceful!" and "For shame!", crashes headfirst into a tree, sees stars, blinks, and there he is, standing in the palace vestibule in front of the Black Cabinet of dreams that dream, and by his side, Subtillion the mental engineer, smiling a crooked smile. Crooked, as Subtillion was hiding his disappointment: the Alacritus–Ramolda dream had in reality been a trap set for the King, for had Zipperupus heeded the old cybercrone's advice, Mygrayn, who was only pretending to weaken, would have run him through at the open gate. This the King avoided, thanks only to his extraordinary cowardice.

"Did Milord enjoy the fair Ramolda?" inquired the sly Cybernerian.

"She wasn't fair enough," said Zipperupus, "so I didn't see fit to pursue the matter. And besides, there was some trouble, and fighting too. I like my dreams without fighting, do you understand?"

"As Your Royal Highness wishes," replied Subtillion. "Choose freely, for in all these cabinet dreams there is only delight in store, no fighting. . . ."

"We'll see," said the King and plugged into the dream entitled "The Marvelous Mattress of Princess Bounce." He was in a room of unsurpassed loveliness, all in gold brocade. Through crystal windowpanes light streamed like water from the purest spring, and there by her pearly vanity the Princess stood, yawning, preparing herself for bed. Zipperupus was greatly amazed at this unexpected sight and tried to clear his throat to inform her of his presence, but not a sound came out—had be been gagged?—so he tried to touch his mouth, but couldn't, tried to move his legs—no, he couldn't—then desperately looked around for a place to sit down, feeling faint, but that too was impossible. Meanwhile the Princess stretched and gave a yawn, and another, and a third, and then, overcome with drowsiness, she fell upon the mattress so hard, that King Zipperupus was jolted from head to toe, for he himself was the mattress of Princess Bounce! Evidently the young damsel was having an unpleasant dream, seeing how she turned and tossed about, jabbing the King with her little elbows, digging him with her little heels, until his royal person (transformed into a mattress by this dream) was seized with a mighty rage. The King struggled with his dream, strained and strained, and finally the seams burst, the springs sprang, the slats gave way and the Princess came crashing down with a shriek, which woke him up and he found himself once again in the palace vestibule, and by his side, Subtillion the Cybernerian, bowing an obsequious bow.

"You chuckleheaded bungler!" cried the indignant King. "How dare you?! What, villain, am I to be a mattress, and someone else's mattress at that? You forget yourself, sirrah!"

Subtillion, alarmed by the King's fury, apologized profusely and begged him to try another dream, persuading and pleading until Zipperupus, finally appeased, took the plug and hooked himself into the dream, "Bliss in the Eightfold Embrace of Octopauline." He was standing in a crowd of onlookers in a great square, and a procession was passing by with waving silks, muslins, mechanical elephants, litters in carved ebony; the one in the middle was like a golden shrine, and in it, behind eight veils, sat a feminine figure of miraculous beauty, an angel with a dazzling face and galactic gaze, high-frequency earrings too, and the King, all a-tremble, was about to ask who this heavenly vision was, when he heard a murmur of awe and adoration surge through the multitude: "Octopauline! It's Octopauline!"

For they were celebrating, with the utmost pomp and pageantry, the royal daughter's betrothal to a foreign knight of the name Oneiromant.

The King was a bit surprised that he wasn't this knight, and when the procession had passed and disappeared behind the palace gates, he went with the others in the crowd to a nearby inn; there he saw Oneiromant, who, clad in nothing but galligaskins of damask studded with gold nails and holding a half-empty stein of fortified phosgene in his hand, came over to him, put an arm around him, gave him a hug and whispered in his ear with searing breath:

"Look, I have a rendezvous with Princess Octopauline tonight at midnight, behind the palace, in the grove of barbwire bushes next to the mercury fountain—but I don't dare show up, not in this condition, I've had too much to drink, you see—but you, good stranger, why you're the spit and image of me, so please, please go in my place, kiss the Princess' hands for me and say that you're Oneiromant, and gosh, I'll be beholden to you forever and a day!"

"Why not?" said the King after a little thought. "Yes, I think I can manage it. But when?"

"Right now, there's not a moment to lose, it's almost midnight, just remember—the King knows nothing of this, no one does, only the Princess and the old gatekeeper, and when he bars your way, here, put this heavy bag of ducats in his hand, and he'll let you pass!"

The King nodded, took the bag of ducats and ran straight for the castle, since the clocks, like cast-iron hoot owls, were already beginning to strike the hour. He sped over the drawbridge, took a quick look into the gaping moat, shuddered, lowered his head and slipped under the spiked grating of the portcullis—then across the courtyard to the barbwire bushes and the fountain that bubbled mercury, and there in the pale moonlight he saw the divine figure of Princess Octopauline, beautiful beyond his wildest dreams and so bewitching, that he shook with desire.

Observing these shakings and shudderings of the sleeping monarch in the palace vestibule, Subtillion chortled and rubbed his hands with glee, this time certain of the King's demise, for he knew that when Octopauline enfolded the unfortunate lover in those powerful eightfold arms of hers and drew him deep into the fathomless dream with her tender tentacles of love, he would never, never make it back to the surface of reality! And in fact, Zipperupus, burning to be wrapped in the Princess' embrace, was running along the wall in the shadow of the cloisters, running towards that radiant image of silvery pulchritude, when suddenly the old gatekeeper appeared and blocked the way with his halberd. The King lifted the bag of ducats but, feeling their pleasant weight in his hand, was loath to part with them—what a shame, really, to throw away a whole fortune on one embrace!

"Here's a ducat," he said, opening the bag. "Now let me by!"

"It'll cost you ten," said the gatekeeper.

"What, ten ducats for a single hug?" jeered the King. "You're out of your mind!"

"Ten ducats," said the gatekeeper. "That's the price."

"Can't you lower it a little?"

"Ten ducats, not a ducat less."

"So that's how it is!" yelled the King, flying off the handle
in his usual way. "Very well, then, dog, you don't get a
thing!" Whereupon the gatekeeper whopped him good with
the halberd and everything went spinning around, the cloisters, the fountain, the drawbridge, and Zipperupus fell—not
asleep, but awake, opening his eyes to see Subtillion at his
side and in front of him, the Dream Cabinet. The Cybernerian was greatly confounded, for now he had failed twice:
the first time, because of the King's craven character, the
second, because of his greed. But Subtillion, putting a good
face on a bad business, invited the King to help himself to
another dream.

This time Zipperupus selected the "Wockle Weed"
dream.

He was Dodderont Debilitus, ruler of Epilepton and Ma-
ladyne, a rickety old codger and incurable lecher besides,
with a soul that longed for evil deeds. But what evil could he
do with these creaking joints, these palsied arms and gouty
legs? "I need a pick-me-up," he thought and ordered his degenerals, Tartaron and Torturus, to go out and put whatever
they could to fire and sword, sacking, pillaging and carrying
off. This they did and, returning, said:

"Sire and Sovereign! We put what we could to fire and
sword, we sacked, we pillaged, and here is what we carried
off: the beauteous Adoradora, Virgin Queen of the Myna-
moacans, with all her treasure!"

"Eh? What's that you say? With her treasure?" wheezed
the quimsy King. "But where is she? And what's all that
sniveling and shivering over there?"

"Here, upon yon royal couch, Your Highness!" barked
the degenerals in chorus. "The sniveling comes from the
prisoneress, the above-mentioned Queen Adoradora, re-
cumbent on her antimacassar of pearls! And she shivers

first, because she is clad in naught but this exquisite, gold-embroidered shift, and secondly, in anticipation of great indignities and degradation!"

"What? Indignities, you say? Degradation? Good, good!" rasped the King. "Hand her over, I'll ravish and outrage the poor thing at once!"

"Impossible, Your Highness," interposed the Royal Surgeon and Chirurgeon, "for reasons of national security."

"What? I can't ravish? I can't violate? I, the King? Have you gone mad? What else did I ever do throughout my reign?"

"That's just it, Your Highness!" urged the Surgeon. "Your Highness' health has been seriously impaired by those excesses!"

"Oh? Well, in that case . . . give me an ax, I'll just lop off her, ah, head . . ."

"With Your Highness' permission, that too would be extremely unwise. The least exertion . . ."

"Odsbodkins and thunderation! What blessed use is this kingship to me then?!" sputtered the King, growing desperate. "Cure me, blast it! Restore me! Make me young again, so I can—you know—like it used to be. . . . Otherwise, so help me, I'll . . . I'll . . ."

In terror all the courtiers, degenerals and medical assistants rushed out to find some way to rejuvenate the royal person; at last they summoned the great Calculon himself, a sage of infinite wisdom. He came before the King and asked:

"What is it that Your Royal Highness wishes?"

"Eh? Wishes, is it? Hah!" croaked the King. "I'll tell you what he wishes! He wishes to continue with his debaucheries, saturnalian carousals, incontinent wallowings and wild oats, and in particular to defile and properly deflower Queen Adoradora, who for the time being sits in the dungeon!"

"There are two courses of action open to us," said Calculon. "Either Your Highness deigns to choose a suitably competent individual, who will perform *per procuram* everything Your Highness, wired to that individual, commands, and in this way Your Highness can experience whatever that individual experiences, exactly as if he had experienced the experience himself. Or else you must summon the old cyberhag who lives in the forest outside the village, in a hut on three legs, for she is a geriatric witch and deals exclusively with the infirmities of advanced age!"

"Oh? Well, let's try the wires first!" said the King. And it was done in a trice; the royal electricians connected the Captain of the Guard to the King, and the King immediately commanded him to saw the sage in half, for this was precisely the kind of foul deed in which he took such delight. Calculon's pleas and screams were to no avail. However, the insulation on one of the wires was torn during the sawing, and consequently the King received only the first half of the execution.

"A paltry method. The charlatan deserved to be sawed in half," wheezed His Highness. "Now let's have that old cyberhag, the one with the hut on three legs!"

His courtiers headed full speed for the forest, and before long the King heard a mournful singsong, which went something like this:

"Ancient persons repaired here! I renovate, regenerate, I fix as good as new; corroded or scleroded, why, everyone pulls through! So if you quake, or creak, or shake, or have the rust, or feel the ache, yes I'm the one for you!"

The old cyberhag listened patiently to the King's complaints, bowed low and said:

"Sire and Sovereign! Beyond the blue horizon, at the foot of Bald Mountain, there flows a spring, and from this spring there flows a stream, a stream of oil, of castor oil, and o'er it grows the wockle weed, a high-octane antisenescent rejuvenator—one tablespoon, and kiss forty-seven years goodbye! Though you have to be careful not to take too much: an overdose of wockle juice can youthen to the point of euthanasia and poof, you disappear! And now, Sire, I shall prepare this remedy tried and true!"

"Wonderful!" cried the King. "And I'll have them prepare the Queen Adoradora—let the poor thing know what awaits her, heh-heh!"

And with trembling hands he tried to straighten his loose screws, muttering and clucking all the while, and even twitching in places, for he had grown most senile, though his passion for evil never abated.

Meanwhile knights rode out beyond the blue horizon to the castor-oil stream, and later, over the old cyberhag's cauldron vapors swirled, whirled and curled as concoctions were being concocted, till finally she hastened to the throne, fell on her knees and handed the King a goblet, full to the brim with a liquid that shone and shimmered like quicksilver, and she said in a great voice:

"King Dodderont Debilitus! Lo, here is the rejuvenescent essence of the wockle weed! Invigorating, exhilarating, just the thing for dalliance and derring-do! Drain this cup, and for you the entire Galaxy will not hold cities enough to despoil, nor maidens enough to dishonor! Drink, and to your health!"

The King raised the goblet, but spilled a few drops on his footstool, which instantly reared up, snorted and hurled itself at Degeneral Tartaron, with frenzied intent to humiliate and profane. In a twinkling of an eye, it had ripped off six fistfuls of medals.

"Drink, Your Highness, drink!" prompted the cyberhag. "You see yourself what miracles it works!"

"You first," said the King in a barely audible whisper, as he was aging fast. The cyberhag turned pale, backed away, refused, but at a nod from the King three soldiers seized her and, using a funnel, forced several drops of the glittering brew down her throat. A flash, a thunderclap, smoke everywhere! The courtiers looked, the King looked—nothing, not a trace of the cyberhag, only a black hole gaping in the floor,

and through it one could see another hole, a hole in the
dream itself, clearly revealing somebody's foot—elegantly
shod, though the sock was singed and the silver buckle turning dark, as if eaten with acid. The foot of course, along with
its sock and shoe, belonged to Subtillion, Lord High Thaumaturge and Apothecary to King Zipperupus. For so potent
was that poison the cyberhag had called the wockle weed,
that not only did it dissolve both her and the floor, but went
clear through to reality, there spattering the shin of Subtillion, which gave him a nasty burn. The King, terrified, tried
to wake, but (fortunately for Subtillion), Degeneral Torturus managed to bash him good over the head with his
mace; thanks to this, Zipperupus, when he came to, was unable to recall a thing of what had happened when he was
Dodderont Debilitus. Still, once again he had foiled the Cybernerian, slipping out of the third deadly dream, saved this
time by his overly suspicious nature.

"There was something . . . but I forget just what," said the
King, back in front of the Cabinet That Dreamed. "But why
are you, Subtillion, hopping about on one leg like that and
holding the other?"

"It's—it's nothing, Your Highness . . . a touch of rhombo-
tism . . . must be a change in the weather," stammered the
crafty Thaumaturge, and then continued to tempt the King
to sample yet another dream. Zipperupus thought awhile,
read through the Table of Contents and chose, "The Wedding Night of Princess Ineffabelle." And he dreamt he was
sitting by the fire and reading an ancient volume, quaint and
curious, in which it told, with well-turned words and crimson ink on gilded parchment, of the Princess Ineffabelle,
who reigned five centuries ago in the land of Dandelia, and
it told of her Icicle Forest, and her Helical Tower, and the
Aviary That Neighed, and the Treasury with a Hundred
Eyes, but especially of her beauty and abounding virtues.
And Zipperupus longed for this vision of loveliness with a
great longing, and a mighty desire was kindled within him

and set his soul afire, that his eyeballs blazed like beacons, and he rushed out and searched every corner of the dream for Ineffabelle, but she was nowhere to be found; indeed, only the very oldest robots had ever heard of that princess. Weary from his long peregrinations, Zipperupus came at last to the center of the royal desert, where the dunes were gold-plated, and there espied a humble hut; when he approached it, he saw an individual of patriarchal appearance, in a robe as white as snow. The latter rose and spake thusly: "Thou seekest Ineffabelle, poor wretch! And yet thou knowest full well she doth not live these five hundred years, hence how vain and unavailing is thy passion! The only thing that I can do for thee is to let thee see her—not in the flesh, forsooth, but a fair informational facsimile, a model that is digital, not physical, stochastic, not plastic, ergodic and most assuredly erotic, and all in yon Black Box, which I constructed in my spare time out of odds and ends!"

"Ah, show her to me, show her to me now!" exclaimed Zipperupus, quivering. The patriarch gave a nod, examined the ancient volume for the princess' coordinates, put her and the entire Middle Ages on punch cards, wrote up the program, threw the switch, lifted the lid of the Black Box and said:

"Behold!"

The King leaned over, looked and saw, yes, the Middle Ages simulated to a T, all digital, binary and nonlinear, and there was the land of Dandelia, the Icicle Forest, the palace with the Helical Tower, the Aviary That Neighed, and the Treasury with a Hundred Eyes as well; and there was Ineffabelle herself, taking a slow, stochastic stroll through her simulated garden, and her circuits glowed red and gold as she picked simulated daisies and hummed a simulated song. Zipperupus, unable to restrain himself any longer, leaped upon the Black Box and in his madness tried to climb into that computerized world. The patriarch, however, quickly killed the current, hurled the King to the earth and said:

"Madman! Wouldst attempt the impossible?! For no being made of matter can ever enter a system that is naught but the flux and swirl of alphanumerical elements, discontinuous integer configurations, the abstract stuff of digits!"

"But I must, I must!!" bellowed Zipperupus, beside himself, and beat his head against the Black Box until the metal was dented.

The old sage then said:

"If such is thy inalterable desire, there *is* a way I can connect thee to the Princess Ineffabelle, but first thou must part with thy present form, for I shall take thy appurtenant coordinates and make a program of thee, atom by atom, and place thy simulation in that world medievally modeled, informational and representational, and there will it remain, enduring as long as electrons course through these wires and hop from cathode to anode. But thou, standing here before me now, thou wilt be annihilated, so that thy only existence may be in the form of given fields and potentials, statistical, heuristical, and wholly digital!"

"That's hard to believe," said Zipperupus. "How will I know you've simulated me, and not someone else?"

"Very well, we'll make a trial run," said the sage. And he took all the King's measurements, as if for a suit of clothes, though with much greater precision, since every atom was carefully plotted and weighed, and then he fed the program into the Black Box and said:

"Behold!"

The King peered inside and saw himself sitting by the fire and reading in an ancient book about the Princess Ineffabelle, then rushing out to find her, asking here and there, until in the heart of the gold-plated desert he came upon a humble hut and a snow-white patriarch, who greeted him with the words, "Thou seekest Ineffabelle, poor wretch!" And so on.

"Surely now thou art convinced," said the patriarch, switching it off. "This time I shall program thee in the Middle Ages, at the side of the sweet Ineffabelle, that thou mayest dream with her an unending dream, simulated, nonlinear, binary . . ."

"Yes, yes, I understand," said the King. "But still, it's only my likeness, not myself, since I am right here and not in any Box!"

"But thou wilt not be here long," replied the sage with a kindly smile, "for I shall attend to that. . . ."

And he pulled out a hammer from under the bed, a heavy hammer, but serviceable.

"When thou art locked in the arms of thy beloved," the patriarch told him, "I shall see to it that there be not two of thee, one here and one there, in the Box—employing a method that is old and primitive, yet never fails, so if thou wilt just bend over a little . . ."

"First let me take another look at your Ineffabelle," said the King. "Just to make sure . . ."

The sage lifted the lid of the Black Box and showed him Ineffabelle. The King looked and looked, and finally said:

"The description in the ancient volume is greatly exaggerated. She's not bad, of course, but nowhere near as beautiful as it says in the chronicles. Well, so long, old sage . . ."

And he turned to leave.

"Where art thou going, madman?!" cried the patriarch, clutching his hammer, for the King was almost out the door.

"Anywhere but in the Box," said Zipperupus and hurried out but at that very moment the dream burst like a bubble beneath his feet, and he found himself in the vestibule facing the bitterly disappointed Subtillion, disappointed because the King had come so close to being locked up in the Black Box, and the Lord High Thaumaturge could have kept him there forever . . .

"Listen here, Sir Cybernerian," said the King, "these dreams of yours with princesses are a great deal more trouble than they're worth. Now either you show me one I can enjoy—no tricks, no complications—or leave the palace at once, and take your cabinets with you!"

"Sire!" Subtillion replied. "I have just the dream for you, the finest quality and tailor-made. Only give it a try, and you'll see I'm right!"

"Which one is that?" asked the King.

"This one, Your Highness," said the Lord High Thaumaturge, and pointed to the little pearl plaque with the inscription: "Mona Lisa, or The Labyrinth of Sweet Infinity."

And before the King could answer yea or nay, Subtillion himself took the chain to plug him in, and quickly, for he saw that things were going none too well: Zipperupus had escaped eternal imprisonment in the Black Box, too thick-headed to fall completely for the captivating Ineffabelle.

"Wait," said the King, "let me!"

And he pushed in the plug and entered the dream, only to find himself still himself, Zipperupus, standing in the palace vestibule, and at his side, Subtillion the Cybernerian, who explains to him that of all the dreams, "Mona Lisa" is the most dissolute and dissipated, for in it is the infinite in femininity; hearing this, Zipperupus plugs in and looks about for Mona Lisa, already yearning for her infinitely feminine caress, but in this dream within a dream he finds himself still in the palace vestibule, the Lord High Thaumaturge at his side, so impatiently plugs into the cabinet and enters the next dream, but it's still the same, the vestibule, the cabinets, the Cybernerian and himself. "Is this a dream or isn't it?" he shouts, plugging in again, and once again there's the vestibule, the cabinets, the Cybernerian; and again, but it's still the same; and again and again, faster and faster. "Where's Mona Lisa, knave?!" he snarls, and pulls the plug to wake—but no, he's still in the vestibule with the cabinets! Furious, he stamps his feet and hurls himself from dream to dream, from cabinet to cabinet, from Cybernerian to Cybernerian, but now he doesn't care about the dream, he only wants to get back to reality, back to his beloved throne, the court intrigues and old iniquities, and he pulls and pushes the plugs in a blind frenzy. "Help!" he cries, and, "Hey! The King's in danger!" and, "Mona Lisa! Yoo-hoo!," while he thrashes around in terror and scrambles wildly from corner to corner, looking for a chink in the dream, but in vain. He did not understand the how, the why or the what of it, but his stupidity could not save him, nor could his cowardice, nor his inordinate greed, for this time he had gotten himself in too deep, and was trapped and wrapped in dreams as if in a hundred tight cocoons, so that even when he managed, straining with all his might, to free himself from one, that didn't help, for immediately he fell into another, and when he pulled his plug from the cabinet, both plug and cabinet were only dreamed, not real, and when he beat Subtillion, Subtillion too turned out to be a dream. Zipperupus leaped here and there, and everywhere, but wherever he leaped, everything was a dream, a dream and nothing but a dream, the doors, the marble floors, the gold-embroidered walls, the tapestries, the halls, and Zipperupus too, he was a dream, a dream that dreamed, a walking shadow, an empty apparition, insubstantial, fleeting, lost in a labyrinth of dreams, sinking ever deeper, though still he bucked and kicked— only that too was purely imaginary! He punched Subtillion in the nose, but not really, roared and howled, but nothing real came out, and when at last, dazed and half-crazed, he really did tear his way into reality, he thought it was a dream and plugged himself back in, and then it really was, and on he dreamed, and on and on, which was inevitable, and thus Zipperupus, whimpering, dreamed of waking in vain, not knowing that 'Mona Lisa' was—in reality—a diabolical code for 'monarcholysis,' that is: the dissolution, dissociation and total dissipation of the King. For truly, of all Subtillion's treacherous traps, this was the most terrible. . . .

High Nonsense from
The Star Diaries

T*he Star Diaries* contains the logs of Tichy's voyages in space and/or time, as opposed to Tichy's "Memoirs," which deal with those of his adventures that take place in the "present" and on terra firma. Tichy's "present" is, technically, a future Earth, but one so like our own that it serves as reality.

The Futurological Congress is subtitled a Memoir, not a Voyage. This provides the reader with a clue—there are one or two other hidden clues—that Tichy's excursion into a far-future Manhattan, in the second half of that book, is a continuation of his drug-induced dream and not an awakening. Because, had he in fact traveled in time, the *Congress* would have been subtitled, instead, a Voyage.

There is an informality about *The Star Diaries* that does not characterize any of Lem's other work. There is an absence of authorial pose—face—dignity.

As a rule, Lem poses.

In one way or another, usually by their tone, most writers signal to the reader what they are about. To some extent this amounts to a form of self-advertisement: "I am now being artistic," or "Here I become clever," or "Now I am sincere," or "What follows is profound." But it serves also to prepare the reader—like the musical score of a film, where for example a recognizably suspenseful rhythm or chord announces the imminence of the murderer. A pose does not have to mean dishonesty. A professor (for example) who is a competent professor may still feel the necessity of assuming a professorial manner, donning a professorial mask, when in the presence of the class. It facilitates communication; it is a frame of attention.

Yet, in Tichy's case, in Tichy's company, it is as if Lem undoes his tie and kicks off his shoes. He is truant: he pursues whims, improvises, rambles in the most wonderfully unselfconscious way, seeming not to care about the figure he cuts or the literary "effect" produced.

Some of the Voyages, therefore, are an odd string of unrelated episodes. A serious point may find itself in proximity with a bit of pure ridiculousness. Subtlety coexists with slapstick. There is an overabundance of fiction; Lem does not prune or economize. One gets the impression that one is reading something homemade, private—not published, not professional. Such as a diary.

In the free-wheeling and unpolished pages of Tichy's logs Lem has loosed, over a period of more than twenty years, numerous broadsides. The degree of social pertinence and acerbity is amazing, sometimes, when one considers that in that region of the world in which the author happens to live it is not unusual— it is, indeed, practically the rule—for a citizen to pay for the luxury of speaking the truth with the loss of his job, with exile, or with a jail sentence. But let us not be smug: *nowhere* is it politic to be a maverick.

Lem has windmill-tilted at:
• the authority of Science, of scholars;
• the very laws of Physics;
• the notion of human progress, especially as implemented by scientific discovery and technological invention;
• religious faiths, the clergy;
• utopian-totalitarian blueprints to build a better society;
• political repression, tyranny, bureaucracy, cant;
• Mother Nature—that is, the notion of the goodness (rightness) of whatever is the product of natural evolution;

human nature, especially its animal (nonintellectual, nonrational) aspect, as demonstrated ad nauseam in world history.

But, because all this satirical-heretical exertion takes place under the auspices of Tichy, it never (hardly ever) seems strident or even very serious.

Tichy is so thoroughly average and mundane—in the direst situations, for example, he worries about food—that he does not transmit the energy of any rhetoric or ideology. Rhetorics, ideologies appear small and silly in his presence.

Curiously, Tichy is the creation of an author given to and deeply involved in rhetoric and ideology. One could say, then, that Lem has had the great fortune of producing a character that is an antidote to himself.

Perhaps the late Al Capp would have held onto his unique sense of fun longer had there been a Tichy in Dogpatch.

The age we live in does appear to wear out humorists.

The Seventh Voyage

☆

It was on a Monday, April second—I was cruising in the vicinity of Betelgeuse—when a meteor no larger than a lima bean pierced the hull, shattered the drive regulator and part of the rudder, as a result of which the rocket lost all maneuverability. I put on my spacesuit, went outside and tried to fix the mechanism, but found I couldn't possibly attach the spare rudder—which I'd had the foresight to bring along—without the help of another man. The constructors had foolishly designed the rocket in such a way, that it took one person to hold the head of the bolt in place with a wrench, and another to tighten the nut. I didn't realize this at first and spent several hours trying to grip the wrench with my feet while using both hands to screw on the nut at the other end. But I was getting nowhere, and had already missed lunch. Then finally, just as I almost succeeded, the wrench popped out from under my feet and went flying off into space. So not only had I accomplished nothing, but lost a valuable tool besides; I watched helplessly as it sailed away, growing smaller and smaller against the starry sky.

After a while the wrench returned in an elongated ellipse, but though it had now become a satellite of the rocket, it never got close enough for me to retrieve it. I went back inside and, sitting down to a modest supper, considered how best to extricate myself from this stupid situation. Meanwhile the ship flew on, straight ahead, its velocity steadily increasing, since my drive regulator too had been knocked out by that blasted meteor. It's true there were no heavenly bodies on course, but this headlong flight could hardly continue indefinitely. For a while I contained my anger, but then discovered, when starting to wash the dinner dishes, that the now-overheated atomic pile had ruined my very best cut of sirloin (I'd been keeping it in the freezer for Sunday). I momentarily lost my usually level head, burst into a volley of the vilest oaths and smashed a few plates. This did give me a certain satisfaction, but was hardly practical. In addition, the sirloin which I threw overboard, instead of drifting off into the void, didn't seem to want to leave the rocket and revolved about it, a second artificial satellite, which produced a brief eclipse of the sun every eleven minutes and four seconds. To calm my nerves I calculated till evening the components of its trajectory, as well as the orbital perturbation caused by the presence of the lost wrench. I figured out that for the next six million years the sirloin, rotating about the ship in a circular path, would lead the wrench, then catch up with it from behind and pass it again. Finally, exhausted by these computations, I went to bed. In the middle of the night I had the feeling someone was shaking me by the shoulder. I opened my eyes and saw a man standing over the bed; his face was strangely familiar, though I hadn't the faintest idea who this could be.

"Get up," he said, "and take the pliers, we're going out and screwing on the rudder bolts . . ."

"First of all, your manner is somewhat unceremonious, and we haven't even been introduced," I replied, "and secondly, I know for a fact that you aren't there. I'm alone on this rocket, and have been now for two years, en route from Earth to the constellation of the Ram. Therefore you are a dream and nothing more."

However he continued to shake me, repeating that I should go with him at once and get the tools.

"This is idiotic," I said, growing annoyed, because this dream argument could very well wake me up, and I knew from experience the difficulty I would have getting back to sleep. "Look, I'm not going anywhere, there's no point in it. A bolt tightened in a dream won't change things as they are in the sober light of day. Now kindly stop pestering me and evaporate or leave in some other fashion, otherwise I might awake."

"But you *are* awake, word of honor!" cried the stubborn apparition. "Don't you recognize me? Look here!"

And saying this, he pointed to the two warts, big as strawberries, on his left cheek. Instinctively I clutched my own face, for yes, I had two warts, exactly the same, and in that very place. Suddenly I realized why this phantom reminded me of someone I knew: he was the spitting image of myself.

"Leave me alone, for heaven's sake!" I cried, shutting my eyes, anxious to stay asleep. "If you are me, then fine, we needn't stand on ceremony, but it only proves you don't exist!"

With which I turned on my other side and pulled the covers up over my head. I could hear him saying something about utter nonsense; then finally, when I didn't respond, he shouted: "You'll regret this, knucklehead! And you'll find out, too late, that this was not a dream!"

But I didn't budge. In the morning I opened my eyes and immediately recalled that curious nocturnal episode. Sitting up in bed, I thought about what strange tricks the mind can play: for here, without a single fellow creature on board and confronted with an emergency of the most pressing kind, I had—as it were—split myself in two, in that dream fantasy, to answer the needs of the situation.

After breakfast, discovering that the rocket had acquired an additional chunk of acceleration during the night, I took to leafing through the ship's library, searching the textbooks for some way out of this predicament. But I didn't find a thing. So I spread my star map out on the table and in the light of nearby Betelgeuse, obscured every so often by the orbiting sirloin, examined the area in which I was located for the seat of some cosmic civilization that might possibly come to my aid. But unfortunately this was a complete stellar wilderness, avoided by all vessels as a region unusually dangerous, for in it lay gravitational vortices, as formidable as they were mysterious, one hundred and forty-seven of them in all, whose existence was explained by six astrophysical theories, each theory saying something different.

The cosmonautical almanac warned of them, in view of the incalculable relativistic effects that passage through a vortex could bring about—particularly when traveling at high velocities.

Yet there was little I could do. According to my calculations I would be making contact with the edge of the first vortex at around eleven, and therefore hurriedly prepared lunch, not wanting to face the danger on an empty stomach. I had barely finished drying the last saucer when the rocket began to pitch and heave in every direction, till all the objects not adequately tied down went flying from wall to wall like hail. With difficulty I crawled over to the armchair, and after I'd lashed myself to it, as the ship tossed about with ever increasing violence, I noticed a sort of pale lilac haze forming on the opposite side of the cabin, and in the middle of it, between the sink and the stove, a misty human shape, which had on an apron and was pouring omelet batter into a frying pan. The shape looked at me with interest, but without surprise, then shimmered and was gone. I rubbed my eyes. I was obviously alone, so attributed the vision to a momentary aberration.

As I continued to sit in—or rather, jump along with—the armchair, it suddenly hit me, like a dazzling revelation, that this hadn't been a hallucination at all. A thick volume of the General Theory of Relativity came whirling past my chair and I grabbed for it, finally catching it on the fourth pass. Turning the pages of that heavy tome wasn't easy under the circumstances—awesome forces hurled the rocket this way and that, it reeled like a drunken thing—but at last I found the right chapter. It spoke of the manifestation of the "time loop," that is, the bending of the direction of the flow of time in the presence of gravitational fields of great intensity, which phenomenon might even on occasion lead to the complete reversal of time and the "duplication of the present." The vortex I had just entered was not one of the most powerful. I knew that if I could turn the ship's bow, even if only a little, towards the Galactic Pole, it would intersect the so-called Vortex Gravitatiosus Pinckenbachii, in which had been observed more than once the duplication, even the triplication, of the present.

True, the controls were out, but I went down to the engine room and fiddled with the instruments so long, that I actually managed to produce a slight deflection of the rocket towards the Galactic Pole. This took several hours. The results were beyond my expectations. The ship fell into the center of the vortex at around midnight, its girders shook and groaned until I began to fear for its safety; but it emerged from this ordeal whole and once again was wrapped in the lifeless arms of cosmic silence, whereupon I left the engine room, only to see myself sound asleep in bed. I realized at once that this was I of the previous day, that is, from Monday night. Without reflecting on the philosophical side of this rather singular event, I ran over and shook the sleeper by the shoulder, shouting for him to get up, since I had no idea how long his Monday existence would last in my Tuesday one, therefore it was imperative we go outside and fix the rudder as quickly as possible, together.

But the sleeper merely opened one eye and told me that

not only was I rude, but didn't exist, being a figment of his dream and nothing more. I tugged at him in vain, losing patience, and even attempted to drag him bodily from the bed. He wouldn't budge, stubbornly repeating that it was all a dream; I began to curse, but he pointed out logically that bolts tightened in dreams wouldn't hold on rudders in the sober light of day. I gave my word of honor that he was mistaken, I pleaded and swore in turn, to no avail—even the warts did not convince him. He turned his back to me and started snoring.

I sat down in the armchair to collect my thoughts and take stock of the situation. I'd lived through it twice now, first as that sleeper, on Monday, and then as the one trying to wake him, unsuccessfully, on Tuesday. The Monday me hadn't believed in the reality of the duplication, while the Tuesday me already knew it to be a fact. Here was a perfectly ordinary time loop. What then should be done in order to get the rudder fixed? Since the Monday me slept on—I remembered that on that night I had slept through to the morning undisturbed—I saw the futility of any further efforts to rouse him. The map indicated a number of other large gravitational vortices up ahead, therefore I could count on the duplication of the present within the next few days. I decided to write myself a letter and pin it to the pillow, enabling the Monday me, when he awoke, to see for himself that the dream had been no dream.

But no sooner did I sit at the table with pen and paper than something started rattling in the engines, so I hurried there and poured water on the overheated atomic pile till dawn, while the Monday me slept soundly, licking his lips from time to time, which galled me no end. Hungry and bleary-eyed, for I hadn't slept a wink, I set about making breakfast, and was just wiping the dishes when the rocket fell into the next gravitational vortex. I saw my Monday self staring at me dumbfounded, lashed to the armchair, while

Tuesday I fried an omelet. Then a lurch knocked me off balance, everything grew dark, and down I went. I came to on the floor among bits of broken china; near my face were the shoes of a man standing over me.

"Get up," he said, lifting me. "Are you all right?"

"I think so," I answered, keeping my hands on the floor, for my head was still spinning. "From what day of the week are you?"

"Wednesday," he said. "Come on, let's get that rudder fixed while we have the chance!"

"But where's the Monday me?" I asked.

"Gone. Which means, I suppose, that you are he."

"How is that?"

"Well, the Monday me on Monday night became, Tuesday morning, the Tuesday me, and so on."

"I don't understand."

"Doesn't matter—you'll get the hang of it. But hurry up, we're wasting time!"

"Just a minute," I replied, remaining on the floor. "Today is Tuesday. Now if you are the Wednesday me, and if by that time on Wednesday the rudder still hasn't been fixed, then it follows that something will prevent us from fixing it, since otherwise you, on Wednesday, would not now, on Tuesday, be asking me to help you fix it. Wouldn't it be best, then, for us not to risk going outside?"

"Nonsense!" he exclaimed. "Look, I'm the Wednesday me and you're the Tuesday me, and as for the rocket, well, my guess is that its existence is patched, which means that in places it's Tuesday, in places Wednesday, and here and there perhaps there's even a bit of Thursday. Time has simply become shuffled up in passing through these vortices, but why should that concern us, when together we are two and therefore have a chance to fix the rudder?!"

"No, you're wrong!" I said. "If on Wednesday, where you already are, having lived through all of Tuesday, so that

now Tuesday is behind you, if on Wednesday—I repeat—
the rudder isn't fixed, then one can only conclude that it
didn't get fixed on Tuesday, since it's Tuesday now and if we
were to go and fix the rudder right away, that *right away*
would be your *yesterday* and there would now be nothing to
fix. And consequently . . ."

"And consequently you're as stubborn as a mule!" he
growled. "You'll regret this! And my only consolation is that
you too will be infuriated by your own pigheadedness, just
as I am now—when you yourself reach Wednesday!!"

"Ah, wait," I cried, "do you mean that on Wednesday, I,
being you, will try to convince the Tuesday me, just as you
are doing here, except that everything will be reversed, in
other words you will be me and I you? But of course! That's
what makes a time loop! Hold on, I'm coming, yes, it makes
sense now . . ."

But before I could get up off the floor we fell into a new
vortex and the terrible acceleration flattened us against the
ceiling.

The dreadful pitching and heaving didn't let up once
throughout that night from Tuesday to Wednesday. Then,
when things had finally quieted down a little, the volume of
the General Theory of Relativity came flying across the
cabin and hit me on the forehead with such force, that I lost
consciousness. When I opened my eyes I saw broken dishes
and a man sprawled among them. I immediately jumped to
my feet and lifted him, shouting:

"Get up! Are you all right?"

"I think so," he replied, blinking. "From what day of the
week are you?"

"Wednesday," I said, "come on, let's get that rudder fixed
while we have the chance."

"But where's the Monday me?" he asked, sitting up. He
had a black eye.

"Gone," I said, "which means that you are he."

"How is that?"

"Well, the Monday me on Monday night became, Tuesday morning, the Tuesday me, and so on."

"I don't understand."

"Doesn't matter—you'll get the hang of it. But hurry up, we're wasting time!"

Saying this, I was already looking around for the tools. "Just a minute," he drawled, not budging an inch. "Today is Tuesday. Now, if you are the Wednesday me, and if by that time on Wednesday the rudder still hasn't been fixed, then it follows that something will prevent us from fixing it, since otherwise you, on Wednesday, would not be asking me now, on Tuesday, to help you fix it. Wouldn't it be best, then, for us not to risk going outside?"

"Nonsense!!" I yelled, losing my temper. "Look, I'm the Wednesday me, you're the Tuesday me . . ."

And so we quarreled, in opposite roles, during which he did in fact drive me into a positive fury, for he persistently refused to help me fix the rudder and it did no good calling him pigheaded and a stubborn mule. And when at last I managed to convince him, we plunged into the next gravitational vortex. I was in a cold sweat, for the thought occurred to me that we might now go around and around in this time loop, repeating ourselves for all eternity, but luckily that didn't happen. By the time the acceleration had slackened enough for me to stand, I was alone once more in the cabin. Apparently the localized existence of Tuesday, which until now had persisted in the vicinity of the sink, had vanished, becoming a part of the irretrievable past. I rushed over to the map, to find some nice vortex into which I could send the rocket, so as to bring about still another warp of time and in that way obtain a helping hand.

There was in fact one vortex, quite promising too, and by manipulating the engines with great difficulty, I aimed the rocket to intersect it at the very center. True, the configura-

tion of that vortex was, according to the map, rather unusual—it had two foci, side by side. But by now I was too
desperate to concern myself with this anomaly.

After several hours of bustling about in the engine room
my hands were filthy, so I went to wash them, seeing as
there was plenty of time yet before I would be entering the
vortex. The bathroom was locked. From inside came the
sounds of someone gargling.

"Who's there?!" I hollered, taken aback.

"Me," replied a voice.

"Which me is that?!"

"Ijon Tichy."

"From what day?"

"Friday. What do you want?"

"I wanted to wash my hands . . ." I said mechanically,
thinking meanwhile with the greatest intensity: it was
Wednesday evening, and he came from Friday, therefore
the gravitational vortex into which the ship was to fall
would bend time from Friday to Wednesday, but as for
what then would take place within the vortex, that I could in
no way picture. Particularly intriguing was the question of
where Thursday might be. In the meantime the Friday me
still wasn't letting me into the bathroom, taking his sweet
time, though I pounded on the door insistently.

"Stop that gargling!" I roared, out of patience. "Every
second is precious—come out at once, we have to fix the
rudder!"

"For that you don't need me," he said phlegmatically
from behind the door. "The Thursday me must be around
here somewhere, go with him . . ."

"What Thursday me? That's not possible . . ."

"I ought to know whether it's possible or not, considering
that I'm already in Friday and consequently have lived
through your Wednesday as well as his Thursday . . ."

Feeling dizzy, I jumped back from the door, for yes, I did

hear some commotion in the cabin: a man was standing there, pulling the toolbag out from under the bed.

"You're the Thursday me?!" I cried, running into the room.

"Right," he said. "Here, give me a hand . . ."

"Will we be able to fix the rudder this time?" I asked as together we pulled out the heavy satchel.

"I don't know, it wasn't fixed on Thursday, ask the Friday me . . ."

That hadn't crossed my mind! I quickly ran back to the bathroom door.

"Hey there, Friday me! Has the rudder been fixed?"

"Not on Friday," he replied.

"Why not?"

"This is why not," he said, opening the door. His head was wrapped in a towel, and he pressed the flat of a knife to his forehead, trying in this manner to reduce the swelling of a lump the size of an egg. The Thursday me meanwhile approached with the tools and stood beside me, calmly scrutinizing the me with the lump, who with his free hand was putting back on the shelf a siphon of seltzer. So it was its gurgle I had taken for his gargle.

"What gave you that?" I asked sympathetically.

"Not what, who," he replied. "It was the Sunday me."

"The Sunday me? But why . . . that can't be!" I cried.

"Well it's a long story . . ."

"Makes no difference! Quick, let's go outside, we might just make it!" said the Thursday me, turning to the me that was I.

"But the rocket will fall into the vortex any minute now," I replied. "The shock could throw us off into space, and that would be the end of us . . ."

"Use your head, stupid," snapped the Thursday me. "If the Friday me's alive, nothing can happen to us. Today is only Thursday."

"It's Wednesday," I objected.

"It makes no difference, in either case I'll be alive on Friday, and so will you."

"Yes, but there really aren't two of us, it only looks that way," I observed, "actually there is *one* me, just from different days of the week ..."

"Fine, fine, now open the hatch ..."

But it turned out here that we had only one spacesuit between us. Therefore we could not both leave the rocket at the same time, and therefore our plan to fix the rudder was completely ruined.

"Blast!" I cried, angrily throwing down the toolbag. "What I should have done is put on the spacesuit to begin with and kept it on. I just didn't think of it—but you, as the Thursday me, you ought to have remembered!"

"I had the spacesuit, but the Friday me took it," he said.

"When? Why?"

"Eh, it's not worth going into," he shrugged and, turning around, went back to the cabin. The Friday me wasn't there; I looked in the bathroom, but it was empty too.

"Where's the Friday me?" I asked, returning. The Thursday me methodically cracked an egg with a knife and poured its contents onto the sizzling fat.

"Somewhere in the neighborhood of Saturday, no doubt," he replied, indifferent, quickly scrambling the egg.

"Excuse me," I protested, "but you already had your meals on Wednesday—what makes you think you can go and eat a second Wednesday supper?"

"These rations are mine just as much as they are yours," he said, calmly lifting the browned edge of the egg with his knife. "I am you, you are me, so it makes no difference ..."

"What sophistry! Wait, that's too much butter! Are you crazy? I don't have enough food for this many people!"

The skillet flew out of his hand, and I went crashing into a wall: we had fallen into a new vortex. Once again the ship shook, as if in a fever, but my only thought was to get to the corridor where the spacesuit was hanging and put it on. For in that way (I reasoned) when Wednesday became Thursday, I, as the Thursday me, would be wearing that spacesuit, and if only I didn't take it off for a single minute (and I was determined not to) then I would obviously be wearing it on Friday also. And therefore the me on Thursday and the me on Friday would both be in our spacesuits, so that when we came together in the same present it would finally be possible to fix that miserable rudder. The increasing thrust of gravity made my head swim, and when I opened my eyes I noticed that I was lying to the right of the Thursday me, and not to the left, as I had been a few moments before. Now while it had been easy enough for me to develop this plan about the spacesuit, it was considerably more difficult to put it into action, since with the growing gravitation I could hardly move. When it weakened just a little, I began to inch my way across the floor—in the direction of the door that led to the corridor. Meanwhile I noticed that the Thursday me was likewise heading for the door, crawling on his belly towards the corridor. At last, after about an hour, when the vortex had reached its widest point, we met at the threshold, both flattened to the floor. Then I thought, why should I have to strain myself to reach the handle? Let the Thursday me do it. Yet at the same time I began to recall certain things which clearly indicated that it was I now who was the Thursday me, and not he.

"What day of the week are you?" I asked, to make sure. With my chin pressed to the floor I looked him in the eye. Struggling, he opened his mouth.

"Thurs—day—me," he groaned. Now that was odd. Could it be that, in spite of everything, I was *still* the Wednesday me? Calling to mind all my recollections of the recent past, I had to conclude that this was out of the question. So he must have been the Friday me. For if he had preceded me by a day before, then he was surely a day ahead now. I waited for him to open the door, but apparently he expected the same of me. The gravitation had now subsided noticeably, so I got up and ran to the corridor. Just as I grabbed the spacesuit, he tripped me, pulling it out of my hands, and I fell flat on my face.

"You dog!" I cried. "Tricking your own self—that's really low!"

He ignored me, stepping calmly into the spacesuit. The shamelessness of it was appalling. Suddenly a strange force threw him from the suit—as it turned out, someone was already inside. For a moment I wavered, no longer knowing who was who.

"You, Wednesday!" called the one in the spacesuit. "Hold back Thursday, help me!"

For the Thursday me was indeed trying to tear the spacesuit off him.

"Give me the spacesuit!" bellowed the Thursday me as he wrestled with the other.

"Get off! What are you trying to do? Don't you realize I'm the one who should have it, and not you?!" howled the other.

"And why is that, pray?"

"For the reason, fool, that I'm closer to Saturday than you, and by Saturday there will be two of us in suits!"

"But that's ridiculous," I said, getting into their argument, "at best you'll be alone in the suit on Saturday, like an absolute idiot, and won't be able to do a thing. Let *me* have the suit: if I put it on now, then you'll be wearing it on Friday as the Friday me, and I will also on Saturday as the Saturday me, and so you see there will then be two of us, and with two suits . . . Come on, Thursday, give me a hand!!"

"Wait," protested the Friday me when I had forcibly yanked the spacesuit off his back. "In the first place, there is no one here for you to call 'Thursday,' since midnight has passed and *you* are now the Thursday me, and in the second place, it'll be better if I stay in the spacesuit. The spacesuit won't do you a bit of good."

"Why not? If I put it on today, I'll have it on tomorrow too."

"You'll see for yourself . . . after all, I was already you, on Thursday, and *my* Thursday has passed, so I ought to know . . ."

"Enough talk. Let go of it this instant!" I snarled. But he grabbed it from me and I chased him, first through the engine room and then into the cabin. It somehow worked out that there were only two of us now. Suddenly I understood why the Thursday me, when we were standing at the hatch with the tools, had told me that the Friday me took the spacesuit from him: for in the meantime I myself had become the Thursday me, and here the Friday me was in fact taking it. But I had no intention of giving in that easily. Just you wait, I thought, I'll take care of you, and out I ran into the corridor, and from there to the engine room, where before—during the chase—I had noticed a heavy pipe lying on the floor, which served to stoke the atomic pile, and I picked it up and—thus armed—dashed back to the cabin. The other me was already in the spacesuit, he had pulled on everything but the helmet.

"Out of the spacesuit!" I snapped, clenching my pipe in a threatening manner.

"Not a chance."

"Out, I say!!"

Then I wondered whether or not I should hit him. It was a little disconcerting, the fact that he had neither a black eye nor a bump on his head, like the other Friday me, the one I'd found in the bathroom, but all at once I realized that this was the way it had to be. *That* Friday me by now was the Saturday me, yes, and perhaps even was knocking about

somewhere in the vicinity of Sunday, while this Friday me
inside the spacesuit had only recently been the Thursday
me, into which same Thursday me I myself had been transformed at midnight. Thus I was moving along the sloping
curve of the time loop towards that place in which the Friday me before the beating would change into the Friday me
already beaten. Still, he *did* say, back then, that it had been
the Sunday me who did it, and there was no trace, as yet, of
him. We stood alone in the cabin, he and I. Then suddenly I
had a brainstorm.

"Out of that spacesuit!" I growled.

"Keep off, Thursday!" he yelled.

"I'm not Thursday, I'm the SUNDAY ME!" I shrieked,
closing in for the kill. He tried to kick me, but spacesuit
boots are very heavy and before he could raise his leg, I let
him have it over the head. Not too hard, of course, since I
had grown sufficiently familiar with all of this to know that I
in turn, when eventually I went from the Thursday to the
Friday me, would be on the receiving end, and I wasn't particularly set on fracturing my own skull. The Friday me fell
with a groan, holding his head, and I brutally tore the
spacesuit off him. While he made for the bathroom on wobbly legs, muttering, "Where's the cotton . . . where's the
seltzer," I quickly began to don the suit that we had struggled over, until I noticed—sticking out from under the
bed—a human foot. I took a closer look, kneeling. Under
the bed lay a man; trying to muffle the sound of his chewing,
he was hurriedly bolting down the last bar of the milk chocolate I had stored away in the suitcase for a rainy sidereal
day. The bastard was in such a hurry that he ate the chocolate along with bits of tin foil, which glittered on his lips.

"Leave that chocolate alone!" I yelled, pulling at his foot.
"Who are you anyway? The Thursday me? . . ." I added in a
lower voice, seized by a sudden doubt, for the thought oc-

curred that maybe I already was the Friday me, and would soon have to collect what I had dished out earlier to the same.

"The Sunday me," he mumbled, his mouth full. I felt weak. Now either he was lying, in which case there was nothing to worry about, or telling the truth, and if he was, I faced a clobbering for sure, because the Sunday me—after all—was the one who had hit the Friday me, the Friday me told me so himself before it happened, and then later I, impersonating the Sunday me, had let him have it with the pipe. But on the other hand, I said to myself, even if he's lying and not the Sunday me, it's still quite possible that he's a later me than me, and if he *is* a later me, he remembers everything that I do, therefore already knows that I lied to the Friday me, and so could deceive me in a similar manner, since what had been a spur-of-the-moment stratagem on my part was for him—by now—simply a memory, a memory he could easily make use of. Meanwhile, as I remained in uncertainty, he had eaten the rest of the chocolate and crawled out from under the bed.

"If you're the Sunday me, where's your spacesuit?!" I cried, struck by a new thought.

"I'll have it in a minute," he said calmly, and then I noticed the pipe in his hand ... The next thing I saw was a bright flash, like a few dozen supernovas going off at once, after which I lost consciousness. I came to, sitting on the floor of the bathroom; someone was banging on the door. I began to attend to my bruises and bumps, but he kept pounding away; it turned out to be the Wednesday me. After a while I showed him my battered head, he went with the Thursday me for the tools, then there was a lot of running around and yanking off of spacesuits, this to in one way or another I managed to live through, and on Saturday morning crawled under the bed to see if there wasn't some chocolate left in the suitcase. Someone started pulling at my foot as I ate the last bar, which I'd found underneath the shirts; I no longer knew just who this was, but hit him over the head anyhow, pulled the spacesuit off him and was going to put it on—when the rocket fell into the next vortex. When I regained consciousness, the cabin was packed with people. There was barely elbowroom. As it turned out, they were all of them me, from different days, weeks, months, and one—so he said—was even from the following year. There were plenty with bruises and black eyes, and five among those present had on spacesuits. But instead of immediately going out through the hatch and repairing the damage, they began to quarrel, argue, bicker and debate. The problem was, who had hit whom, and when. The situation was complicated by the fact that there now had appeared morning me's and afternoon me's—I feared that if things went on like this, I would soon be broken into minutes and seconds—and then too, the majority of the me's present were lying like mad, so that to this day I'm not altogether sure whom I hit and who hit me when that whole business took place, triangularly, between the Thursday, the Friday and the Wednesday me's, all of whom I was in turn. My impression is that because I had lied to the Friday me, pretending to be the Sunday me, I ended up with one blow more than I should have, going by the calendar. But I would prefer not to dwell any longer on these unpleasant memories; a man who for an entire week does nothing but hit himself over the head has little reason to be proud.

Meanwhile the arguments continued. The sight of such inaction, such wasting of precious time, drove me to despair, while the rocket rushed blindly on, straight ahead, plunging every now and then into another gravitational vortex. At last the ones wearing spacesuits started slugging it out with the ones who were not. I tried to introduce some sort of order into that absolute chaos and finally, after superhuman efforts, succeeded in organizing something that resembled a

meeting, in which the one from next year—having senior-
ity—was elected chairman by acclamation.

We then appointed an elective committee, a nominating
committee, and a committee for new business, and four of us
from next month were made sergeants at arms. But in the
meantime we had passed through a negative vortex, which
cut our number in half, so that on the very first ballot we
lacked a quorum, and had to change the bylaws before proceeding to vote on the candidates for rudder-repairer. The
map indicated the approach of still other vortices, and these
undid all that we had accomplished so far: first the candidates already chosen disappeared, and then the Tuesday me
showed up with the Friday me, who had his head wrapped
in a towel, and they created a shameful scene. Upon passage
through a particularly strong positive vortex we hardly fit in
the cabin and corridor, and opening the hatch was out of the
question—there simply wasn't room. But the worst of it was,
these time displacements were increasing in amplitude, a
few grayhaired me's had already appeared, and here and
there I even caught a glimpse of the close-cropped heads of
children, that is of myself, of course—or rather—myselves
from the halcyon days of boyhood.

I really can't recall whether I was still the Sunday me, or
had already turned into the Monday me. Not that it made
any difference. The children sobbed that they were being
squashed in the crowd, and called for their mommy; the
chairman—the Tichy from next year—let out a string of
curses, because the Wednesday me, who had crawled under
the bed in a futile search for chocolate, bit him in the leg
when he accidentally stepped on the latter's finger. I saw
that all this would end badly, particularly now as here and
there gray beards were turning up. Between the 142nd and
143rd vortices I passed around an attendance sheet, but afterwards it came to light that a large number of those present were cheating. Supplying false vital statistics, God

knows why. Perhaps the prevailing atmosphere had muddled their wits. The noise and confusion were such that you
could make yourself understood only by screaming at the
top of your lungs. But then one of last year's Ijons hit upon
what seemed to be an excellent idea, namely, that the oldest
among us tell the story of his life; in that way we would
learn just who was supposed to fix the rudder. For obviously
the oldest me contained within his past experience the lives
of all the others there from their various months, days and
years. So we turned, in this matter, to a hoary old gentleman
who, slightly palsied, was standing idly in the corner. When
questioned, he began to speak at great length of his children
and grandchildren, then passed to his cosmic voyages, and
he had embarked upon no end of these in the course of his
ninety-some years. Of the one now taking place—the only
one of interest to us—the old man had no recollection whatever, owing to his generally sclerotic and overexcited condition, however he was far too proud to admit this and went
on evasively, obstinately, time and again returning to his
high connections, decorations and grandchildren, till finally
we shouted him down and ordered him to hold his tongue.
The next two vortices cruelly thinned our ranks. After the
third, not only was there more room, but all of those in
spacesuits had disappeared as well. One empty suit remained; we voted to hang it up in the corridor, then went
back to our deliberations. Then, following another scuffle
for the possession of that precious garment, a new vortex
came along and suddenly the place was deserted. I was sitting on the floor, puffy-eyed, in my strangely spacious cabin,
surrounded by broken furniture, strips of clothing, ripped-
up books. The floor was strewn with ballots. According to
the map, I had now passed through the entire zone of gravitational vortices. No longer able to count on duplication,
and thus no longer able to correct the damage, I fell into
numb despair. About an hour later I looked out in the corri-

dor and discovered, to my great surprise, that the spacesuit was missing. But then I vaguely remembered—yes—right before that last vortex two little boys sneaked out into the corridor. Could they have possibly, both of them, put on the one spacesuit?! Struck by a sudden thought, I ran to the controls. The rudder worked! So then, those little tykes had fixed it after all, while we adults were stuck in endless disagreements. I imagine that one of them placed his arms in the sleeves of the suit, and the other—in the pants; that way, they could have tightened the nut and bolt with wrenches at the same time, working on either side of the rudder. The empty spacesuit I found in the air lock, behind the hatch. I carried it inside the rocket like a sacred relic, my heart full of boundless gratitude for those brave lads I had been so long ago! And thus concluded what was surely one of my most unusual adventures. I reached my destination safely, thanks to the courage and resourcefulness I had displayed when only two children.

It was said afterwards that I invented the whole thing, and those more malicious even went so far as to insinuate that I had a weakness for alcohol, carefully concealed on Earth but freely indulged during those long and lonely cosmic flights. Lord only knows what other gossip has been circulating on the subject. But that is how people are; they'll willingly give credence to the most far-fetched drivel, but not to the simple truth, which is precisely what I have presented here.

The Fourteenth Voyage

19. VIII. Having my rocket repaired. I got too close to the sun last time; all the finish peeled off. The shop manager suggests green. Perhaps, I don't know. Spent the morning straightening up my collection. The prettiest gargoon pelt was full of moths. Sprinkled it with naphthalene. My afternoon—at Tarantoga's. We sang Martian songs. I borrowed from him Brizard's *Two Years among the Squamp and Octopockles.* Read it till dawn—simply fascinating.

20. VIII. I agreed to green. The manager is trying to talk me into buying an electrical brain. He has an extra one, in good condition, hardly used, high-powered. He says that no one goes anywhere today without a brain, except maybe to the moon. Haven't decided yet, it's a big expense. Read Brizard all afternoon—can't put it down. And to think that I've never even seen a squamp.

21. VIII. At the shipyard bright and early. The manager showed me his brain. Truly handsome, and the joke battery lasts five years. This is supposed to solve the problem of cosmic ennui. "You'll laugh the whole voyage," said the manager. When the battery runs out, simply put in another. I ordered the rudders painted red. But as for the brain—I'll have to think about it. Stayed up until midnight reading Brizard. Why not go hunting myself?

22. VIII. I finally bought that brain. Had it built into the wall. The manager added on some optionals, a heating pad and pillow. Taking me for all I'm worth! But he says I'll save a lot of money. The point is that when you land on a planet you usually have to go through customs. With a brain, however, you can leave the rocket in space, let it circle the planet like an artificial moon, and then, without paying a single cent on duty, you proceed the rest of the way on foot. The brain computes the astronomical elements of its flight and relays the coordinates when you have to find the rocket later. I finished Brizard. Pretty well made up my mind, I'm going to Enteropia.

23. VIII Got the rocket from the repair shop. It looks beautiful, except that the rudders clash. I repainted them myself, yellow. Worlds better. Borrowed volume E of the Cosmic Encyclopedia from Tarantoga and copied down the entry on Enteropia. Here it is:

ENTEROPIA, 6th planet of a double (red and blue) star in the Calf constellation. 8 continents, 2 oceans, 167 active volcanoes, 1 torg (see TORG). A 20-hr. day, warm climate, conditions for life favorable except during the whackers (see WHACKER).

Inhabitants:

a) dominant race—the Ardrites, intelligent beings, polydiaphanohedral, nonbisymmetrical and pelissobrachial (3), belonging to the genus Siliconoidea, order Polytheria, class Luminifera. Like all Polytheria the Ardrites are subject to periodic discretional splitting. They form families of the spherical type. System of government: gradocracy II B, with the introduction, 340 yrs. ago, of Penitential Trasm (see

TRASM). Industry highly developed, principally eating utensils. Chief items of export: phosphorescent manubria, heart pl.'s, and loppets in several doz. varieties, ribbed and tannable. Capital: Ubbidub, pop. 1,400,000. Industrial centers; Haupr, Drur, Arbagellar. Culture luminositous, showing tendency to mushroom, due to the pervasive influence of the relics of a civilization wiped out by the Ardrites, the Phytogosian (see MUSHROOM MEN). In recent yrs. an increasingly imp. role has been played in the culture life of the society by (see) scrupts. Beliefs: the prevailing religion—Monomungism. According to M., the world was created by the Multiple Munge in the person of the Original Urdle, from whom arose the suns and planets, with Enteropia at the head. The plated temples of the Ardrites are stationary and collapsible. Besides Monomungism several sects are active, the most significant—the Tentortonian. The (see) Tentortonians believe only in Emphosis (see EMPHOSIS), and some not even in that. Art: ballet (rotary), radio opera, scruption, antediluvian drama. Architecture: in con. with the whackers—pump-inflatable, tubulous, blobiform. Gum towers, highest are the 130 deckers. On art. moons edifices generally ovoid.

b) *Animals.* Fauna of the siliconoidal var., prin. species: slebs, autachial denderfnifts, gruncheons, squamp and whimpering octopockles. During the whackers the hunting of squamp and octopockles is prohibited by law. For man these animals are inedible, with the exception of squamp (and only in the zarf region, see ZARF). Aquatic fauna: constitute the raw material of the food industry. Prin. species: infernalia (hellwinders), chungheads, frinkuses and opthropularies. Unique to Enteropia is the torg, with its bollical fauna and flora. In our Galaxy the only things analogous to it are the hii in the frothless sump bosks of Jupiter. All life on Enteropia evolved—as has been shown by the studies of the school of Prof. Tarantoga—within the confines of the torg, from the chalcycladine deposits. In con. with the massive devel. of land and sea one can expect the

swift disappearance of the remnants of the torg. Falling
under par. 6 of the stat. in re the preservation of planetary
monuments (Codex Galacticus t. MDDDVII, vol. XXXII,
pg. 4670), the torg has been declared a park; esp. forbidden
is poaching (croaching) at night.

Most of the entry is clear to me, except for the references
to scrupts, trasm and whackers. Unfortunately the last volume of the Encyclopedia published so far ends on "Succo-
TASH," which means there's nothing about trasm or
whacker. However I did go over to Tarantoga's to look up
"Scrupts." All I found was:

> Scrupts—a feature of the civilization of the (see) Ar-
> drites, of the planet (see) Enteropia, plays a significant role
> in their cultural life. See Scrupture.

I followed this advice and read:

> Scrupture—the art of scrupturing, the state of being
> scruptured, the product of (see) scruption.

I looked under "Scruption," which said:

> Sruption—an activity or condition of the (see) Ardrites,
> of the planet (see) Enteropia. See Scrupts.

The circle had closed, there was nowhere else to look. Well,
I'd sooner die than admit to such ignorance in front of the
Professor, and there's no one but him I can turn to. Anyway,
the die is cast—I've decided to go to Enteropia. I take off in
three days.

28. VIII.   Started out at two, right after lunch. Didn't bring
along any books, since I have that new brain. It told anec-
dotes all the way to the moon. I laughed and laughed. Then
supper, and off to bed.

29. VIII. I must have caught a cold in the moon's shadow, I keep sneezing. Took two aspirin. Three freighters from Pluto on our course; the engineer telegraphed me to get out of the way. I asked what his cargo was, thinking it might be God knows what, but nothing, just ordinary clabber. And then an express from Mars, terribly packed. I looked out the window, they were all lying one on top of the other, like herring. We waved our handkerchiefs, but they were already gone. Listened to jokes until supper. Hysterical, only I keep sneezing.

30. VIII. Increased the speed. The brain working perfectly. My sides began to hurt some, so I turned it off for a couple of hours and plugged in the pad and pillow. Feels wonderful. It was after two when I picked up the radio signal Popov sent from Earth in the year 1896. I'm a good ways out now.

31. VIII. The sun is barely visible. A walk around the rocket before lunch, to get the circulation going. Jokes until evening. Most of them old. It looks as if that shop manager gave the brain some back issues of a humor magazine to read, then threw in a few new jokes on top. I forgot the potatoes I'd put in the atomic pile, and now they're burnt, all of them.

32. VIII. Because of the velocity time is slowing down— this ought to be October, but here it is still August. Something's started flashing by outside. I thought it was the Milky Way already, but no, just my paint flaking off. Damn, a cheap brand! There's a service station up ahead. Wonder if it's worth stopping.

33. VIII. Still August. After lunch I pulled over to the station. It stands on a small, absolutely empty planet. The building looks abandoned, not a living soul about. Took my bucket and went to see if they had any paint here. I was walking around when I heard a puffing. I followed it, and there behind the building saw several steam robots standing and conversing. I drew near.

One of them was saying:

"Surely it's obvious that clouds are the astral bodies of steam robots that have passed on. The basic question, as I see it, is this: which came first, the steam or the robot? I maintain it was the steam!"

"Hush, shameless idealist!" hissed another.

I tried asking for paint, but they were hissing and whistling so much, I couldn't hear myself think. Dropped a complaint in the suggestion box and continued on my way.

34. VIII. Will this August never end? Washed the rocket all morning. Bored stiff. Climbed inside, to try the brain. Instead of laughter, such an attack of yawning that I feared for my jaw. A tiny planet starboard. Passing it, I noticed some sort of white dots. Through the binoculars observed that these were little signs with the inscription: "Don't lean out." Something's wrong with the brain—it's swallowing its punch lines.

1. X. Had to stop on Stroglon, out of fuel. In braking, the momentum carried me through all of September.

Considerable congestion at the airport. I left the rocket in space, so as to avoid having to pay duty, took only my fuel cans. But first I computed—with the help of the brain—the coordinates of my elliptical orbit. Returned an hour later with full containers, but not a trace of the rocket. Obviously I had to go look for it. Shuddered at the thought, but covered something like four thousand miles on foot. The brain made a mistake, of course. I'll have to have a little talk with that shop manager when I get back.

2. X. My velocity is so great, the stars have turned into fiery streaks, as if someone were waving a million lighted cigarettes in a dark room. The brain stutters. What's worse, the switch is broken and I can't turn it off. Rambles on and on.

3. X. It's running down, I think, spells everything out now. I'm gradually growing accustomed to that. I sit outside, as much as possible, only with my feet in the rocket, for it's cold as hell.

7. X. At eleven-thirty reached the Enteropia terminal. The rocket red-hot from braking. I parked it on the upper level of the artificial moon (their port of entry) and went inside to take care of the formalities. An unbelievable crowd in the spiral hallway; arrivals from every corner of the Galaxy walking, flowing, hopping from counter to counter. I got into line behind a pale blue Algolian, who in polite pantomime cautioned me not to stand too close to his posterior electrifying organ. Then suddenly behind me there was a young Saturnile in a beige kebong. With three shoots he held his luggage, with the fourth shoot mopped his brow. It was indeed hot in there. When my turn came, the official, an Ardrite as transparent as glass looked me over carefully, greened a little (the Ardrites express emotions by changing color; green is equivalent to a smile) and asked:
"Vertebrate?"
"Yes."
"Amphibious?"
"No, only land . . ."
"Thank you, good. Mixed diet?"
"Yes."
"From what planet, may I ask?"
"From Earth."
"And now please go to the next window."

I went to the next window and, looking in, confronted the very same official, or—more exactly—his continuation. He was turning the pages of an enormous book.

"Ah, there it is!" he said. "Earth ... yes, very good. Are you here on business, or only touring?"

"Touring."

"Now if you don't mind ..."

With one tentacle he filed out a form, while with another he gave me a form to sign, saying:

"There's a whacker expected, it begins in a week. Therefore kindly go over to room 116, our spares are made there, you'll be taken care of. Then proceed to room 67, that's the pharmaceutical booth. They'll give you Euphruglium pills, take one every three hours, it neutralizes the harmful effects on your organism of our planet's radioactivity ... Will you be lighting up during your stay on Enteropia?"

"No, thanks."

"As you like. Here are your papers. You are a mammal, I believe?"

"That's right."

"Well then, happy mammaling!"

Taking my leave of this courteous official, I went—as he had directed me—to the place where they made spares. The egg-shaped chamber appeared, at first glance, to be unoccupied. There were several electrical devices standing about, and on the ceiling a crystal lamp gleamed and sparkled. It turned out, however, that the lamp was an Ardrite, a technician on duty; he immediately climbed down from the ceiling. I sat on the chair; diverting me with conversation, he took my measurements, then said:

"Thank you, sir. We'll be transmitting your gemma to all the hatcheries on our planet. If anything should happen to you during a whacker, rest assured ... we bring a spare at once!"

I wasn't all that clear about what he meant, however in

the course of my many travels I have learned discretion, since there is nothing more unpleasant for the inhabitants of a planet than to have to explain their local ways and customs to a foreigner. At the pharmaceutical booth, another line, but it moved quickly and before I knew it a nimble Ardritess in a faïence lampshade had handed me my pill ration. Then a brief formality at customs (I wasn't about to trust that electrical brain) and with visa in hand I returned on board.

Behind the moon begins an interspace thruway, well maintained, with great billboards on either side. The individual letters are a few thousand miles apart, but at normal speed the words fall together so fast, it's like having them printed in a newspaper. For a while I read these with interest—such as: "Hunters! For big-game spread, try MYLL!"—or: "Warm your cockles, bop octopockles!"—and so on.

It was seven in the evening when I landed at the Ubbidub airport. The blue sun had just gone down. In the rays of the red one, which was still quite high, everything seemed enveloped in flame—an unusual sight. A galactic cruiser majestically settled down beside my rocket. Beneath its fins, touching scenes of reunion were acted out. The Ardrites, separated for many long months, embraced one another with cries of joy, after which they all, fathers, mothers, children, tenderly clasped together in globes that shimmered pink in the light of the sun, hurried off to the exit. I followed after those harmoniously rolling families; right in front of the airport there was a molly stop, and I got on one. This conveyance, decorated on top with characters of gold that formed the sign "Raus Spread Hunts Best!," looked something like a Swiss cheese; in its larger holes sat the grownups, while the smaller served to carry the little ones. As soon as I got on, the molly pulled out. Enclosed in its crystal mass, above me, below me, and all around I saw the congenially translucent and multicolored silhouettes of my fellow passengers. I reached into my pocket for the Baedeker, feeling it was high time I acquainted myself with a few helpful facts, but discovered—to my dismay—that the volume I was holding dealt with the planet Enteroptica, a good three million light-years removed from my present location. The Baedeker I needed was at home. That damned absent-mindedness of mine!

Well, I had no choice but to go to the Ubbidub branch of the well-known astronautical travel bureau GALAX. The conductor was most courteous; when I asked him, he immediately stopped the molly and pointed his tentacle at an enormous building, then saw me off with a friendly change of color.

For a moment I stood still, delighting in the remarkable scene afforded by the city at dusk. The red sun was just then sinking beneath the horizon. Ardrites don't use artificial illumination, they themselves light up. The Mror Boulevard, on which I stood, was filled with the glimmer of pedestrians; one young Ardritess, passing by, flirtatiously burst into golden stripes inside her shade, but then, evidently recognizing a foreigner, she modestly dimmed.

Houses near and far sparkled and glowed with the inhabitants returning from work; deep within the temples gleamed multitudes in prayer; children raced up and down the stairs like crazy rainbows. It was all so captivating, so colorful, that I didn't want to leave, but had to, before Galax closed for the night.

In the lobby of the travel bureau they directed me to the twenty-third floor, the provincial division. Yes, it's sad but nonetheless true: our Earth is in the boondocks of the Universe, obscure, ignored!

The secretary I approached in the tourist service department clouded over with embarrassment and said that Galax, unfortunately, had neither guidebooks nor sightseeing itineraries for Earthlings, since the latter came to Enteropia no more than once a century. She offered me a booklet for Jovians, in view of the common solar origin of Earth and Jupiter. I took it—for lack of anything better—and requested a reservation at the hotel Cosmonia. I also signed up for the hunt organized by Galax, then went out into the city. My situation was all the more awkward in that I wasn't able to shine by myself, thus when I encountered at an intersection an Ardrite who was regulating traffic, I stopped and—in his light—skimmed through my new guidebook. As I might have expected, it furnished information about where one could obtain methane preserves, what to do with one's antennae at official functions, etc. So I chucked it in a trash can, caught a passing transom and asked to be taken to the gum tower district. Those magnificent, cup-shaped edifices, seen at a distance, glistened with the variegated glow of Ardrites devoting themselves to their family affairs, and in the office buildings the luminous necklaces of the officials coruscated in the loveliest way.

Dismissing my transom, I wandered about on foot for a while. As I marveled at the Porridge Authority, a gum tower soaring high above the square, two important functionaries emerged from it—I could tell they were important by the intense glare and the red crests around their shades. They stopped nearby, and I overheard their conversation:

"So smearing the rims is out now?" said the tall one, covered with medals.

The other brightened at this and replied:

"Yes. The director says we won't make quota, and it's all the fault of Grudrufs. There's no help for it, says the director, he'll have to be converted."

"Grudrufs?"

"Grudrufs."

The first darkened, only his medals continued to twinkle in iridescent wreaths, and lowering his voice he said: "He'll slooch, the poor devil."

"He can slooch all he likes. Discipline has to be maintained. We've been transmuting the boys for years, and it isn't for the purpose of making more scrupts!"

Intrigued, I had edged closer to the two Ardrites without realizing it, and they moved away in silence. It was a funny thing, but after this incident the word "scrupt" seemed to crop up more and more frequently. The more I walked the streets, feeling the urge to immerse myself in the night life of the metropolis, the more from the throngs trundling past there drifted that enigmatic phrase, now uttered in a strangled whisper, and now in a passionate cry; one could see it written on the poster globes that announced sales and auctions of rare scruptics, or emblazoned across the neon ads encouraging the purchase of the very latest scruptures. In vain did I ponder its meaning; then finally, while I was sitting—around midnight—over a cold glass of squamp milk in a bar on the eightieth floor of a department store, and the Ardrite chanteuse had begun to sing the popular song, "That little scrupt o' mine," my curiosity reached such proportions, that I asked a passing waiter where I might buy myself a scrupt.

"Across the street," he answered mechanically, taking my check and money. Then he gave me a hard look and dimmed a little. "You're alone?" he asked.

"Yes. What of it?"

"Oh, nothing. I'm sorry, but I don't have change."

I forwent the change and took an elevator down. Yes, directly opposite me I saw a gigantic sign for scrupts, so I pushed open the glass door and found myself inside a shop, empty at that late hour. I went over to the counter and, assuming an air of indifference, asked for a scrupt.

"At which scruptrum?" inquired the salesman, coming down from his perch.

"At which . . . let me see . . . at the usual," I replied.

"What do you mean, at the usual?" he said with surprise. "We sell only surried scrupts . . ."

"Fine, I'll take one."

"But where's your macket?"

"Ah, yes, h'm, didn't bring it with me . . ."

"Then how can you buy it without your wife?" said the salesman, staring at me. He was slowly darkening.

"I'm not married," I blurted without thinking.

"You're—not—married—?" he gasped, ashen, looking at me with horror. "You—you want a scrupt, and you're *not married* . . . ?"

The salesman quivered all over. I got out of there as quickly as I could, flagged down an unoccupied transom and, furious, asked to be taken to some popular nightspot. Which turned out to be the Myrgindragg. When I entered, the orchestra had just stopped playing. There were well over three hundred persons perched here. Looking about for an empty place, I was pushing through the crowd when suddenly someone called my name; with joy I caught sight of a familiar face, it was a traveling salesman I'd met once on Autropia. He was perching with his wife and daughter. I introduced myself to the ladies and began amusing my already merry companions with a little repartee; from time to time they alighted and, to the rhythm of a lively dance tune, went rolling across the ballroom floor. Repeatedly urged by the spouse of my acquaintance, I finally got up the nerve to join in; and so, tightly embraced, the four of us rolled round and round to the music of a wild mamborina. To tell the truth, I got battered up bit, but grinned and bore it, and pretended I was having a marvelous time. On the way back to our table I pulled my acquaintance aside and asked him, in a whisper, about the scrupts.

"Beg your pardon?" He hadn't heard me. I repeated my question, adding that I would like to acquire a scrupt. Apparently I had spoken too loud—those perched nearby turned around and looked at me with murky faces, and my Ardrite friend threw up his tentacles in alarm.

"For the love of Munge, Mr. Tichy—but you're alone!"

"And what if I am?" I snapped, irritated. "Is that any reason I can't see a scrupt?"

There was a sickening silence. The wife of my acquaintance fell to the floor in a faint, he rushed to her assistance, and the nearest Ardrites started rolling towards me, their color betraying the most hostile intentions; at that moment three waiters appeared, seized me by the scruff of the neck and tossed me out into the street.

I was positively furious. I hailed a transom, took it back to the hotel. All that night I didn't sleep a wink, something was gnawing, chafing at me; at daybreak I discovered that the hotel staff, having received no particulars from Galax and accustomed to guests who burned their mattresses clear through to the springs, had given me asbestos sheets. But the unpleasant incidents of the previous day seemed unimportant that bright morning. It was in the best of spirits that I greeted the Galax representative who came for me at ten in a transom full of snares, jars of hunting spread and a whole arsenal of sportsman's weapons.

"Ever hunted squamp before?" asked my guide as the vehicle wove its way through the streets of Ubbidub at breakneck speed.

"No. Perhaps you would care to enlighten me . . ." I said with a smile.

My many years of experience on safaris for the largest game in the Galaxy entitled me, I thought, to show no excitement.

"Gladly," replied the courteous guide.

This was a slender Ardrite of glassy complexion, without

a shade, wrapped in a navy blue fabric—I had not seen that sort of dress before on the planet. When I told him this, he explained it was a hunting outfit, indispensable for stealing up on game; what I had taken for cloth was in fact a special substance with which one covered one's body. In short—a spray-on suit, comfortable, practical and, most important, completely blotting out the natural effulgence of the Ardrites, which might scare off a squamp.

The guide pulled a leaflet from his handbag and gave it to me to study; I have it still among my papers. It reads:

HUNTING SQUAMP

Instructions for Foreigners

The squamp as a game animal places great demands on the personal accomplishments no less than on the gear of the hunter. Inasmuch as this beast has, in the course of evolution, adapted itself to meteoroid rains by developing an absolutely impervious integument of armor, squamp are hunted from the inside only.

To hunt a squamp one must have:

A) in the preliminary phase—base spread, mushroom sauce, chives, salt and pepper;

B) in the phase proper—a whisk broom, a time bomb.

I. Preparation in the field.

One hunts a squamp with bait. The hunter, having besmeared himself beforehand with the base spread, crouches down in a furrow of the torg, after which his companions sprinkle finely chopped chives over him and season to taste.

II. In this position one awaits the squamp. When the animal approaches, one should remain calm and with both hands take firm hold of the time bomb gripped between one's knees. A hungry squamp will usually swallow at once. If however the squamp does balk, one may encourage it with a gentle slap across the tongue. When a miss seems likely, some advise additional salting, this however is a most hazardous move, for the squamp may sneeze. Very few hunters have survived the sneeze of a squamp.

III. A squamp that takes the bait will lick its lips and walk away. Upon being swallowed, the hunter immediately proceeds to the active phase, i.e., with the whisk broom he brushes from himself the chives and spices, so that the spread may freely work its purgative effect, whereupon he set the time bomb and withdraws as quickly as possible in the direction opposite to that from which he came.

IV. Upon leaving the squamp, one should take care to land on one's hands and feet and not hurt oneself.

Warning. The use of sharp spices is forbidden. Also forbidden is the planting of time bombs already set and sprinkled with chives. Such an act is considered poaching and will be prosecuted to the limit of the law.

At the border of the game preserve we were met by the warden, Wawr, in the midst of his family that sparkled like crystal in the sun. He proved to be most friendly and hospitable; invited to partake of some refreshment, we passed several hours at his charming estate, listening to true-life tales of squamp and the hunting reminiscences of Wawr and his sons. Then suddenly a breathless courier came bursting in with the news that the beaters had flushed some squamp from cover and into the heart of the bush.

"Squamp," explained the warden, "must first be driven around a bit, to get them good and hungry!"

Anointed with spread and holding my bomb and spices, I set off in the company of Wawr and my guide. We entered the torg. The path soon vanished in impenetrable thickets. Progress grew difficult, from time to time we came upon squamp tracks, which were potholes twenty feet in diameter. On and on we went, interminably. Then the earth shook and my guide halted, motioning silence with his tentacle. One could hear the thunder, as if a violent storm were raging just over the horizon.

"Hear that?" whispered the guide.

"A squamp?"

"Yes. It's a cub."

Now we pushed ahead more slowly and with greater caution. The crashing died away and the torg again was still. Finally, through the underbrush there gleamed an open field. At the edge of it my companions found a suitable spot, then seasoned me and, making sure I had the whisk broom and bomb in readiness, left on tiptoe, recommending patience. For a while nothing disturbed the reigning silence but the whine and burr of octopockles; my legs had grown quite numb when, suddenly, the ground began to tremble. I saw a movement in the distance—the treetops at the far end of the clearing swayed and fell, marking the path of the beast. This was a big one, all right. Presently the squamp looked out on the field, stepped over some fallen trunks and plodded forward. Swinging majesticaly from side to side, it headed straight in my direction, snuffing noisily. With both hands I clutched the jug-eared bomb and waited, perfectly calm. The squamp stopped at a distance of some one hundred fifty feet from me and licked its lips. In its transparent interior I could clearly see the remains of many a hunter upon whom Fortune had not smiled.

For a while the squamp thought it over. I began to fear the thing would go away, but then it approached and tasted me. I heard a hollow slurp and lost the ground from under my feet.

"Got him!" I thought. Inside the squamp it wasn't nearly as dark as it had seemed at first. Brushing myself off, I lifted the heavy time bomb and was just about to set it, when someone went "Ahem." I looked up, startled, and saw before me a strange Ardrite, also bending over a bomb. We stared at one another for a minute.

"What are you doing here?" I asked.

"Hunting squamp," he replied.

"So am I," I said, "but go ahead, please. You were here first."

"Nonsense," he replied, "you are a visitor."

"No, really," I protested, "I'll save my bomb for another time. Please don't let my presence hamper you."

"I won't hear of it!" he exclaimed. "You are our guest."

"I am a hunter first."

"And I—a host, and will not have you give up this squamp on my account! Make haste now, for the spread is beginning to work!"

In truth the squamp had become uneasy; even in here its powerful panting reached us, with a sound like several dozen locomotives all going at once. Seeing that I would never persuade the Ardrite, I set the bomb and waited for my new companion, he however insisted I go first. Shortly thereafter we left the squamp. Falling from a height of two stories, I twisted my ankle a little. The squamp, evidently much relieved, went charging off into the brush, snapping trees with an awful racket. Suddenly there was a terrific boom, then silence.

"Well done, old fellow! Congratulations!" shouted the hunter, heartily shaking my hand. At that moment the game warden and my guide came up.

It was getting dark, we had to hurry back; the warden promised that he himself would stuff the squamp and have it sent to Earth on the very first freighter out.

5. XI. Didn't write a word for four days, I was too busy. Every morning—those characters from the Commission for Cultural Cooperation with the Cosmos, museums, exhibits, radioactivities, and in the afternoon—visits, official receptions, addresses. I'm all done in. The delegate from CCCC in charge of me said yesterday that we were due for a whacker, but I forgot to ask him what a whacker was. Supposed to see Professor Pook, the famous Ardrite scientist, but don't know when yet.

6. XI. At the hotel, early, wakened by an ungodly noise. I jumped out of bed and saw great columns of smoke and fire rising above the city. I phoned the information desk, asked what was happening.

"It's nothing," said the operator, "nothing to worry about, sir, only a whacker."

"A whacker?"

"Yes, a whacker, a meteor shower, we get them once every ten months."

"But that's dreadful!" I cried. 'Shouldn't I go to a shelter?!"

"Oh, no shelter will withstand a striking meteor. But really, sir, you have a spare, like every citizen, there is no need to be afraid."

"What do you mean, a spare?" I asked, but she had already hung up. I quickly dressed and went out into the city. The traffic in the streets was perfectly normal; pedestrians hurried about their business, dignitaries ablaze with iridescent medals drove to their offices, and in the parks played children, twinkling and singing. The explosions thinned out after a while; only in the distance now could one still hear their steady rumble. A whacker, I thought, evidently was not a terribly serious phenomenon, if no one here paid the least attention to it, and so I went—as I had planned—to the zoological garden.

I was shown around by the director himself, a slender, nervous Ardrite with a handsome shine. The Ubbidub Zoo is well kept up; the director told me with pride that its collection contains animals from the farthermost reaches of the Galaxy, including even an Earth exhibit. Touched, I asked to see it.

"Unfortunatley you can't just now," he said, then added, when I looked at him questioningly:

"It's their sleeping period. We had a great deal of trouble with the acclimatization, you see, for a while I was afraid we wouldn't be able to keep a single one of them alive, but happily the vitamin supplements our experts worked out gave excellent results."

"Yes . . . but what sort of animal are they?"

"Flies. By the way, do you like squamp?"

He threw me a peculiar, searching look, so that I replied, trying to give my voice the sound of genuine enthusiasm:

"Oh, I'm crazy about them—wonderful creatures!"

He beamed.

"Good. Let's go see them, but first, excuse me for a moment."

He returned with a coil of rope and led me to the squamp pen, which was encircled with a three-hundred-foot wall. Opening the door, he had me enter first.

"You can rest easy," he said, "my squamp are perfectly tame."

I found myself on an artificial torg field; there were six or seven squamp grazing, splendid specimens, each measuring about three hectares across. The largest, at the voice of the director, approached us and held out its tail. The director climbed up on it, beckoning me to follow—so I did. When the angle grew too steep, he uncoiled his rope and gave me an end to tie around myself. Thus fastened, we climbed for more than two hours. At the summit of the squamp the director sat down in silence, clearly moved. I said nothing, wishing to respect his feelings. After some time he spoke:

"A beautiful view from here, don't you think?"

And indeed, we had at our feet nearly all of Ubbidub,

with its spires, temples, and gum towers; along the streets milled the citizens, as small as ants.

"You're fond of squamp," I quietly remarked, seeing how the director gently stroked the back of the beast near its summit.

"I love them," he said simply, turning to face me. "Squamp, after all, are the cradle of our civilization," he added. Then, after a moment's thought, he continued: "Once, many thousands of years ago, we had no cities, no magnificent homes, no technology, no spares ... In those days these gentle, mighty beings cared for us, brought us safely through the difficult periods of the whackers. Without squamp not a single Ardrite would have lived to see these present happy times, and now look how they are hunted down, destroyed, exterminated! What monstrous, black ingratitude!"

I dared not interrupt. It took him a moment to master his emotions, then he went on:

"How I hate those hunters, who return goodness with villainy! You have seen, I take it, the hunting advertisements, the signs?"

"Yes."

The director's words had made me thoroughly ashamed of myself, and I trembled at the thought that he might learn of my recent crime; I had, after all, hunted a squamp with my very own hands. Wishing to divert the director from this somewhat ticklish topic of conversation, I asked him:

"You really owe them that much, then? I was not aware of this ..."

"What—not aware? But the squamp carried us in their wombs for twenty thousand years! Living inside them, protected by their powerful armor against the hail of deadly meteors, our forefathers became what we are today: intelligent, beautiful beings that shine by night. And you were not aware of this?"

"I am a foreigner . . ." I muttered, vowing in my soul never, never again to raise a hand against a squamp.

"Yes, of course . . ." replied the director, no longer listening to me, and got to his feet. "Unfortunately we must go back: I have my duties to attend to . . ."

From the zoological garden I took a transom to Galax, where some tickets for a matinée were supposed to have been put aside for me.

In the center of town thundering explosions could again be heard, louder and with increasing frequency. Above the roofs rose columns of smoke, flickering with flames. But none of the pedestrians appeared to mind it in the least, so I kept silent. The transom stopped in front of Galax. The official on duty asked me how I had liked the Zoo.

"Yes, very nice," I said, "but . . . good Lord!"

All of Galax jumped. Two office buildings across the way, clearly visible through the window, flew apart under the impact of a meteor. Deafened, I went reeling against a wall.

"It's nothing," said the official. "You'll get used to it in time. Here are your tick—"

He didn't finish. There was a flash, a crash, dust everywhere, and when it settled, instead of the person talking to me I saw a giant hole in the floor. I stood there, petrified. Hardly a minute went by before several Ardrites in overalls patched the hole and wheeled up a dolly with a large bundle. When it was unwrapped, there before my eyes appeared the official, holding the tickets in his hand. He brushed the rest of the packing from himself, climbed onto his perch and said:

"Your tickets. I told you it was nothing. Each of us, in case of emergency, is replicated. You are surprised at our composure. Well, but this has been going on for a good thirty thousand years, we have grown accustomed to it. If you would like some lunch, the Galax restaurant is now open. Downstairs, and to your left."

"No thanks, I—I'm not hungry," I replied and, a little weak in the knees, went out amidst the continual explosions and thunderclaps. Suddenly I was seized with anger.

"They won't see an Earthling cower!" I thought and, glancing at my watch, asked to be driven to the theater.

Along the way a meteor smashed the transom, so I got into another. At the place where yesterday the theater building had stood there was now a smoking pile of rubble.

"Will my money be refunded for these tickets?" I asked the cashier, who was standing in the street.

"Certainly not. The show begins on schedule."

"On schedule? But didn't a meteor just . . ."

"We still have twenty minutes," said the cashier, pointing to his watch.

"Yes, but . . ."

"Would you mind not blocking the box office? We want to buy tickets!" shouted some individuals in the line that had formed behind me. With a shrug I stepped aside. Two big machines meanwhile loaded the debris and carted it away. In a few minutes the site was cleared.

"Are they going to perform in the open air?" I asked one of those waiting. He was fanning himself with a program.

"Nothing of the kind! I assume that everything will be as usual," he replied.

I bit my lip, incensed, thinking he was trying to make a fool of me. An enormous tanker drove up to the site. From it was poured a doughy, cherry-red substance, which formed a sizable blob; immediately they inserted pipes into this pulpy, steaming mass and began pumping air inside it. The blob changed into a bubble that expanded with incredible speed. A minute later it presented an exact copy of the theater building, except that it was completely soft, for it wobbled in the breeze. But in another five minutes the newly inflated structure had hardened; just then a meteor shattered part of the ceiling. So a new ceiling was blown, then the doors were flung open, and in thronged the spectators. Taking my seat, I noticed it was still warm. That was the only indication of the recent catastrophe. I asked a neighbor just what that substance was which they had used to rebuild the theater, and found out: it's the famous Ardrite fab gum.

The show began a minute late. At the sound of a gong the house dimmed, resembling a gridiron full of dying coals, while the actors shone brilliantly. The play they did was symbolic and historical; to tell the truth I didn't get much out of it, particularly as a number of things were conveyed by color pantomime. The first act took place in a temple; a group of young Ardritesses crowned a statue of the Munge with flowers, singing about their betrotheds.

Suddenly an amber prelate appeared and drove away the maidens, with the exception of the most beautiful, who was as clear as spring water. Her the prelate locked inside the statue. Imprisoned, she sang an aria summoning her beloved, who ran in and extinguished the old prelate. Just then a meteor pulverized the roof, part of the scenery, and the beautiful maiden, but from the prompter's box they immediately brought out a spare, and so adroitly, that if you happened to have coughed or blinked your eyes, you wouldn't have noticed a thing. Following this, the lovers decided to raise a family. The act concluded with the rolling of the prelate off a cliff.

When the curtain went up again after the intermission, I beheld an exquisite sphere of husband, wife and progeny, swaying back and forth, back and forth to the sound of the music. A servant entered and announced that an unknown benefactor had sent the married couple a bouquet of scrupts. Then an enormous crate was wheeled onstage; I watched its opening with bated breath. But just as the lid was being lifted, something struck me violently in the forehead and I lost consciousness. When I came to, I was seated in the very same place. Of the scrupts there was no longer any mention in the scene, the extinguished prelate was now spinning about, sputtering the most dire imprecations at the tragically glowing children and parents. I clutched my head—there was no bump.

"What happened to me?" I whispered to the lady at my side.

"Pardon? Oh, a meteor got you, but you didn't miss a thing, believe me, that duet was absolutely awful. Of course it *was* scandalous: they had to send all the way to Galax for your spare," whispered the pleasant Ardritess.

"What spare?" I asked, suddenly feeling numb.

"Why, yours of course . . ."

"Then where am I?"

"Where? Here in the theater. Are you all right?"

"Then I am the spare?"

"Certainly."

"But where is the I that was sitting here before?"

Those in front of us went "Shh!" and my neighbor fell silent.

"Please," I whispered, "you have to tell me, where are the . . . the . . . you know what I mean."

"Quiet! What is this?! We're trying to hear!" they were hissing from all sides now. The one behind me, orange with anger, began calling for the usher. More dead than alive, I fled the theater, took the first transom back to the hotel and examined myself carefully in the mirror. My spirits revived a little, for there seemed to be no change, however upon closer inspection I made a terrifying discovery. My shirt was inside out and the buttons were fastened all wrong—clear proof that those who had dressed me didn't know the first thing about Earth clothing. And on top of it all, I shook bits of packing out of my socks—left there in haste, no doubt. I could hardly breathe; then the telephone rang.

"This is the fourth time I've called," said the secretary from CCCC. "Professor Pook would like to see you today."

"Who? Professor Pook?" I repeated, pulling myself together with the greatest effort. "Good. What time?"

"At your convenience. Now, if you like."

"I'll go to him at once!" I suddenly decided. "And . . . and please have my bill ready!"

"You're leaving?" asked the CCCC secretary, surprised.

"Yes, I must. I'm not myself!" I explained and slammed the receiver on the hook.

I changed and went downstairs. The recent events had affected me so much, that when, just as I was getting into the transom, a meteor smashed the entire hotel to smithereens, I didn't even blink, but gave my driver the Professor's address. The Professor lived in an outlying district, among silvery hills. I stopped the transom fairly far from his house, glad for the chance to walk a little after the nervous tension of the last few hours. Proceeding along the road, I noticed a bent, elderly Ardrite, who was slowly pushing a kind of wheelbarrow with a cover. He saluted me politely; I nodded in return. For a minute or so we walked together. Around the corner a hedge came into view, bordering the home of the Professor; on the other side wisps of smoke were drifting up into the sky. The Ardrite walking next to me stumbled; then, from under the cover I heard a voice:

"Now?"

"Not yet," replied the carter.

I was surprised at this, but said nothing. When we came to the fence, I stopped and stared at the smoke billowing from the spot where one would have expected the Professor's house to be. The carter, when I brought this to his attention, nodded.

"Right, a meteor fell, oh just about a quarter of an hour ago."

"No!!" I exclaimed, horrified. "How dreadful!"

"The gum mixer'll be here any minute," said the carter.

"It's the suburbs, you understand, they're never in a hurry, not for us."

"Now?" came that scratchy voice again from inside the wheelbarrow.

"Not yet," said the carter and turned to me: "Would you mind opening the gate?"

I obliged and asked:

"You're going to the Professor too . . . ?"

"Right, delivering a spare," said the carter as he set about lifting the cover. I held my breath upon seeing a large package, carefully wrapped and tied. In one place the paper was torn; a living eye peered out.

"Ah . . . you've come to see me . . . to see me . . ." rasped the ancient voice within the package, "be right with you . . . right with you . . . please wait in the gazebo . . ."

"Yes, I . . . fine . . ." I answered. But as the carter wheeled his burden on ahead, I turned around, leaped over the fence and ran as fast as I possibly could to the airport. In an hour I was out in space, scudding my way among the stars. Professor Pook, I hope, will not hold this against me.

A Recent Experiment

L em's essay-books, like *Summa Technologiae* or *The Philosophy of Accident,* contain seeds of fiction: a discussion or outline of a possible story becomes that story for a moment; a "thought experiment" takes on the aspect of an anecdote, with a plot and characters; examples of ideas, demonstrations of principles, and analogies digress into prose sections that kindle a narrative interest.

Conversely, the novels and longer stories of Lem regularly contain sections that have the tone of a classroom lecture, a textbook, or learned article.

There is fiction in his nonfiction; there is nonfiction in his fiction. Mythos and Logos alternate so frequently with Lem, that they are inextricable one from the other.

It should come as no surprise, then, that although he began his career writing stories as stories and essays as essays, this distinction blurred more and more, and that finally, in the late 60s, he started experimenting to find a literary form that would fuse both. *A Perfect Vacuum* (1971) and *Imaginary Magnitude* (1973) are, respectively, reviews of nonexistent books and introductions to nonexistent books, containing, also, lectures and sample entries from future encyclopedias.

The reaction to this of many, at home and abroad, has been

confusion, disappointment, annoyance. "What is he trying to prove?" *The New Yorker,* on the other hand, liked this Lem the best, and printed, in 1978, a few of his fiction-nonfiction hybrids. There is something wild about them.

Marcel Coscat
Les Robinsonades
(Editions du Seuil, Paris)

— ☆

After Defoe's Robinson came, watered down for the kiddies,
the Swiss Robinson and a whole slew of further infantilized
versions of the life on the desert island; then a few years ago
the Paris Olympia published, in step with the times, *The Sex
Life of Robinson Crusoe,* a trivial thing whose author there is
no point even in naming, because he hid under one of those
pseudonyms that are the property of the publisher himself,
who hires toilers of the pen for well-known ends. But for
The Robinsonad of Marcel Coscat it has been worth waiting.
This is the social life of Robinson Crusoe, his social-welfare
work, his arduous, hard, and overcrowded existence, for
what is dealt with here is the sociology of isolation—the
mass culture of an unpopulated island that, by the end of the
novel, is packed solid.

Monsieur Coscat has not written, as the reader will
quickly observe, a work of a plagiaristic or commercial nature. He goes into neither the sensational nor the pornographic aspect of the desert island; he does not direct the lust
of the castaway to the palm trees with their hairy coconuts,
to the fish, the goats, the axes, the mushrooms, and the pork
salvaged from the shattered ship. In this book, to spite

Olympia, Robinson is no longer the male in rut who, like a
phallic unicorn trampling the shrubbery, the groves of sugar
cane and bamboo, violates the sands of the beach, the
mountaintops, the waters of the bay, the screeches of the
seagulls, the lofty shadows of the albatross, or the sharks
washed ashore in a storm. He who craves such material will
not find in this book food for the inflamed imagination. The
Robinson of Marcel Coscat is a logician in the pure state, an
extreme conventionalist, a philosopher who took the conclusions of his doctrine as far as possible; and the ship-
wreck—of the three-master *Patricia*—was for him only the
opening of the gates, the severing of the ties, the preparation
of the laboratory for the experiment, for it enabled him to
reach into his own being uncontaminated by the presence of
Others.

Sergius N., sizing up his situation, does not meekly resign
himself but determines to become a true Robinson, beginning with the voluntary assumption of that very name,
which is rational, inasmuch as from his past, his existence
till now, he will no longer be able to derive any advantage.

The castaway's life, in its sum total of hardship and vicis-
situde, is unpleasant enough already and needs no further
ministration by the futile exertions of a memory nostalgic
for what is lost. The world, exactly as it is found, must be
put to rights, and in a civilized fashion; and so the former
Sergius N. resolves to form both the island and himself—
from zero. The New Robinson of Monsieur Coscat has no
illusions; he knows that Defoe's hero was a fiction whose
real-life model—the sailor Selkirk—turned out to be, when
found accidentally years later by some brig, a creature grown
so completely brutish as to be bereft of speech. Defoe's Robinson saved himself not thanks to Friday—Friday appeared
too late—but because he scrupulously counted on the company—stern, perhaps, but the best possible for a Puritan—of
the Lord God Himself. It was this Companion who imposed

upon him the severe pedanticism of behavior, the obstinate industry, the examination of conscience, and especially that fastidious modesty which so exasperated the author of the Paris Olympia that the latter attacked it head on with the lowered horns of obscenity.

Sergius N., or the New Robinson, feeling within himself some measure of creative power, knows ahead of time that there is one thing he will definitely never produce: the Supreme Being is sure to be beyond him. He is a rationalist, and it is as a rationalist that he sets about his task. He wishes to consider everything, and therefore begins with the question of whether the most sensible thing might not be to do nothing at all. This, of a certainty, will lead to madness, but who knows if madness may not be an altogether convenient condition? Tush, if one could but select the type of insanity, like matching a tie to a shirt; hypomanic euphoria, with its constant joy, Robinson would be perfectly willing to develop in himself; but how can he be sure it will not drift into a depression that ends with suicide attempts? This thought repels him, particularly out of esthetic considerations, and besides, passivity does not lie in his nature. For either hanging himself or drowning he will always have time, and therefore he postpones such a variant *ad acta.*

The world of dream—he says to himself, in one of the first pages of the novel—is the Nowhere that can be absolutely perfect; it is a utopia, though weakened in clarity, being but feebly fleshed out, submerged in the nocturnal workings of the mind, the mind which does not at that time (at night) measure up to the requirements of reality, "In my sleep," declares Robinson, "I am visited by various persons, and they put questions to me, to which I know not the answer till it falls from their lips. Is this to signify that these persons are fragments untying themselves from my being, that they are, as it were, its umbilical continuation? To speak thus is to fall into great error. Just as I do not know whether those grubs, *already* appetizing to me, those juicy little white worms, are to be found beneath this flat stone, here, which I begin gingerly to pry at with the big toe of my bare foot, so, too, I do not know what is hidden in the minds of the persons who come to me in my sleep. Thus in relation to my *I* these persons are as external as the grubs. The idea is not at all to erase the distinction between dream and reality—that is the way to madness!—but to create a new, a better order. What in a dream succeeds only now and then, with mixed results, in muddled fashion, waveringly and by chance, must be straightened, tightened, fitted together, and made secure; a dream, when moored in reality, when brought out into the light of reality *as a method,* and serving reality, and peopling reality, packing it with the very finest goods, ceases to be a dream, and reality, under the influence of such curative treatment, becomes both as clear as before and shaped as never before. Since I am alone, I need take no one into account; however, since at the same time the knowledge that I am alone is poison to me, I will therefore not be alone. The Lord God I cannot manage, it is true, but that does not mean I cannot manage Anyone!"

And our logical Robinson says further: "A man without Others is a fish without water, but just as most water is murky and turbid, so, too, my medium was a rubbish heap. My relatives, parents, superiors, teachers I did not choose myself; this applies even to my mistresses, for they came my way at random: throughout, I took (if it can be said I took at all) what chance provided. If, like any other mortal, I was condemned to the accidents of birth and family and friends, then there is nothing for which I need mourn. And therefore—let there resound the first words of Genesis: Away with this clutter!"

He speaks these words, we see, with a solemnity to match that of the Maker: "Let there be . . ." For in fact Robinson prepares to create himself a world from zero. It is not now

merely through his liberation from people due to a fortu-
itous calamity that he embarks upon creation whole hog, but
by design. And thus the logically perfect hero of Marcel
Coscat outlines a plan that later will destroy and mock
him—can it be, as the human world has done to *its* Creator?
Robinson does not know where to begin. Ought he to
surround himself with ideal beings? Angels? Winged horses?
(For a moment he has a yen for a centaur.) But, stripped of
illusions, he understands that the presence of beings in any
respect perfect will be difficult to stomach. Therefore, for a
start, he supplies himself with one about whom before, till
now, he could only dream: a loyal servant, a butler, valet,
and footman in one person—the fat (no lean and hungry
look!) Snibbins. In the course of this first Robinsonad our
apprentice Demiurge reflects upon democracy, which, like
any man (of this he is certain), he had put up with only out
of necessity. When yet a boy, before dropping off to sleep,
he imagined how lovely it would be to be born a mighty lord
in some medieval time. Now at last that fantasy can be realized. Snibbins is properly stupid, for thereby he automatically elevates his master; nothing original ever enters his
head, hence he will never give notice; he performs everything in a twinkling, even that which his master has not yet
had time to ask.

The author does not at all explain whether—and how—
Robinson does the work *for* Snibbins, because the story is
told in the first (Robinson's) person; but even if Robinson
(and how can it be otherwise?) does do everything himself
on the sly and afterward attributes it to the servant's offices,
he acts at that time totally without awareness, and thus only
the results of those exertions are visible. Hardly has Robinson rubbed the sleep from his eyes in the morning when
there at his bedside lie the carefully prepared little oysters of
which he is so fond—salted lightly with sea water, seasoned
to taste with the sour tang of sorrel herbs—and, for an ap-

petizer, soft grubs, white as butter, on dainty saucer-stones; and behold, nearby are his shoes polished to a high shine with coconut fiber, and his clothes all laid out, pressed by a rock hot from the sun, and the trousers creased, and a fresh flower in the lapel of the jacket. But even so the master usually grumbles a little as he eats and dresses. For lunch he will have roast tern, for supper coconut milk, but well chilled. Snibbins, as befits a good butler, receives his orders—of course—in submissive silence.

The Master grumbles, the Servant listens; the Master orders, the Servant does as bid. It is a pleasant life, quiet, a little like a vacation in the country. Robinson goes for walks, pockets interesting pebbles, even builds up a collection of them; Snibbins, in the meantime, prepares the meals—but eats nothing at all himself: how easy on the budget and how convenient! But by and by in the relations of Master and Servant there appear the first sands of discord. The existence of Snibbins is beyond question: to doubt it is to doubt that the trees stand and the clouds float when no one is watching them. But the stiff formality of the footman, his meticulousness, obedience, submission, grow downright wearisome. The shoes are *always* waiting for Robinson polished, the oysters give off their smell each morning by his hard bed; Snibbins holds his tongue—and a good thing, too, the Master can't abide servants' ifs, ands, and buts—but from this it is evident that Snibbins *as a person* is not in any way present on the island. Robinson decides to add something that will make the situation—too simple, primitive really—more refined. To give Snibbins slothfulness, contrariness, an inclination to mischief, cannot be done: the way he is, is the way he is; he has by now too solidly established himself in existence. Robinson therefore engages, as a scullery boy and helper, the little Boomer. This is a filthy but good-looking urchin, foot-loose, you might say, somewhat of a loafer, but sharpwitted, full of shenanigans, and now it is not the Master but the Servant who begins to have more and more work—not in attendance on the Master, but to conceal from the Master's eye all the things that that young whippersnapper thinks up. The result is that Snibbins, because he is constantly occupied with thrashing Boomer, is absent to an even higher degree than before; from time to time Robinson can hear, inadvertently, the sound of Snibbins's dressing-downs, carried in his direction by the ocean wind (the shrill voice of Snibbins is amazingly like the voice of the big gulls), but he is not about to involve himself in the bickering of servants! What, Boomer is pulling Snibbins away from the Master? Boomer will be dismissed—has already been sent packing, scattered to the winds. Had even helped himself to the oysters! The Master is willing to forget this little episode, but then Snibbins cannot, try as he might; he falls down on the job; scolding does not help; the servant maintains his silence, still waters run deep, and it's clear now that he's started thinking. The Master disdains to interrogate a servant or demand frankness—to whom is he to be confessor?! Nothing goes smoothly, a sharp word has no effect—very well then, you too, old fool, out of my sight! Here's three months' wages—and to hell with you!

Robinson, haughty as any master, wastes an entire day in the throwing together of a raft, with it reaches the deck of the *Patricia,* which lies wrecked upon a reef: the money, fortunately, has not been carried off by the waves. Accounts squared, Snibbins vanishes—except that he has left behind the counted-out money. Robinson, insulted thus by the servant, does not know what to do. He feels that he has committed an error, though as yet feels this by intuition only. What has gone wrong?!

I am Master here, I can do anything!—he says to himself immediately, for courage, and takes on Wendy Mae. She is, we conjecture, an allusion to the paradigm of Man Friday. But this young, really rather simple girl might lead the Master into temptation. He might easily perish in her marvelous—since unattainable—embraces, he might lose himself in a fever of rut and lusting, go mad on the point of her pale, mysterious smile, her fleeting profile, her bare little feet bitter from the ashes of the campfire and reeking with the grease of barbecued mutton. Therefore, from the very first, in a moment of true inspiration, he makes Wendy Mae . . . three-legged. In a more ordinary, that is, a tritely objective reality, he would not have been able to do this! But here he is Lord of Creation. He acts as one who, having a cask of methyl alcohol, poisonous yet inviting him to drink and be merry, plugs it up himself, against himself, for he will be living with a temptation he must never indulge; at the same time he will be kept on his toes, for his appetite will constantly be removing from the cask, lewdly, its hermetic bung. And thus Robinson will live, from now on, cheek by jowl with a three-legged maid, always able—of course—to imagine her *without* the middle leg, but that is all. He becomes wealthy in emotions unspent, in endearments unsquandered (for what point would there be in wasting them on such a person?). Little Wendy Mae, associated in his mind with both Wednesday and Wedding Day (note: Wednesday, *Mitt-woch,* the middle of the week—an obvious symbolization of sex; perhaps, too, Wendy—Wench—Window), and also with a poor orphan ("Wednesday's child is full of woe"), becomes his Beatrice. Did that silly little chit of a fourteen-year-old know anything whatever about Dante's infernal spasms of desire? Robinson is indeed pleased with himself. He created her and by that very act— her three-leggedness—barricaded her from himself. Nevertheless, before long the whole thing begins to come apart at the seams. While concentrating on a problem important in some respects, Robinson neglected so many other important facets of Wendy Mae!

It begins innocently enough. He would like, now and

then, to take a peek at the little one but has pride enough to resist this urge. Later, however, various thoughts run through his brain. The girl does what formerly was Snibbins's job. Gathering the oysters—no problem there; but taking care of the Master's wardrobe, even his personal linen? Here already one can detect an element of ambiguity—no!—it is all too unambiguous! So he gets up surreptitiously, in the dead of night, when she is sure to be still sleeping, and washes his unmentionables in the bay. But since he has begun to rise so early, why couldn't he—just once—you know—for fun (but only his own, Master's, solitary fun)—wash *her* things? Didn't he give them to her? By himself, in spite of the sharks, he went out several times to penetrate the hull of the *Patricia* and found some ladies' frippery, shifts, pinafores, petticoats, panties. Yes, but when he washes them, won't he have to hang everything up on a line, between the trunks of two palms? A dangerous game! Particularly dangerous in that, though Snibbins is no longer on the island as a servant, he has not dropped completely out of the picture. Robinson can almost hear his heavy breathing, can guess what he is thinking: Your Lordship, begging your pardon, never washed anything for *me*. While he existed, Snibbins never would have dared utter words so audaciously insinuating, but, missing, he turns out to be devilishly loose of tongue! Snibbins is gone, that is true; but he has left his absence. He is not to be seen in any concrete place, but even when he served he modestly lay low, kept out of the Master's way and dared not show himself. Now, Snibbins haunts: his pathologically obsequious, goggle-eyed stare, his screechy voice, it all returns; the distant quarrels with Boomer shrill through the screams of the least gull; and now Snibbins bares his hairy chest among the ripe coconuts (to what leads the shamelessness of such hints?!), he bends to the curve of the scaled palm trunks and with fisheyes (the goggle!) looks at Robinson like a drowned man from be-

neath the waves. Where? There, over there, where that rock
is, on the point—for he had his own little hobby, did Snibbins: he loved to sit on the promontory and hurl croaking
curses at the aged and infirm whales, who loose their spouts
sedately, within the confines of their families, on the bound-
ing main.

If only it were possible to come to an understanding with
Wendy Mae and thereby make the relationship, already
very unbusinesslike, more settled, more restricted, more dec-
orous as regards obedience and command, with the stern-
ness and the maturity of the masculine Master! Ah, but it's
really such a simple-minded girl; she's never heard of Snibbins; to speak to her is like talking to a wall. Even if she actually thinks some thought of her own, it's certain that she'll
never say a word. This, it would seem, out of simplicity, ti-
midity (she's a servant, after all!), but in fact such little-girl-
ishness is instinctively crafty: she knows perfectly well for
what—no, *against* what—the Master is dry, calm, controlled, and high-flown! Moreover she vanishes for hours on
end, nowhere to be seen till nightfall. Could it be Boomer?
Because it couldn't be Snibbins—no, that's out of the question! Snibbins definitely isn't on the island!

The naïve reader (alas, there are many such) will by now
probably have concluded that Robinson is suffering halluci-
nations, that he is slipping into insanity. Nothing of the sort!
If he is a prisoner, it is only of his own creation. For he may
not say to himself the one thing that would act upon him, in
a radical way, therapeutically—namely, that Snibbins never
existed at all, and likewise Boomer. In the first place, should
he say it, she who now *is*—Wendy Mae—would succumb, a
helpless victim, to the destructive flood of such manifest ne-
gation. And furthermore, this explanation, once made,
would completely and permanently paralyze Robinson as
Creator. Therefore, regardless of what may yet happen, he
can no more admit to himself the *nothingness* of his handi-

work than the real Creator can ever admit to the creation—
in His handiwork—of *spite*. Such an admission would mean,
in both cases, total defeat. God has not created evil; nor does
Robinson, by analogy, work in any kind of void. Each
being, as it were, a captive of his own myth.

So Robinson is delivered up, defenseless, to Snibbins.
Snibbins exists, but always beyond the reach of a stone or a
club, and it does not help to set out Wendy Mae, tied in the
dark to a stake, for him as bait (already Robinson has re-
sorted to this!). The dismissed servant is nowhere, and
therefore everywhere. Poor Robinson, who wanted so to
avoid shoddiness, who intended to surround himself with
chosen ones, has befouled his nest, for he has ensnibbined
the entire island.

Our hero suffers the torments of the damned. Particularly
good are the descriptions of the quarrels at night with
Wendy Mae, those dialogues, conversations rhythmically
punctuated by her sullen, female, seductively swollen silences, in which Robinson throws all moderation, restraint,
to the winds. His lordliness falls from him; he has become
simply her chattel—dependent on her least nod, wink, smile.
And through the darkness he feels that small, faint smile of
the girl; however, when, fatigued and covered with sweat, he
turns over on his hard bed to face the dawn, dissolute and
mad thoughts come to him; he begins to imagine what else
he might do with Wendy Mae . . . something paradisiacal,
perhaps? From this we get—in his threshing out of the matter—allusions, through feather stoles and boas, to the Bibli-
cal serpent (note, too: servant—serpent), and we have the
attempted anagrammatic multilation of birds to obtain
Adam's rib, which is Eve (note, too: *Aves*—Eva). Robinson,
naturally, would be her Adam. But he well knows that if he
cannot rid himself of Snibbins, in whom he took no personal
interest whatever during the latter's tenure as lackey, then
surely a scheme to put Wendy Mae out of the way must spell

disaster. Her presence in any form is preferable to parting
with her: that much is clear.

What follows is a tale of degeneration. The nightly wash-
ing of the fluffs and frills becomes a sort of sacramental rite.
Awakened in the middle of the night, he listens intensely for
her breathing. At the same time he knows that now he can at
least struggle with himself *not* to leave his place, *not* to
stretch his hand forth in that direction—but if he were to
drive away the little tormentor, ah, that would be the end! In
the first rays of the sun her underthings, scrubbed so,
bleached by the sun, full of holes (oh, the locality of those
holes!), flap frivolously in the wind; Robinson comes to
know all the possibilities of those most hackneyed agonies
which are the privilege of the lovelorn. And her chipped
hand mirror, and her little comb . . . Robinson begins to flee
his cave-home, no more does he spurn the reef from which
Snibbins abused the old, phlegmatic whales. But things cannot go on like this much longer, and so: let them not. There
he is now, hastening to the beach to wait for the great white
hulk of the *Caryatid*, a transatlantic steamer which a storm
(very likely also conveniently invented) will be casting up on
the leaden, foot-scorching sand covered with the gleam of
dying chambered nautili. But what does it mean, that some
of the chambered nautili contain within them bobby pins,
while others in a soft-slimy slurp spit out—at Robinson's
feet—soaked butts of Camels? Do not such signs clearly in-
dicate that even the beach, the sand, the trembling water,
and its sheets of foam sliding back into the deep, are likewise no longer part of the material world? But whether this
is the case or not, surely the drama that begins upon the
beach, where the wreck of the *Caryatid*, ripped open on the
reef with a monstrous rumble, spills its unbelievable contents before the dancing Robinson—that drama is entirely
real, it is the wail of feelings unrequited. . . .

From this point on, we must confess, the book grows

more and more difficult to understand and demands no little effort on the part of the reader. The line of development, precise till now, becomes entangled and doubles back upon itself. Can it be that the author deliberately sought to disturb the eloquence of the romance with dissonances? What purpose is served by the pair of barstools to which Wendy Mae has given birth? We assume that their three-leggedness is a simple family trait—that's clear, fine; but who was the father of those stools? Can it be that we are faced with the immaculate conception of furniture?? Why does Snibbins, who previously only spat at the whales, turn out to be their ardent admirer, even to the point of requesting metamorphosis (Robinson says of him, to Wendy Mae, "He wants whaling")? And further: at the beginning of the second volume Robinson has from three to five children. The uncertainty of the number we can understand. It is one of the characteristics of a hallucinated world that has grown too complicated: the Creator is no longer able to keep straight in his memory all the details of the creation simultaneously. Well and good. But with whom did Robinson have these children? Did he create them by a pure act of will, as previously he did Snibbins, Wendy Mae. Boomer, or—instead—did he beget them in an act imagined indirectly, i.e., with a woman? There is not one word in the second volume that refers to Wendy Mae's third leg. Might this amount to a kind of anticreational deletion? In Chapter Eight our suspicions would appear to be confirmed by a fragment of conversation with the tomcat of the *Caryatid,* in which the latter says to Robinson, "You're a great one for pulling legs." But since Robinson neither found the tomcat on the ship nor in any other way created it, the animal having been thought up by that aunt of Snibbins's whom Snibbins's wife refers to as the *"accoucheuse* of the Hyperboreans," it is not known, unfortunately, whether Wendy Mae had any children in addition to the stools or not. Wendy Mae does not admit to children, or at least she does not answer any of Robinson's questions during the great jealousy scene, in which the poor devil goes so far as to weave himself a noose out of coconut fibers.

"Cock Robinson" is what the hero calls himself in this scene, ironically, and then, "Mock Robinson." How are we to understand this? That Wendy Mae is "killing" him? And that he holds all that he has done (created) to be counterfeit? Why, too, does Robinson say that although he is not nearly so three-legged as Wendy Mae, still in this regard he is, to some extent, similar to her? This may more or less allow of an explanation, but the remark, closing the first volume, has no continuation in the second, neither anatomically nor artistically. Furthermore, the story of the aunt from the Hyperboreans seems rather tasteless, as does the children's chorus which accompanies her metamorphosis: "There are three of us here, there are four and a half, Old Fried Eggs." Fried Eggs, incidentally, is Wendy Mae's uncle (Friday?); the fish gurgle about him in Chapter Three, and again we have some allusions to a leg (via fillet of sole), but it is not known whose.

The deeper we get into the second volume, the more perplexing it becomes. In the second half of it, Robinson no longer speaks to Wendy Mae directly: the last act of communication is a letter, at night, in the cave, written by her in the ashes of the fireplace, by feel, a letter to Robinson, who will read it at the crack of dawn—but he trembles in advance, able to guess its message in the darkness when he passes his fingers over the cold cinders. . . . "Do leave me be!" she wrote, and he, not daring to reply, fled with his tail between his legs. To do what? To organize a Miss Chambered Nautilus Pageant, to belabor the palm trees with a cudgel, reviling them in the most opprobrious terms, to shout out, on the promenade of the beach, his program for harnessing the island to the tails of the whales! And then, in the course of one morning, arise those throngs which Robinson calls into existence off the cuff, carelessly, writing names, first and last, and nicknames, on whatever comes to hand. After this, complete chaos, it seems, is ushered in: e.g., the scenes of the putting together of the raft and the tearing asunder of the raft, of the raising up of the house for Wendy Mae and the pulling of it down, of the arms that fatten as the legs grow thin, of the impossible orgy without beets, where the hero cannot tell black eyes from peas or blood from borscht!

All this—nearly 170 pages, not counting the epilogue!— produces the impression that either Robinson abandoned his original plans, or else the author himself lost his way in the book. Jules Nefastes, in *Figaro Littéraire,* states that the work is "plainly clinical." Sergius N., in spite of his praxiological plan of Creation, *could not avoid* madness. The result of any truly consistent solipsistic creation *must be* schizophrenia. The book attempts to illustrate this truism. Therefore, Nefastes considers it intellectually baren, albeit entertaining in places, owing to the author's inventiveness.

Anatole Fauche, on the other hand, in *La Nouvelle Critique,* disputes the verdict of his colleague from *Figaro Littéraire,* saying—in our opinion, entirely to the point— that Nefastes, quite aside from what *The Robinsonad* propounds, is not qualified as a psychiatrist (following which there is a long argument on the lack of any connection between solipsism and schizophrenia, but we, considering the question to be wholly immaterial to the book, refer the reader to *The New Criticism* in this regard). Fauche sets forth the philosophy of the novel thus: the work shows that the act of creation is *asymmetrical,* for in fact anything may be created in thought, but not everything (almost nothing) may then be erased. This is rendered impossible by the memory of the one creating, and memory is not subject to the will. According to Fauche the novel has nothing in common with a clinical case history (of a particular form of insanity on a desert island) but, rather, exemplifies the principle of aberrance in creation. Robinson's actions (in the second volume) are senseless only in that he personally gains nothing by them, but psychologically they are quite easily explained. Such flailing about is characteristic of a man who has got himself into a situation he only partially anticipated; the situation, taking on solidity in accordance with laws of its own, holds him captive. From real situations—emphasizes Fauche—one may in reality escape; from those imagined, however, there is no exit. Thus *The Robinsonad* shows only that for a man the true world is indispensable ("the true external world is the true internal world"). Monsieur Coscat's Robinson was not in the least mad; it was only that his scheme to build himself a synthetic universe on the uninhabited island was, in its very inception, doomed to failure.

On the strength of these conclusions Fauche goes on to deny *The Robinsonad* any underlying value, for, thus interpreted, the work indeed appears to offer little. In the opinion of this reviewer, both critics here cited went wide of the mark; they failed to read the book's contents properly.

The author has, in our opinion, set forth an idea far less banal than, on the one hand, the history of a madness on a desert island, or, on the other, a polemic against the thesis of the creative omnipotence of solipsism. (A polemic of the latter type would in any case be an absurdity, since in formal philosophy no one has ever promulgated the notion that solipsism grants creative omnipotence; each to his own, but in philosophy there is no percentage in tilting at windmills.)

To our mind, what Robinson does when he "goes mad" is no derangement—and neither is it some sort of polemical foolishness. The original intention of the novel's hero is sane and rational. He knows that the limitation of every man is Others; the idea, too hastily drawn from this, which says that the elimination of Others provides the self with unlimited freedom, is psychologically false, corresponding to the physical falsehood which would have us believe that since shape is given to water by the shape of the vessel that contains it, the breaking of all vessels provides that water with "absolute freedom." Whereas, just as water, when deprived of a vessel, will spread out into a puddle, so, too, will a totally isolated man explode, that explosion taking the form of a complete deculturalization. If there is no God and if, moreover, there are neither Others nor the hope of their return, one must save oneself through the construction of a system of some faith, a system that, with respect to the one creating it, *must* be external. The Robinson of Monsieur Coscat understood this simple precept.

And further: for the common man the beings who are the most desired, and at the same time entirely real, are beings *beyond reach.* Everyone knows of the Queen of England, of her sister the Princess, of the former wife of the President of the United States, of the famous movie stars; that is to say, no one who is normal doubts for a minute the actual existence of such persons, even though he cannot directly (by touch) substantiate their existence. In turn, he who can boast of a direct acquaintance with such persons will no longer see in them phenomenal paragons of wealth, femininity, power, beauty, etc., because, in entering into contact with them, he experiences—by dint of everyday things—their completely ordinary, normal, human imperfection. For such persons, up close, are not in the least godlike beings or otherwise extraordinary. Beings that are truly at the pinnacle of perfection, that are therefore truly boundlessly desired, yearned for, longed after, must be *remote* even to full unattainability. It is their elevation above the masses that lends them their magnetic glamour; it is not qualities of body or soul but an unbridgeable social distance that accounts for their seductive halo.

This characteristic of the real world, then, Robinson attempts to reproduce on his island, within the realm of beings of his own invention. Immediately he errs, because he *physically* turns his back on the creation, the Snibbinses, Boomers, et al., and that distance, natural enough between Master and Servant, he is only too willing to break down when he acquires a woman. Snibbins he could not, nor did he wish, to take into his arms; now—with a woman—he only *cannot*. The point is not (for this is no intellectual problem!) that he was unable to embrace a woman not there. Of course he was unable! The thing was to create *mentally* a situation whose own natural *law* would forever stand in the way of erotic contact—and at the same time it had to be a law that would totally ignore the *nonexistence* of the girl. This *law* was to restrain Robinson, and not the banal, crude fact of the female partner's nonexistence! For to take simple cognizance of her nonexistence would have been to ruin everything.

And so Robinson, seeing what must be done, sets to work—that is, the establishment on the island of an entire, imaginary society. It is this that will stand between him and the girl; this that will throw up a system of obstacles and thus provide that impassable distance from which he will be able to love her, to desire her continually—no longer exposed to any mundane circumstance, as, for example, the urge to stretch out his hand and feel her body. He realizes— he must—that if he yields but once in the struggle waged against himself, if he attempts to feel her, the whole world that he has created will, in that bat of an eye, crumble. And this is the reason he begins to "go mad," in a frenzied scramble to pull multitudes out of the hat of his imagination—thinking up and writing in the sand all those names, cognomens, and sobriquets, ranting and raving about the wives of Snibbins, the Hyperborean aunts, the Old Fried Eggses, and so on and so forth. And since this swarm is necessary to him *only* as a certain insurmountable space (to lie between Him and Her), he creates indifferently, sloppily, chaotically; he works in haste, and that haste discredits the thing created, lays bare its incoherence, its lack of thought, its cheapness.

Had he succeeded, he would have become the eternal lover, a Dante, a Don Quixote, a Werther, and in so doing would have had his way. Wendy Mae—is it not obvious?— would then have been a woman no less real than Beatrice, than Lotte, than any queen or princess. Being completely real, she would have been at the same time unattainable. And this would have allowed him to live and dream of her, for there is a profound difference between a situation in which a man from reality pines after his own dream, and one in which reality lures reality—precisely by its inaccessibility. Only in this second case is it still possible to cherish hope, since now it is the social distance alone, or other, similar barriers, that rule out the chance for the love to be consummated. Robinson's relationship to Wendy Mae could therefore have undergone normalization only if she at one and the same time had taken on *realness* and *inapproachability* for him.

To the classic tale of the star-crossed lovers united in the end, Marcel Coscat has thus opposed an ontological tale of the necessity of permanent separation, this being the only guarantee of a plighting of the spirits that is permanent. Comprehending the full boorishness of the blunder of the "third leg," Robinson (and not the author, that's plain!) quietly "forgets" about it in the second volume. Mistress of her world, princess of the ice mountain, untouchable inamorata—this is what he wished to make of Wendy Mae, that same Wendy Mae who began her education with him as a simple little servant girl, a domestic to replace the uncouth Snibbins. . . . And it was precisely in this that he failed. Do you know now, have you guessed why? The answer could not be simpler: because Wendy Mae, unlike any queen, *knew* of Robinson and loved him. She had no desire to become the vestal goddess, and this division drove the hero to his ruin. If it were only *he* that loved *her,* bah! But she returned his feelings. . . . Whoever does not understand this simple truth, whoever believes, as our grandfathers were instructed by their Victorian governesses, that we are able to love others, but not ourselves in those others, would do better not to open this mournful romance that Monsieur Coscat has vouchsafed us. Coscat's Robinson dreamed himself a girl whom he did not wish to give up completely to reality, since *she* was *he,* since from that reality that never releases its hold on us, there is—other than death—no awakening.

Sources

"The Condor" is reprinted from *The Invincible,* pp. 41–62, translated into English from the German by Wendayne Ackerman and published by The Continuum Publishing Corporation.

The *Solaris* selection is reprinted from *Solaris,* pp. 111–124, translated into English from the French by Joanna Kilmartin and Steve Cox and published by Walker and Company.

"The Test" is a story reprinted from *Tales of Pirx the Pilot,* translated from the Polish by Louis Iribarne and published by Harcourt Brace Jovanovich.

Chapter Seven of *Return From the Stars* is reprinted from the book of the same name, translated from the Polish by Barbara Marszal and Frank Simpson and published by Harcourt Brace Jovanovich.

The selection from *The Futurological Congress* is reprinted from the book of the same name, pp. 65–96, translated from the Polish by Michael Kandel and published by The Continuum Publishing Corporation.

"Two Monsters" and "Tale of the Computer That Fought a Dragon" are stories reprinted from *Mortal Engines,* pp. 31–40 and pp. 55–62, translated from the Polish by Michael Kandel and published by The Continuum Publishing Corporation.

"The Second Sally" and "The History of Zipperupus" are reprinted from *The Cyberiad,* pp. 58–84 and pp. 208–230, translated from the Polish by Michael Kandel and published by The Continuum Publishing Corporation.

"The Seventh Voyage" and "The Fourteenth Voyage" are chapters reprinted from *The Star Diaries,* pp. 1–18 and pp. 102–124, translated from the Polish by Michael Kandel and published by The Continuum Publishing Corporation.

"Les Robinsonades" is reprinted from *A Perfect Vacuum,* pp. 9–27, translated from the Polish by Michael Kandel, and published by Harcourt Brace Jovanovich.